MAN OF
THE WORLD

MAN OF THE WORLD
THE TRAVELS OF WINSTON CHURCHILL

ROBIN CROSS

AMBERLEY

First published 2024

Amberley Publishing
The Hill, Stroud
Gloucestershire, GL5 4EP

www.amberley-books.com

Copyright © Robin Cross, 2024

The right of Robin Cross to be identified as
the Author of this work has been asserted in
accordance with the Copyright, Designs and
Patents Act 1988.

ISBN 978 1 3981 1855 3 (hardback)
ISBN 978 1 3981 1856 0 (ebook)

British Library Cataloguing in Publication Data.
A catalogue record for this book is available
from the British Library.

1 2 3 4 5 6 7 8 9 10

Typesetting by SJmagic DESIGN SERVICES, India.
Printed in the UK.

CONTENTS

I

YOUNG MAN IN A HURRY

Winston Spencer Churchill was born two months prematurely early on the morning of Monday, 30 November 1874 in a bleak bedroom in Blenheim Palace, the ancestral home of his grandfather, the Seventh Duke of Marlborough. His father, Lord Randolph Churchill, the Duke's third son, had expected that the baby would be delivered in his fashionable rented house in Charles Street, Mayfair, but the house was not yet ready for occupation, necessitating a stay at the vast Baroque pile that is Blenheim Palace. Here his wife Jennie had a fall while out with a shooting party, and a subsequent bumpy ride in a pony carriage brought on her labour pains. Her baby was delivered a day later by a Woodstock country doctor. As he was to demonstrate from an early age, the new-born child was a "a young man in a hurry".

There was no doubt that he was following in his father's footsteps. Lord Randolph had been elected as a Member of Parliament for Woodstock in February 1874 at the age of 25. It was the start of a glittering but short-lived political career which promised much but ultimately delivered little, save a reputation for a savagely cutting wit. In April of that year Churchill married Jennie Jerome, the 20-year-old daughter of a New York financial buccaneer, in the British Embassy in Paris. Neither Randolph nor Jennie proved ideal parents to Winston and his brother Jack, who was born in 1880. Their father was a distant figure, who rarely spoke to his sons. Jennie, who was described by an admirer as looking more like a panther than a woman, possessed a personality with which it was equally difficult to connect. In his book *My Early Life*, Churchill recalled: "She shone for me like the Evening Star. I loved her dearly – but at a distance." During his childhood the woman to whom Churchill felt closest was his nurse, Mrs Everest, a homely woman who hailed from Chatham in Kent. She regaled the youngster with tales of her upbringing in the "Garden of England" with its abundant clusters of hop and fruit farms. Churchill always wanted to live in this demi-paradise and after acquiring the Chartwell estate in 1922 he was able to fulfil this boyhood dream.

From 1876 to 1879 the Churchills spent much of their time in Ireland, where Churchill's father was serving as secretary to his father, who had been appointed by Prime Minister Benjamin Disraeli as Lord-Lieutenant, a largely symbolic role. They lived in a house called "Little Lodge", a stone's throw from the Lord-Lieutenant's's residence. One of Churchill's earliest childhood memories is the dread Mrs Everest had of the Fenians, an umbrella term for the Irish Republican Brotherhood, the clandestine political organisation dedicated to the establishment of an independent Irish republic. Everest impressed on the infant Churchill the wickedness of these people who would stop at nothing to achieve their goal. On a walk together, with Churchill mounted on a donkey, Everest spotted what she thought was the approach of a menacing column of Fenians. Many years later Churchill recalled that the "Fenians" were probably a Rifle Brigade formation on a route march. In the general panic the donkey threw off Churchill who was badly concussed. Such was his introduction to Irish politics.

The young Churchill's introduction to education was at the hands of a formidable creature, the "Governess". Mrs Everest had done her best to soften the advent of this alarming personage by providing her charge with a book entitled *Reading Without Tears*. Never has a volume been so misnamed. The alphabet and ordeal by simple arithmetic proved another trial for Winston, to say nothing of the Latin and Greek which confronted him at the first of the preparatory schools, Saint George's, Ascot, a boutique Eton, to which he was sent as a boarder. Nevertheless, these years also saw a budding fascination with the English language and its literature, rather than the Lays of Ancient Rome, which would stand him in good stead as he grew into adulthood. Less stimulating for the sensitive seven-year-old boy was his first headmaster's morbid enthusiasm for flogging his pupils with a birch on the flimsiest excuse and his dogged promotion of sporting prowess, all-too-common features of private education that survived well into the second half of the 20th century. High Church chapel sermons were not to Churchill's taste, nor that of the Low Church Mrs Everest, who detected in them the mark of the dreaded Fenians, Papists to a man. The unhappy Churchill consoled himself with books, particularly Robert Louis Stephenson's *Treasure Island*, a gift from his father. In the school holidays he devoted much time to the marshalling of his 1,500-strong army of lead soldiers, fighting famous battles on the floor of his playroom.

After two-and-a-half years of misery, Churchill fell ill and was moved to a "dame school" in Brighton, where he received the kindness and sympathy singularly absent from Saint James. His health remained fragile and during his three years in Brighton he was almost carried away by double pneumonia. Nevertheless, freed from the tyranny of Latin and Greek, he enjoyed History and French – he remained an engagingly creative Francophone for the rest of his life – and was introduced to riding and swimming, both of them great passions with him as a young man. Sadly, the dame school did not prepare Churchill well when he came to sit the entrance examination for Harrow. He was unable to answer a single question in the Latin paper, which was handed in as a blank foolscap to the headmaster Mr Welldon.

This did not hinder Churchill's entry to Harrow in 1887. However, this was a fatal year for his father, who had reached the peak of his Parliamentary career as Chancellor of the Exchequer before resigning after just 11 months in office. He had clashed with Lord Salisbury's Cabinet over the swingeing cuts he had proposed to make to the Army and Navy budgets, ironically similar to measures which his son would also recommend as Minister of War after World War I. Randolph Churchill fully expected to be rapidly reinstated, but although he remained a Member of Parliament he was never recalled to Cabinet. Thereafter he entered an agonising and undiagnosed physical decline, possibly caused by a brain tumour or tertiary syphilis. He died in the small hours of 24 January 1895.

Churchill spent his first year at Harrow in the lowest form. Far from being discouraged, he delighted in his "dunce" status. Under the guidance of a talented teacher, Mr Somervell, he absorbed all the elements of English parsing and analysis, the foundation of his career as a writer. In *My Early Life* he reflected: "Naturally I am biased in favour of boys learning English. I would make them all learn English; and then I would let the cleverer ones learn Latin as an honour, and Greek as a treat. But the only thing I would whip them for is not knowing English. I would whip them hard for that." Eventually, Churchill gravitated to Harrow's Army Class, peopled by those students destined for the military academies at Sandhurst and Woolwich. In this ambition he had been encouraged by his father who, impressed by his son's toy soldier army while simultaneously underestimating his intelligence, had privately concluded that his son was not bright enough to study for the Bar. It took Churchill three attempts, the third aided by a Cromwell Road crammer, to gain a place at Sandhurst in 1893 as a cavalry cadet. Here his rudimentary grasp of Latin and Greek was no bar to advancement. Lectures and study on Tactics, Fortifications, Topography, Military Law and Administration filled his days in addition to Drill, Gymnastics and Riding. In *My Early Life* he recalled that the cadets were never taught anything about bombs or hand grenades as they were now considered obsolete weapons of war.

Churchill's years at Sandhurst came at a time when a revolution in warfare was fast gathering pace, heralded by the invention of the internal combustion engine and the Maxim machine gun, quick-firing artillery, the establishment of mature national rail networks, the development of the all-big-gun battleship and the arrival of sophisticated communications technology. Air warfare was still a small cloud on the horizon. At Sandhurst in the 1890s there was little insight into these massive shifts in the tectonic plates of the military world. In Europe the industrial muscle and manpower reserves of the continental powers enabled them to assemble huge conscript armies, which could be mobilised as acts of political policy to achieve national ends. The German Army, drawing on a reserve of 4.3 million trained men organised in 25 corps, comprised 87 infantry and 11 cavalry divisions. In contrast, the British Regular Army numbered some 213,555 men, supplemented by 83,000 Reserves, 108,000 Militia, 9,200 Yeomanry and 231,000 Volunteers. It had one cavalry division. The Army's principal overseas task was to act as a colonial police force and had not fired on a European enemy since the Crimean War in the 1850s. Military strategists did not envisage a war on the continent of Europe which would involve Britain. Nevertheless, cavalry cadet Churchill consoled himself at Sandhurst in the knowledge that within the British Empire there were "still savages and barbarous people" to subdue: Zulus, Afghans and the Dervishes of the Sudan. Perhaps there might be a revolt in India.

In March 1895 Churchill was gazetted to the Fourth Hussars. Newly joined officers were obliged to undergo the same painful six months of basic training in horsemanship required of the regiment's recruits. They were also introduced to regimental drill, a spectacle which Churchill found intoxicating. He recalled:

> There is a thrill and charm of its own in the glittering jingle of a cavalry squadron manoeuvring at a trot; and this deepens into joyous excitement when the same evolutions are performed at a gallop. The stir of the horses, the clank of their equipment, the thrill of motion, the tossing plumes, the sense of incorporation in a living machine, the suave dignity of the uniform – all combine to make a cavalry drill a fine thing in itself.

Another fine thing which made a great impression on the 21-year-old Churchill was the Regimental Mess: "Twenty or thirty officers, all magnificently attired in blue and gold, assembled round a table upon which shone the plate and trophies gathered by the regiment in two hundred years of sport and campaigning. It was like a State banquet. In an all-pervading air of glitter, affluence and ceremony and veiled discipline, an excellent and lengthy dinner was served to the strains of the regimental string band."

The Hussars' commanding officer, Colonel Brabazon, an Irishman who had spent his life in the British Army, was a throwback to a vanished age, a commanding figure sporting a bristling moustache of which Kaiser Wilhelm II would have been proud. In the style of the swells who had fought at Waterloo, Brabazon drawled his Rs as Ws and could boast a colourful albeit switchback career. Straitened finances had forced him to leave the Grenadier Guards to serve as a "gentleman volunteer" in the 1874 Ashanti campaign and then, his commission regained, with an infantry regiment of the Line. Finally restored to a cavalry regiment, the Tenth Hussars, Brabazon fought in the Afghan War at the end of the 1870s and in the Sudan with Kitchener in the early 1880s. A celebrated and possibly apocryphal story about him concerned an encounter with the stationmaster at Aldershot. Brabazon enquired, "Where is the London twain?" to which he received the reply, "It has gone, Colonel." "Gone! Bwing me another!" Having received two brevets for his overseas service,[1] Brabazon was technically superior to the commanding officer of the Tenth Hussars. This officer, dissatisfied with the performance of Brabazon's squadron, ordered it home to barracks. This rankled with Brabazon, and when a few weeks later the Hussars were brigaded for manoeuvres with another cavalry regiment, he pulled rank with his Colonel,

---

1. A brevet was given to a commissioned officer as a higher rank as a reward for gallantry or meritorious conduct. It did not necessarily carry the authority, precedence or pay of the real rank.

assuming command of the Regiment and ordering his discomfited CO to "take his wegiment home".

When he arrived with Fourth Hussars, Brabazon alarmed the Mess President with the blunt enquiry, "And what chemist do you get this champagne from?" It was left to Sir Evelyn Wood, the Commandant at Aldershot, to get the better of Brabazon, who over the years had stealthily introduced a number of sartorial irregularities to the uniforms worn by the Regiment. The tenacious Wood found his weak spot, a small beard under his lower lip, contrary to Queen's Regulations: "The chin and underlip are to be shaved (except by pioneers, who will wear beards)." Brabazon was ordered to appear on the next parade "shaved in accordance with regulations". The matter was never mentioned in the Regiment and Brabazon never spoke to Wood again.

Churchill, swayed by Brabazon's tales of real soldiering, was impatient with the peace-time routine of the Hussars, however glittering, and yearned for the taste of combat. Contemplating his five months of winter leave, his eye lit upon the guerilla war in the Spanish colony of Cuba that had broken out in February 1895. Sir Henry Woolff, the British Ambassador in Madrid and an old friend of the Churchill family, provided Churchill and his companion in the adventure, Reginald Barnes, with the necessary introductions. Churchill and Barnes arrived in Cuba via New York in November 1895. Churchill was entranced with the island, the "Pearl of the Antilles", with its luxuriant vegetation, temperate climate and abundance of the very finest cigars. The two British subalterns were received with the greatest courtesy and took an armoured train to meet the Spanish Captain General, Marshal Martinez Campos, at Santa Clara, some 150 miles from the Cuban capital Havana.

At Santa Clara they were entrusted to the care of a staff officer, Lieutenant Juan O'Donnell, the descendant of an Irish "Wild Goose", who invited them to join a mobile column led by General Valdez which had recently set off for Sancti Spiritus, 40 miles away. However, they were discouraged from setting off immediately with the warning that the elusive rebels were everywhere and nowhere. Fifty horsemen could go where they pleased; two would not travel more than five miles before falling foul of an ambush. To rendezvous with the column, they had to take the train and then a boat to the coastal town of Tuna. Here they made contact with General Valdez and a column comprising 3,000 infantry, two squadrons of cavalry and mule-borne artillery. The General welcomed his guests with a shower of compliments, stressing the importance of this British gesture of support. Through an interpreter the two subalterns replied that it was "awfully kind of him and that the march would be awfully jolly".

The column set off at dawn the next morning. Churchill was in a high state of anticipation:

We are on our horses, in uniform; our revolvers are loaded ... in the half-light, long files of armed and laden men are shuffling off towards the enemy. He may be very near; perhaps he is waiting for us a mile away. We cannot tell; we know nothing of the qualities either of our friends or foes. We have nothing to do with their quarrels ... What is it then that we do want? It is the lure of youth – adventure for adventure's sake. You might call it tomfoolery.

After a five-hour march a halt was called for a siesta. The officers and the two British subalterns ate a hearty stew and drank "runcotelle" (rum cocktails), the latter not a regular feature of the Hussars' commissary. The march continued uneventfully for several days through magnificent scenery. Churchill was struck by the determination of the Spanish officers to preserve the integrity of their country, an observation chiming with his views about Ireland, prompting him to question his previous sympathies with the Cuban rebels. Nevertheless, he could not see how the colonialists could win. The sheer cost of maintaining the Cuban garrisons, some quarter of a million men, over the Atlantic Ocean could not be indefinitely shouldered by as poor a country as Spain. The rebels were well supplied with guns, ammunition and, as Churchill noted, a cost-free weapon of war, the machete, deadly in an ambush. With a keen eye to the military history which he had absorbed at Sandhurst, Churchill noted that the Spanish column "moved like Napoleon's convoys in the Peninsula, league after league, day after day, through a world of impalpable hostility, slashed here and there by fierce onslaught".

One morning, during a halt for breakfast, a volley of shots rang out, fatally wounding Churchill's horse and whistling past a few feet from his head. Skirmishers tracked the column through open country and jungle, the deep crack of their Remington rifles contrasting with the rattle of the column's magazine-fed weapons. Bullets ripped through the thatch of a hut where Churchill was sleeping uneasily in a hammock. He consoled himself with the fact that next to him, and providing some sort of protection, was an extremely fat officer in another hammock. Breaking once more into open country, the column's commander prepared for a set-piece encounter with a body of rebels defending a position in front of a long low hill on the edge of a dense jungle. Two companies were despatched to envelop the flanks of the rebels' defensive line while the General, his staff and his two British guests advanced some 50 yards behind. The column's artillery was pushed forward in the centre while a detachment of cavalry was deployed on the right of the Spanish line. A fierce firefight ensued. Churchill recalled the surreal sounds of battle: "There were sounds about us sometimes like a sigh, sometimes like a whistle, and at others like the buzz of an offended hornet." The General and his entourage watched as the infantry closed with the enemy and shot smacked into the palm trees all around them. After several sharp exchanges of fire the rebels melted away into the jungle behind their position, which was soon occupied by the Spanish column. Churchill had enjoyed his baptism of fire, but all the evidence suggested that there would be no speedy end to the fighting in Cuba. Another guerrilla war lay four years ahead of him, in South Africa.

At the beginning of October 1896, Churchill arrived in India after a 23-day voyage on a troop ship. On coming ashore in Bombay, the accident-prone young man slipped and fell heavily, dislocating his shoulder, an injury which was to plague him for the rest of his life. At the rest-camp in Poona he and his fellow-officers selected the servants – butler, dressing boy and head groom – who would provide their young charges with a degree of luxury unimaginable today: "For a humble wage, justice and a few kind words, there was nothing they would not do. Their world became bounded by the commonplace articles of your wardrobe and other small possessions. No toil was too hard, no hours were too long, no dangers too great for their unruffled calm or their unfailing care. Princes could live no better than we."

Within 48 hours, Churchill had fallen under the spell of Imperial India, and this infatuation explains much of his stubborn resistance, as a politician, to the moves many years later to grant Dominion status and then post-war independence to the subcontinent. Inside the elder statesman there remained the careless young subaltern sipping sundowners on the veranda of a bungalow in the cool of an Indian evening. The Hussars were stationed in a military cantonment outside Bangalore on the plateau of Southern India, an area approximately the size of France. Their barracks were large, cool and colonnaded, connected by tree-lined avenues. At 3,000 feet above sea level the climate was tolerable for Churchill and his two companions, Reginald Barnes and Hugo Baring, who pooled their resources to rent a substantial bungalow wreathed in purple bougainvillea and standing in two acres of rose garden. Here they built stables for thirty polo ponies.

The sport of polo was central to the life of a young cavalry officer in India. In Poona, home of the Poona Light Horse, Churchill and his companions had opened negotiations for the purchase of a string of polo ponies and had convinced their Regimental Polo Club to purchase the Light Horse's entire stud, some 25 ponies. The ponies would form the nucleus of a team to compete in the prestigious Inter-Regimental Tournament, which had never been won by a cavalry regiment stationed in Southern India. This was a task which would absorb much of Churchill's energies for the next two years. Polo apart, a minimum of military duties required Churchill's attention. Every morning he was woken at dawn and neatly shaved in bed by one of his servants. An hour later the Regiment was on parade before 90 minutes of drilling and manoeuvring. After bathing in his bungalow and breakfasting in the Regimental Mess, he would repair to the stables and orderly room for another hour and a half, by which time the heat discouraged any perambulation through the expanses of the cantonment. Cantering about on hacks from one destination to another was now the order of the day. By eleven in the morning all the British troops in the cantonment were under shelter, venturing out in the blistering heat for lunch before retiring for a sleep until five in the afternoon, when the slumbering station roused itself for polo. Churchill usually managed to play at least eight chukkas before walking back to his bungalow and a hot bath. Dinner, eaten to the sounds of the Regimental Band and the clinking of ice-filled glasses, followed at 8.30pm. Later, if not corralled for a game of whist with senior officers, a young subaltern could enjoy a cigar and the quiet contemplation of the cool of the evening before retiring to bed. As Churchill observed, "Such was the long Indian day as I knew if for three years; and not such a bad day either."

In one crucial respect Churchill was markedly different from the majority of his fellow officers. He became an autodidact, writing to his mother to request a wide range of books covering history, philosophy, economics and politics. Jennie responded willingly, and every month a package arrived in Bangalore containing volumes to stimulate her son's intellectual awakening: among them Gibbon's *Decline and Fall of the Roman Empire*; Lord Macaulay's *Critical and Historic Essays*; Aristotle's *Politics*; Darwin's *Origin of Species*; and Adam Smith's *Wealth of Nations*. Churchill's crash course in self-improvement also prompted him to question the religious beliefs he had unquestioningly absorbed at Harrow, a passing phase which was to a large extent later dispelled by his frequent brushes with mortal danger. He also studied Parliamentary debates, studiously noting the cut and thrust of arguments on political matters large and small.

Churchill's single-minded consumption of literary landmarks was matched only by his exceptional eagerness to see more action. In July 1897 while he was on leave in England and enjoying horse racing at Goodwood, he heard that a punitive expedition by three brigades was to be mounted against rebellious Pathan tribesmen in the Swat Valley on India's border with Afghanistan. It was to be led by the magnificently named Brigadier-General Sir Bindon Blood, whom Churchill had met in Surrey in 1896. Blood, a veteran of the Northwest Frontier and a descendant of Colonel Thomas Blood, who in 1671 attempted to steal the Crown Jewels from the Tower of London, had informed Churchill that if he commanded another expedition on the Indian frontier, he would let him join it. Cutting short his leave, Churchill hastened back to India to be met in Bombay by a telegram from Blood: "Very difficult; no vacancies; come up as a correspondent; will try to fit you in. BB."

Undeterred, Churchill sought and gained permission from his Regiment in Bangalore to join the expedition and then started on the 2,000-mile journey by rail to join Blood's brigades, five days in unforgiving heat in a shuttered carriage fitfully cooled by a damp wheel of wet straw operated by its occupant. Churchill broke the journey in Rawalpindi, joining a sing-song with the city's Dragoon Guards garrison to salute the Motherland: "Great White Mother, far across the sea / Ruler of the Empire may she ever be / Long may she reign, glorious and free / in the Great White Motherland."

Six days after leaving Bangalore, he was making his way in blistering heat in a pony cart over the dusty plain below the ascent to the disputed Malakand Pass, the summit of which had been secured by Blood three years earlier. When he arrived at Blood's headquarters, he was told the General was presently at the head of a flying column dealing with another local uprising. Churchill used the days before Blood returned in the melancholy but practical acquisition at an auction of kit belonging to a recently deceased officer. While waiting for Blood, he also developed a liking for whisky, a drink he had previously abhorred and for which he now developed a lifelong fondness.

Blood returned, having just despatched with a revolver at point-blank range a knife-wielding assailant at a meeting with tribesmen. His brigades, the 8,000-strong Malakand Field Force, then advanced into hostile territory, rustling the tribesmen's cattle for rations and cutting their crops for forage. The Force was accompanied by a contingent of Political Officers, deeply resented by the Army, which had scant time for their attempts to patch up deals with the local tribes before the fighting began, as it always did. Churchill's participation in Blood's expedition, accomplished with an extraordinary energy beyond almost all junior officers, fulfilled two purposes: the existential thrill of fighting enthralled him, as did the simultaneous and subsequent writing about it. He had already sent despatches to the *Daily Graphic* about his experiences in Cuba. From the Northwest Frontier he supplied *The Daily Telegraph* with copy on Blood's campaign, much of which formed the basis of an 1898 book, the stimulating but atrociously edited *The Malakand Field Force*, which he dedicated to General Blood. The General's punitive expedition, a series of skirmishes climaxing in the relief of the garrison holding the besieged camp at Malakand South, gave Churchill an exhilarating taste of fighting on the Northwest Frontier. He was profoundly impressed by its savage scenery and the harsh code of the Pathan tribesmen, according to which nothing was ever forgotten and very few debts were left unpaid. He observed that while the Pathans had enthusiastically welcomed the introduction by the British of the breech-loading rifle to their traditional way of life and waging war, they had rejected with equal vigour the Raj's "civilising" mission, particularly the building of roads into their heartland.

The Malakand Field Force's brief campaign had sparked a series of convulsions on the Indian frontier and in September 1897 the Afridi tribe rose up in revolt in Tirah, a mountainous region to the east of the Khyber Pass. The Government of India decided to despatch an expedition to the Afridi stronghold, the Tirah Maidan, situated on a flat plain accessible only through gorges cut deep in the heights which surround it. This was to be accomplished by a force of some 35,000 men. Churchill was desperate to play a part in the forthcoming campaign but was forced to kick his heels in Bangalore. Here he embarked on writing a novel, *Savrola*: "I chose as a theme a revolt in some imaginary Balkan or South American Republic, and traced the fortunes of a liberal leader who overthrew an arbitrary Government only to be swallowed up by a socialist revolution." The principal character in *Savrola* is clearly modelled on himself and another, a nurse, is loosely based on Mrs Everest. The heroine of the story, Lucile, has some parallels with Lady Randolph Churchill. It took Churchill two months to write *Savrola*, clearly borrowing from Anthony Hope's *Prisoner of Zenda*, and it was originally published in serial form in *Macmillan's Magazine* before going into several subsequent book editions. Churchill later confessed, "I have consistently urged my friends to abstain from reading it."

The Tirah expeditionary force was being demobilised when Churchill's attention was drawn to another trouble spot, the Sudan in north-east Africa. The first British engagement with Sudan ended in 1885 with the murder in Khartoum of General Gordon by the Dervish army of the Mahdi. By 1896 the British were drawn back into the region by the tyrannical rule of the Mahdi's successor, the Khalifa. It was feared that if the government did not intervene, an imperial rival, possibly the French, might step in and establish colonial rule. Command of an expedition of reconquest was given to General Sir Herbert Kitchener, Sirdar (Commander) of the Egyptian Army. Churchill was well aware that his pursuit of combat had aroused a degree of hostility in Army circles. He had been dubbed a "medal hunter" and a "self-advertiser", and this had been brought to the attention of Kitchener, who refused Churchill's initial request, which was favoured by the War Office, to take part in the Sudan campaign.

In London in the early summer of 1896, Churchill mobilised the forces at his disposal. His mother wrote to Kitchener, who replied with icy politeness that he already had more than enough officers for the campaign, all of whom had better qualifications than her son. It was now the end of June and Kitchener's campaign in Sudan was to be launched early in August. Help then promised to come from an unexpected quarter. The Prime Minister, Lord Salisbury, had read *The Malakand Field Force* and wanted to meet its author. An audience was arranged in an enormous room overlooking Horse Guards Parade. The two men talked for over half an hour, at the end of which

Salisbury observed: "I hope you will allow me to say how much you remind me of your father, with whom such important days of my political life were lived. If there is anything at any time that I can do which would be of assistance to you, pray do not fail to let me know."

Churchill pondered this offer for several days before approaching Sir Schombergh McDonell, Salisbury's Private Secretary and another family friend, to seek the Prime Minister's endorsement. However, Salisbury declined to intercede on Churchill's behalf, and it was left to the wife of Sir Francis Jeune, an eminent judge and another acquaintance of the Churchills, to swing the matter Winston's way. She told Churchill that she had heard Sir Evelyn Wood, now the Adjutant-General, expressing at a dinner party the opinion that Kitchener was exceeding his authority in rejecting the appointment of junior officers recommended by the War Office. Churchill, reasoning that the substantial and purely British element of Kitchener's task force, of which he intended to be a member attached by agreement with his own regiment to the 21st Lancers, was the responsibility of the War Office, not that of the Sirdar. Churchill urged her to have a word with Sir Evelyn Wood, and two days later he received a message from the War Office informing him that he had been attached as a supernumerary Lieutenant to the 21st Lancers for the Sudan campaign. The terms on which he was to serve were brutally frank. He was to proceed at his own expense and were he to be killed or wounded in the fighting, or for any other reason, no charge would be made on Army funds.

Churchill set off for the Sudan from Marseilles at the end of July aboard a filthy French steamer. Throughout the voyage he fretted that Kitchener might suddenly countermand the War Office, but the Sirdar had many more things on his mind than the fate of Lieutenant Churchill. Before leaving London, Churchill had also secured a commission from the *Morning Post* to pay him £15 a column for reports on the campaign. Within a week he was in Cairo, travelling thence by train to Assiout and on by paddle-steamer to Assouan, where he disembarked and rode by horse around the cataract at Philae. Re-embarked on another steamer, he moved on to Wadi Halfa, where he took a military train across 400 miles of desert to the base camp of Kitchener's army on the River Nile. The arduous fortnight's journey had been accomplished in the highest spirits, marred only by Churchill's fear of a last-minute recall from the battle front. He kept a weather eye out for any forbidding staff officers. He need not have worried. He later learned that when news reached the Sirdar of Churchill's appointment by the War Office, he had merely shrugged his shoulders before moving on to matters of greater moment.

In *My Early Life* Churchill left a vivid although partial picture of the Battle of Omdurman, fought outside Khartoum on 2 September 1898. Kitchener's army closed on the city on 28 August. During the day the heat was intense, burning through the Lancers' thick uniforms, spine pads and pith helmets. The canvas water bags hanging from their saddles were drained by mid-afternoon. In the cool of the evening Churchill and his comrades were able to slake their thirst from the waters of the Nile. They were convinced that the Dervishes would not give battle but would slink away. Perhaps these fearsome warriors were figments of the Sirdar's imagination. These doubts were dispelled around nine o'clock on the morning of 1 September. Churchill, on patrol with his squadron, spotted a dark smear on the horizon. A sergeant-major riding back from an advanced position, confirmed that the enemy was in sight. He had seen "a good army, quite a good army". Churchill was ordered up to the outpost line where he was told to report to Kitchener who was riding ahead of the infantry, some six miles behind the Lancers.

After cantering for 40 minutes, he intercepted Kitchener, who was leading a battle array of five infantry brigades marching in open columns echeloned back towards the Nile and followed by the artillery and camel-borne supply chains. On the great river were heavily laden supply boats towed by paddle steamers and white-painted gunboats stripped down for action. Disappearing into the desert haze were squadrons of Egyptian cavalry and columns of the Camel Corps. Churchill picked out Kitchener riding under the Egyptian flag and a Union Jack with his headquarters staff. He intercepted the Sirdar and his entourage and saluted. The Sirdar turned towards him and Churchill noted, "The heavy moustache, the queer rolling look of the eyes, the sunburnt and almost purple cheeks and jowls made a vivid manifestation upon the senses."

Churchill briefed the Sirdar on the approach of the enemy, estimating that they were probably some 90 minutes distant. Kitchener nodded assent before the column moved on, leaving Churchill, his duty discharged, to enjoy a bully beef lunch with some officers of Army Intelligence led by their Chief, General Wingate, while around them troops were assembling thornbush barricades, *zaribas*, in anticipation of battle. The mood among the officers sitting around their biscuit box table was one of relaxed confidence. They might have been enjoying an alfresco Derby Day picnic on Epsom Downs. Churchill found himself next to Baron von Tiedemann, a representative of the German General Staff and there as an observer, who remarked, "This is the First of September, our great day and now your great day, Sedan[2] and Sudan." Churchill then turned to General Wingate and asked if there was going to be a battle that day or tomorrow. Wingate replied with the greatest insouciance, "No, here now in an hour or two." Wingate was wrong. Omdurman was fought on the following day, 2 September. On the evening before the battle Churchill had wandered down to the Nile and talked from the river bank with men from one the gunboats commanded by a Lieutenant Beatty, who as a Vice-Admiral later commanded the Royal Navy battle cruiser squadron at Jutland in 1916. At the end of the exchange a bottle of champagne was generously tossed towards the shore, Churchill had to wade in and fish it from the water.

The Battle of Omdurman was a one-sided clash between the modern and medieval worlds. The Dervishes deployed some relatively effective firearms, but they were no match for Kitchener's bolt-action Lee-Enfields, Maxim machine guns and quick-firing artillery, the last of which began tearing holes in the battle array

---

2. A reference to the Battle of Sedan (1 September 1870) a decisive Prussian victory over the French in the Franco-Prussian War.

of up to 50,000 Dervishes at a range of two miles. When the Dervishes launched their charge, rifles and Maxims finished the job. On the right of the British line the 21st Lancers clashed with a body of Dervishes after launching a gallant but culpably reckless charge over unreconnoitered and hazardous ground. In this action Churchill subsequently claimed to have despatched with his Mauser pistol a possible five Dervishes, an unlikely tally from a total of 23 enemy killed in the incident. The heat of battle distorts to a greater or lesser extent the perception of the majority of those caught up in it. This in no way questions Churchill's valour at Omdurman, during which he managed to avoid having "a hair of my horse or a stitch of my clothing being touched; very few can say the same." One perhaps was Captain Douglas Haig, another of the Lancers and in 1915 appointed Commander-in-Chief of the British Army in France. By then soldiering had become a very different phenomenon. British casualties at Omdurman had been 47, while mounds of dead Dervishes littered the desert. On the first day of the Battle of the Somme in July 1916, British dead and wounded were some 60,000.

It was now time for the hero of Omdurman to enter politics. In the summer of 1899 Churchill stood as a Conservative, and lost, in a by-election held in the Lancashire town of Oldham. He returned to London "with those feelings of deflation which a bottle of champagne, or even soda-water, represents when it has been half-emptied and left uncorked for the night". Fortunately for Churchill, another war was at hand to restore his considerable ego. There was a long-simmering conflict in South Africa between the British and the Boers (the Dutch/Afrikaans word for farmer). The Cape of Good Hope had been colonised by the Dutch but after 1814 the British had acquired it by purchase. When the British abolished slavery in 1834, the Dutch settlers decided that their overlords were mad and tried to get away from them for ever by uprooting themselves and moving northward in what became known as the Great Trek.

Eventually, the Boers were granted two independent states, the Orange Free State and the Transvaal. However, diamonds and gold in considerable quantities were soon discovered in Boer territory. The Boers lost control of the diamonds but were determined to keep their hands on the gold deposits. Foreigners, including the British, were denied the most basic rights in the Boer territories. A half-hearted attempt to assert themselves by the British in 1881 had been seen off by the Boers, who treated subsequent British threats with contempt. By 1899 there was stalemate. The Boer leader Paul Kruger, a veteran of the Great Trek, would not give way to the British.

The Boers armed themselves and were met with a British ultimatum which in turn prompted a Boer invasion of British territory in October 1899. By mid-October Churchill was bound for South Africa on a Castle Line steamer, the *Dunnotra Castle*. He had in his pocket a deal he had struck with the *Morning Post* in September promising him £250 a month for a four-month assignment plus all expenses. Also aboard with Churchill were ample supplies of alcohol (claret at two shillings a bottle, whisky at four and vintage champagne at nine) and the burly, red-faced General Sir Redvers Buller, commander of the British First Army Corps. The *Dunnotra Castle*, Churchill, Buller, his staff and his two warhorses Ironmonger and Biffin were given a rousing send-off by an excited dockside crowd, who sang "Rule Britannia" and "For He's a Jolly Good Fellow".

On the voyage to South Africa Churchill had obtained from a fellow-passenger, Lord Gerard, one of Buller's aides de camp, the promise of a commission and attachment to a Yeomanry regiment, the Lancashire Hussars. This made his position as a serving officer and a newspaper correspondent decidedly ambiguous. However, there could be no doubt that he was not a non-combatant, as he would later claim. By the time that he arrived at the front, the British had been pushed on to the back foot by the Boers. At the town of Estcourt in Natal he encountered an old acquaintance from the Northwest Frontier, Captain (later General) Aylmer Haldane, who was about to set off on an armoured train, unescorted by cavalry, on 15 November to reconnoitre a likely axis of advance. Churchill joined him in spite of his misgivings about Haldane's mission. While formidable to a trackside observer, an armoured train is a remarkably vulnerable instrument of war, certain to be stranded in hostile country by a blown bridge or a blocked defile. Moreover, the train's engine was located in the middle with trucks fore and aft. One hundred and fifty men were positioned in six trucks, three on each side of the engine, plus a 7pdr naval gun.

The penetration into Boer territory was short-lived. After crawling along for some 14 miles, Boer horsemen were spotted in the distance. The train withdrew, at a faster pace, its occupants exchanging fire with an encircling force of Boers before the front trucks were derailed. Churchill presided over the successful clearing of the track back to Estcourt, to which the train trundled carrying some 50 wounded. It was without Churchill, who had been suddenly confronted by a mounted and armed Boer to whom he surrendered. Churchill and his comrades were taken to Pretoria where they were imprisoned in a school which had been converted into a prison camp.

Churchill remained a prisoner of war for just over three weeks. When his implausible appeal to be released as a non-combatant was turned down, he offered to give his parole that he would not undertake any military duties or supply the British Army with any information he may have learned about Boer dispositions. He was in fact simultaneously planning a wildly ambitious scheme in which he and some fellow officers would overpower their jailors, seize their arms and liberate the 2,000 men held at another nearby prisoner of war camp before taking over Pretoria, the Boer capital, and capturing its government, thus bringing the war to its end. This madcap plan had been firmly quashed by senior officers, leaving Churchill free to discuss a more modest escape venture alongside two of the camp's inmates, Captain Haldane, his companion on the armoured train, and a Lieutenant Brockie, a Regimental Sergeant Major who was posing as an officer.

Churchill's customary impatience and self-centredness took him out of the camp with relative ease. Failing to rendezvous with Haldane and Brockie,[3] he pressed on alone. His goal was Lourenco Marques in Portuguese East Africa, some 280 miles away. He covered the first leg of the journey by jumping a goods train carrying coal, a risky feat considering his dislocated shoulder. Resuming his trek on foot but without much of a plan, he then had his first stroke of luck. Stumbling on a colliery in the small hours, he knocked on the door of one of its outlying buildings and woke its English mine manager, John Howard. The Englishman quickly saw through Churchill's clumsily fabricated explanation of his presence but invited him in and offered his unexpected and famished guest the remains of his mutton supper. This was Churchill's first stroke of good fortune. Howard proved a friendly face in a hostile sea of Boers. Moreover, his assistant, another Englishman, hailed from Oldham. Churchill spent the next few days hidden in one of the colliery's rat-infested mineshafts, fortified by Howard's whisky and reading Robert Louis Stevenson's *Kidnapped* by candlelight, until the hue and cry raised after his escape died down. Early on the morning of 19 December, he was concealed under a tarpaulin in a truck on another train carrying bales of wool belonging to a local merchant, Charles Burnham. The latter had decided to travel on the train, time spent securing Churchill's safe passage by the discreet disbursement of bribes. Churchill remained over 60 agonising hours in this uncomfortable haven, sustained by cold roast chicken and bottles of tea, while the goods train was shunted to and fro on its interminable journey. Finally, the fugitive spotted, through chinks in his truck's side, officials in Portuguese uniforms on the station platform at Ressana Garcia.

Churchill clambered out of the truck and made his way to the British consulate where he was initially rebuffed before he angrily declared his identity. Thereafter "every resource of hospitality and welcome was at my disposal. A hot bath, clean clothing, an excellent dinner, means of telegraphing – all I could want." Less

---

3. Brockie later initiated an unsuccessful legal action against Churchill's account of his escape.

welcome was the news in the papers which Churchill eagerly devoured. They detailed the events of what became known as "Black Week", severe tactical reverses suffered by the British Army at Stornberg, Magersfontein and Colenso. Churchill, now rapidly elevated to the status of popular hero, was eager to rejoin the Army and the fray.

2

QUITE A HERO

Winston Churchill arrived by boat in Durban on 23 December 1899, there to find himself famous, He addressed a milling crowd in front of the town hall and slept that night at the residence of the Governor General of Natal in Pietermaritzburg, rejoining the Army on the following day. Buller gave Churchill a lieutenant's commission in the South African Light Horse, a regiment of over 700 men fielding a battery of mobile Colt machine guns. The regiment had been raised in South Africa by Colonel (later General) Julian "Bungo" Byng of the 10th Hussars, who appointed Churchill his assistant adjutant with freedom to go where he pleased when the formation was not fighting and also to continue his journalism. Buller added, "You will have to do as much as you can for both jobs. But you will get no pay for ours." Some veterans of the Light Horse were to achieve subsequent eminence. Along with Byng, William Birdwood and Hubert Gough would become Army commanders in the First World War, not all of them distinguished, and several others led divisions. With a bird's feather symbolically stuck in his slouch hat, Churchill was a happy young man.

Churchill saw action at Spion Kop, where a bullet passed through his jaunty plume, and the relief of Ladysmith, before obtaining leave of absence from the Light Horse to resume his activities as a correspondent with Lord Roberts, who had supplanted Buller as Commander-in-Chief in South Africa in January 1900. There was, however, a delay in granting Churchill the relevant press pass. Roberts, an intensely religious man, had taken offence at an article written by Churchill which was heavily critical of a trite sermon preached on the eve of an engagement in the war by an Army chaplain. Churchill, never short of friends in high places, enlisted the help of Sir Ian Hamilton,[4] Roberts' aide de camp (ADC), to resolve the matter and the pass was issued, but with a warning against reckless and uncharitable criticism. Thereafter Churchill was studiously ignored by the Commander-in-Chief. Nor did he exchange a single word with General Sir John French, commander of the cavalry division to which he was subsequently attached. The general, it seemed, was unhappy with Churchill's ambiguous status as subaltern and war correspondent. The two men established friendlier relations in 1914 when French commanded the British Expeditionary Force in France.

Churchill had also attracted considerable criticism at home for a piece he had filed in the *Morning Post* from Durban in January 1900 following his escape. In his report he had observed of the Boers:

It is foolish not to recognise that we are fighting a formidable and terrible adversary. The high qualities of the burghers [Boers] increase their efficiency ... We must face the facts. The individual Boer, mounted in suitable country is worth three to five regular soldiers. The power of modern rifles is so tremendous that frontal attacks must often be repulsed. The extraordinary mobility of the enemy protects his flanks. The only way of treating the problem is either to get men equal in character and intelligence as riflemen or, failing the individual, huge masses of troops. The advance of an army of

---

4. Later General Sir Ian Hamilton, hapless commander of British forces at Gallipoli. His command there came to an end after journalists, among them the Australian Keith Murdoch, father of Rupert, leaked the truth about the scale of the Dardanelles disaster. He never again held a senior military appointment.

80,000 men in force, covered by 150 guns in line, would be an operation beyond the Boers' capacity to grapple with, but columns of 15,000 are only strong enough to suffer loss. It is a perilous policy to dribble out reinforcements and to fritter away armies.

Churchill was with French's division in the days before the British capture of Johannesburg at the end of May 1900. In *My Early Life* he left a vivid picture of the fighting on the approaches to the city, a harbinger of things to come:

> The Boers, buried amid the jagged outcropping rocks of the ridges, defied bombardment and had to be dislodged by the bayonet. The Gordon Highlanders, with a loss of nearly a hundred killed and wounded, performed the arduous task, while at the same time French's mounted forces tried rather feebly to turn the enemy's right flank and rear. I had myself a fortunate escape in this fight. After the ridge had been taken by the Highlanders, General Smith-Dorrien,[5] who commanded one of Sir Ian Hamilton's brigades, wished to bring his artillery immediately on to the captured position, and as time was short, determined to choose the place himself. Inviting me to follow him, he cantered forward alone across the rolling slopes. The Boers had, according to their usual custom, lighted the dry grass, and long lines of smoke blotted out the landscape in various directions. In these baffling veils we missed the left flank of the Gordon Highlanders on the ridge, and coming through the smoke curtain with its line of flame, found ourselves only a few score yards from the enemy. There was an immediate explosion of rifle fire. The air

---

5. Horace Smith-Dorrien had a distinguished record against the Zulus and the Boers but as commander of II Corps at the Second Battle of Ypres was forced to resign in the spring of 1915, principally because of the hostility of the C-in-C British Expeditionary Forces, Sir John French.

all round us cracked with the whiplash sound of close-range bullets. We tugged our horses' heads round and plunged back into our smoke curtains. One of our horses was grazed by a bullet, but otherwise we were uninjured.

Churchill led a charmed life. Later, in civilian clothes, he bicycled insouciantly around Johannesburg where a dwindling band of Boers held on, before reporting to Roberts, who greeted his news of the ongoing Boer withdrawal with a twinkle in his eye.

The Boer War lasted three years and was to absorb colossal amounts of British and Imperial manpower, some 450,000 men of whom 100,000 became casualties. The War Office calculated that over 400,000 horses, mules and donkeys were "expended" during the conflict, which had cost the taxpayer more than £200 million. Relative Boer losses were just as high, with 7,000 deaths among 87,000 Boers, including 2,000 foreign volunteers. There are no precise figures for the death of Boer men, women and children in the so-called concentration camps introduced by the British as a means of controlling the South African interior, but estimates run as high as 28,000. These were the cost of the sharp lessons administered to the British Army during the conflict which brought about significant changes in tactics, marksmanship, training, camouflage and uniforms and underlined the importance of railways in any future war.

Long before the Boer War was brought to an end in 1902, Churchill was back in England, landing in Southampton in early July 1900 and relaunching his political career. While still in South Africa he had been approached with an offer to stand as a Conservative in the prosperous seaside town of Southport, on the face of it a seemingly safe Conservative seat.[6] Churchill, however, opted to stand again in the decidedly less prosperous Oldham and secured a narrow majority in what was dubbed the "Khaki Election" that

---

6. Southport was by no means safe, falling to the Liberal Party in 1898 and retained in a by-election in the following year.

autumn. He had wisely decided to play down his earlier admiration for the Boers while simultaneously playing up his own adventures in the South African campaign. He was also enlisted by Arthur Balfour, Leader of the House of Commons, to address a packed meeting in his own constituency in Manchester. Balfour was on his feet when Churchill arrived. On his entrance, "The whole meeting rose and shouted at my entry. With his great air [Balfour] presented me to the audience. After this I never addressed any but the greatest meetings. Five or six thousand electors – all men – brimming with interest, thoroughly acquainted the main objects, crowded into the finest halls, with venerable pillars of the party and many-a-year members of Parliament sitting as supporters on the platform!"

The new Parliament met on 3 December, but one of its newest members was notably absent. On 1 December, Churchill had sailed for New York. Churchill's reverence for the House of Commons never wavered to the end of his days, but he also had a lifetime habit of living above his means. A lecture tour in North America had been arranged while he warmed up with a well-remunerated nationwide progress which took in London, Edinburgh, Liverpool, Belfast, Dublin. Birmingham, Brighton, Bristol, Manchester and Windsor. Churchill also cannily secured the services of the great and the good to chair the meetings: Field Marshal Lord Wolseley, then C-in-C of the British Army, introduced him at the inaugural meeting in St James's Hall in London, and titled gentlemen of equivalent distinction agreed to set the ball rolling at each of Churchill's chosen venues. He was scrupulous in tracking the successive takings which, with two exceptions, reached the equivalent of £5,000 in today's money.

Churchill's progress through America was less successful. His disagreeable American agent, a Major Pond, struck a series of bad bargains, prompting Churchill to write to his mother that "He is a Vulgar Yankee impresario and poured a lot of very mendacious statements into the ears of the reporters ..." A more likely explanation of Churchill's unease was the fact that the British war in South Africa was unpopular with the American public. He was happier when the tour took him to Canada and a Christmas stay in

Ottawa with the Governor-General, the Earl of Minto. Churchill was in Winnipeg when he heard of the death of Queen Victoria on 22 January, news which he did not allow to overshadow his satisfaction with the box-office receipts on the Canadian leg of his lecture tour. Often later described as the last of the Victorians, it would seem that Churchill was more of an Edwardian at heart.

He returned to England on 10 February 1901, took his Parliamentary oath of loyalty to Edward VII on 14 February, and made his maiden speech four days later immediately after David Lloyd George, an MP of eleven years standing, had just spoken in support of the Boers. Churchill had prepared meticulously for the speech and, foreshadowing many later speeches good, bad and indifferent, had virtually learned it by heart. In it he argued that it should be made "easy and honourable" for the Boer, whom he characterised as a mixture squire and peasant, to surrender and "painful and perilous" for him to continue fighting. H.W. Massingham, writing in the Liberal-supporting *Daily News*, observed:

> Mr Churchill does not inherit his father's voice – save for the slight lisp. Address, accent, appearance do not help him. But he has one quality – intellect. He has an eye – and he can judge and think for himself. Parts of the speech were faulty enough – there was claptrap with the wisdom and insight but such remarks [squires and peasants and honourable peace] showed that this young man has kept his critical faculty through the glamour of association with our arms.

In politics it pays to have an enemy, and in Churchill's case it was the hapless St John Brodrick, Secretary of State for War, whom he had in his sights for the first major speech he made in the Commons on 12 May 1901. It took Churchill six weeks to prepare and learn it by heart. The theme was national security and the plans Brodrick had for the formation of six Army Corps, three of which would be held ready for despatch abroad. Churchill launched a withering attack on Brodrick's policy: "The Secretary of State for War knows – and none better than he – that it will not make us secure, and that if we went to war with any Great Power his three Army Corps would scarcely serve as a vanguard. If we are hated, they will not make us loved. If we are in danger, they will not make us safe. They are enough to irritate; they are not enough to overawe. Yet, while they cannot make us invulnerable, they may very likely make us venturesome."

This early demonstration of the cutting edge of rhetoric was both an asset and a disadvantage. As his Liberal Party colleague Charles Masterman observed of Churchill a few years later: "An idea enters from outside. It then rolls around the hollows of his brain, collecting strength like a snowball. Then after whirling winds of rhetoric, he becomes convinced that it is right." This worked well for Churchill in the days before he became a Minister in 1906 but was a far less effective device during the Dardanelles disaster in 1915 and Churchill's dog days in the 1930s, when his warnings about the threat from Nazi Germany were seen as repetitious and went largely unheeded.

As a young politician Churchill was driven by intense personal ambition rather than any specific ideology. He rapidly made enemies on the Right and the Left. In 1903 the social reformer Beatrice Webb observed after meeting Churchill for the first time that "he was bound to be unpopular – too unpleasant a flavour with his restless, self-regarding personality and lack of moral and intellectual refinement." But she also spotted qualities in Churchill: "… his pluck, courage, resourcefulness, and great tradition may carry him far unless he knocks himself to pieces like his father." He was unmistakeably a man on the make as the Liberal journalist A. G. Gardiner noted five years later: "He has that scorn of concealment that belongs to a caste which never doubts itself." By then Churchill had switched parties and had become a junior Minister in Sir Henry Campbell Bannerman's Liberal government. Churchill never had a permanent commitment to a single party, whether Conservative or Liberal. Party to him was as essential as a horse is to a rider, an instrument to facilitate his progress. The major fault line in his relationship with the Conservatives was the argument between the advocates of Protectionism and Free Trade. Simply stated, the former is an economic doctrine which restricts international trade through the use of tariffs, quotas and other forms of government intervention. Free Trade is a largely theoretical policy by which government imposes no tariffs, taxes or duties over imports or quotas over exports. Churchill, who was no economist, was wholly in favour of Free Trade while the Conservative Party was in favour of forms of Protectionism. The bitter schisms which were opened up in the Conservative Party by this difference in dogma anticipated those of the 1990s over British membership of the European Union. In 1906 they led to a dégringolade for the Conservatives in the General Election of that year.

Three years earlier Churchill had stated his position in a letter, never sent, to the Prime Minister Arthur Balfour: "I am utterly opposed to anything which will alter the Free Trade character of this country; and I will consider such an issue superior in importance to any other now before us." He had crossed the floor of the House of Commons to join the Liberals in 1904, and in December 1905 was rewarded with a junior ministerial post as Under-Secretary for the Colonies. He was now sitting for the single-seat constituency of North-West Manchester, Oldham having declined to renominate him. To his friend Edward Marsh,[7] Churchill observed of his new constituents: "Fancy living in one of those streets – never seeing anything beautiful – never eating anything savoury – never saying anything clever!"

At the Colonial Department the Secretary of State was the Earl of Elgin, who had first met Churchill in Bangalore when Elgin was Viceroy. The two men were contrasting characters: Churchill loquacious and bumptious, forever propelled forward by his flair for florid phrasemaking, Elgin a man of precious few words. It was during this phase of his Parliamentary career that Churchill deployed the famous phrase "terminological inexactitude". Churchill had used this expression in a House of Commons debate on 22 February 1906 about the employment of indentured Chinese labour in South Africa. When challenged whether this practice amounted to slavery,

---

7. Churchill's private secretary

Churchill sidestepped the convention that an MP cannot call another Member a liar by replying, "At least that word in its full sense could not be applied without a risk of terminological inexactitude."

At this early stage in his Parliamentary career, Churchill already nursed ambitions to have a seat in Cabinet. He was a consummate breaker of ceilings. However, he had sensible second thoughts about this, as Elgin was already in the Cabinet and would have resisted any attempt to elevate his junior to a place beside him. When in April 1908 Churchill became President of the Board of Trade, succeeding David Lloyd George, he achieved Cabinet rank at the age of 33. At the Board of Trade, Churchill threw himself with characteristic energy into a sustained programme of social reform. His achievements included the establishment of Labour exchanges in 1909; measures to curb the excesses of "sweated labour"; and The Miners Accidents Act of 1910. It was a striking demonstration of how much, in the words of William Beveridge, "the personality of a Minister in a few critical months may change the course of social legislation." Charles Masterman, who was to later work with Churchill at the Home Office, remained sceptical of Churchill's motives, observing that "he desired in Britain a state of things where a benign upper class dispensed benefits to an industrious, bien pensant and grateful working class."

These were hectic years for Churchill, both politically and personally. On 15 August 1908 his engagement to Clementine Hozier[8] was announced and five weeks later the couple married at St Margaret's, Westminster. Although this was an "out of season" date there were 1,300 guests. Most politicians were away but Lloyd George, Churchill's closest ally in his welfare crusade and now Chancellor of the Exchequer, was the only signatory of

---

8. Clementine was the daughter of the notably promiscuous Lady Blanche Hozier (née Ogilvy), the wife of Henry Hozier, a former Guards officer. It is unlikely that Hozier was her father. Possible candidates include Bertram Mitford, later the first Lord Redesdale, and Captain William Middleton, an officer in the 12th Lancers, who died in a steeple-chasing accident at the age of 46.

the register who was not a member of the family. Churchill and Lloyd George had been spotted in animated discussion before the ceremony, which befitted two of the greatest British politicians of the 20th century. Dean Welldon, Churchill's headmaster at Harrow and formerly Bishop of Calcutta, gave the address. Lord Hugh Cecil, a former member of the "Hughligan" group of mildly mutinous and high-living Conservatives in which Churchill had once played a part, was the groom's best man. On these occasions, personal and class loyalties overrode Party affiliation.

In accordance with contemporary constitutional arrangements, appointment to the Cabinet required electoral confirmation by the Member's constituency. This was normally a matter of course and often conducted unopposed. Not so for Churchill. In April 1908 he was defeated at the poll in Manchester, but rebounded shortly afterwards in the vacant seat of Dundee, a constituency seen as "safe for life". His campaign marked a significant change of political emphasis, with a full-frontal attack on Socialism: "Socialism seeks to pull down wealth. Liberalism seeks to raise up poverty. Socialism would destroy private interests; Liberalism would preserve private interests in the only way in which they can be safely and justly preserved, namely by reconciling them with public right. Socialism would kill enterprise; Liberalism would rescue enterprise from the trammels of privilege and preference."

Churchill was temperamentally unable to stick to his departmental brief, often taking a Prime Ministerial rather than a Ministerial overview of policy. In the summer of 1908, he formed an alliance with Lloyd George, the Chancellor of the Exchequer, to attack the government's costly warship-building programme embodied in the revolutionary "all-big-gun" battleship HMS *Dreadnought*, which had been launched in 1906. *Dreadnought* was designed to make all other battleships obsolete, and this it did, albeit only temporarily. It was not long before Germany, Austria, France and Italy embarked on their own "Dreadnought" programmes, sparking an arms race which would reach a climax at the Battle of Jutland in 1916. Ironically, Churchill would soon become the greatest booster of the *Dreadnought* idea, but for the moment he did not anticipate any threat from the *Kriegsmarine* or Kaiser Wilhelm II, whom he had accompanied on German military manoeuvres in September 1906 while he was President of the Board of Trade. In August 1908, Churchill told an audience in Swansea: "I think it is greatly to be deprecated that persons should try to spread the belief in this country that war between Germany and Great Britain is inevitable. It is all nonsense. There are no collisions of primary interests – big, important interests – between Great Britain and Germany in any quarter of the globe." This glowing endorsement of peaceful relations was in part prompted by Churchill's admiration of Germany's social welfare schemes.

Churchill and Lloyd George's scepticism about the *Dreadnought* programme was largely the result of their conviction that the nation could not afford ambitious programmes of social reform and a fleet of new battleships. In the end it got both, but the passing of Lloyd George's People's Budget of 1909 endured a stormier passage. In the winter of 1909, its provision of social insurance, to be partly paid for by land and income taxes, was rejected by the House of Lords. In the subsequent election of January 1910, the Liberal and Conservative Parties were tied at 273 seats each. Prime Minister Herbert Asquith needed the support of the Labour Party, with 42 seats, and the Irish Nationalists. Labour support was only forthcoming if Asquith stripped the Lords of its power of veto.[9] By April, the country was gripped by a full-blown political crisis. Asquith had discussed with the new King, George V, the creation of up to 300 new peers to obliterate the anti-Government majority in the Lords. Churchill, still at the Board of Trade, had carefully considered the matter and had devised his own solution. Essentially, it involved the abolition of the House of Lords and the creation of an elected Second Chamber of 150 members, which would have no power over money bills but could delay

---

9. The House of Lords' power of veto was removed by the Parliament Act of 1911 after the struggle to pass Lloyd George's "People's Budget" of 1909.

other legislation for years. Any deadlock could then be resolved by a joint sitting of both Houses and a majority vote. Churchill's proposal did not find favour with any of the combatants in the war of the veto, but it did lead in February 1910 to the offer of a new job, that of Home Secretary.

Then as now, the job of Home Secretary involves a myriad of responsibilities. Some, like the oversight of policing, prison reform and the criminal law, loom large; others, like the care of wild birds or the determination of which towns in England and Wales can call themselves cities, fell lower down the scale of importance. However, as former Prime Minister Harold MacMillan once told an interviewer, Home Secretaries must be prepared for anything to come off the deck at them at any moment. Importance is seldom determined with the advantage of careful foresight but depends on "events, dear boy, events". In the 20 months Churchill spent as Home Secretary there was no shortage of events, in most of which he was at the centre of the action, a position in which he was usually happy to find himself.

A significant part of Churchill's time as Home Secretary was occupied with business he had initiated at the Board of Trade. He remained the driving force behind the passage of the Mines Act of 1911 mentioned earlier. This was at a time when coal mining was a vital plank in the British economy and employed over a million men working in often dangerous conditions. In addition to the major disasters which hit the headlines, the steady attrition rate on the health of miners who survived their one in twenty chances of being killed in a pit accident took a terrible toll. The Act seems modest by the standards of today but was nonetheless significant, raising the minimum age for employment in the mines from thirteen to fourteen, regulating the use of machinery in the galleries and increasing the size and powers of the mines inspectorate.

Churchill also actively pursued a policy of prison reform. In 1910 during a long summer holiday he had drafted what was in effect a Criminal Justice Bill but had failed to find a place for it in the legislative timetable. Nevertheless, his reforming energy found an administrative outlet in the Home Office, the result, some argued, of the three weeks he had spent as a prisoner of the Boers. This is highly unlikely. His zeal sprang from his natural sympathies with the underdog provided, of course, that he remained at all times top dog. In characteristically melodramatic form, Churchill kicked off his campaign by escorting the Chairman of the Prison Commissioners, the exotically named Sir Evelyn Ruggles-Brice, to the opening night of Galsworthy's social conscience play, *Justice*. He followed up by consulting a friend, the Orientalist poet and libertine Wilfred Scawen Blunt, who had spent two months in solitary confinement for chairing an anti-eviction meeting in Ireland. With the playwright and poet's strictures ringing in is ears, Churchill set about improving the lot of the inmates of His Majesty's prisons.

Fired by his deep scepticism about the value of locking people up, Churchill aimed to keep them out of prison in the first place. As a result, the figures for debtors and drunks placed behind bars fell swiftly, from 100,000 in 1908 to less than 2,000 ten years later. This "soft" attitude towards offenders attracted much criticism from the hard Right press and the hangers and floggers in the House of Commons, among them Earl Winterton who led a fierce attack on the Home Secretary. Churchill reminded him, "I wanted to draw attention of the country … to the evil by which 7,000 lads of the poorer classes are sent to gaol every year for offences for which, if the noble lord had committed them at college, he would not have been subjected to the slightest degree of inconvenience." Occasionally, Churchill's charitable instincts got the better of him. Both he and Lloyd George tripped themselves up in the case of David Davies, the "Dartmoor Shepherd", a man of seemingly unimpeachable rectitude who had been sentenced to penal servitude for stealing money from a church poor box. Churchill succeeded in obtaining Davies's release to a farm in Wales while Lloyd George made a much-publicised speech, contrasting his wretched lot with that of the aristocratic "plunderers of the poor." Unfortunately, Davies, an habitual offender, was within 24 hours busy breaking and entering a nearby property and was soon back in gaol. Unabashed, Churchill pressed on with his earnest endeavours.

One morbid aspect of Churchill's duties, the execution of the death penalty, tested his nerve almost to the limit. At the Home Secretary's office there was a daily reminder of this duty, a device not unlike a snooker marker that traced the expiring life span of those sentenced to death at the conclusion of their trial. In Edwardian England a death sentence was handed down with great regularity, so there was no relief from this harbinger of doom. During his time as Home Secretary, Churchill employed his prerogative of mercy in 21 of the 43 cases which landed on his desk. He was scrupulous in examining each one and thinking them through, as is evidenced in memoranda sent to his Permanent Under-Secretary. If the Home Secretary was on holiday, the task was delegated to the Foreign Secretary. In August 1910 this fell to Edward Grey who wrote to Churchill informing him that there was no evidence to contradict his recommendations that the hanging should proceed but confessing that "... on the night before the two men were hung I kept meditating upon the sort of night they were having, till I felt that I ought not to let them hang unless I were hung too."

In Edwardian England there was little or no public debate about capital punishment. The campaign for women's suffrage attracted greater controversy. Here, Churchill found himself in deep water. His own views on the topic were, for the time, unexceptionable. He was privately in favour of limited female suffrage, the limits defined by property qualification, but in public he was reduced to fence-sitting. In the Dundee General Election of December 1910 he was reported as warning women "not to build any undue hopes on any words he might say". This inflamed the suffragette wing of the women's movement who attempted to disrupt his meetings. These women were members of the Women's Social and Political Union (WSPU) formed in 1903 by Emmeline Pankhurst and from 1905 committed to direct action – stone-throwing and window-smashing – rather than the employment of constitutional means to achieve the ends desired by the moderate suffragists. Churchill considered the suffragettes' tactics "anti-democratic" and castigated them as liars and terrorists and an insult to womanhood.

In 1910 a Conciliation Bill giving about a million women the vote, not a measure favoured by Prime Minister Asquith and opposed by Churchill and Lloyd George, failed to make its way on to the statute book, prompting a march in November on the House of Commons by some 300 suffragettes in groups of 10. Outside Parliament they were met by hostile male bystanders and a large body of police drafted in from Whitechapel and the East End. They were not given a friendly welcome and were jostled and manhandled by the police in a six-hour running battle. Four men and 115 women were arrested but no charges were brought. There were calls for a public inquiry into the "Black Friday" incident, but Churchill would not budge. In the Commons he subsequently denied that the police were acting under orders from the Home Office: "There is no truth in the statement that the police had instructions which led them to terrorise and maltreat the women." Subsequently, Churchill suggested the holding of a referendum to settle the issue of women's suffrage, but Asquith would have none of it. The outbreak of war in 1914 put the problem on the back burner.

The early months of Churchill's spell as Home Secretary plunged the Home Office into a series of industrial disputes, one of which, the coal strike at the Welsh town of Tonypandy, still resonates today. In the autumn of 1910, the Cambrian Combine, owners of the coal mine at Tonypandy, had locked out their workforce. Unrest followed in which a miner, Samuel Rhys, died after suffering a fractured skull. In early November, Churchill authorised the despatch to Tonypandy of constabulary, and infantry and cavalry formations. Their arrival was followed by rioting and looting, to which the police aggressively responded. The behaviour of the troops was more circumspect and their commander exercised restraint. The police did not and, as one historian has noted, resembled that of army of occupation rather than the force of law and order. The strike did not end until August 1911 and left a permanent stain on Churchill's reputation. When in 1940 Churchill negotiated with the Labour Party leader Clement Attlee over the formation of the wartime Coalition

Government, Attlee reminded him that Tonypandy had not been forgotten. In the General Election of 1950, when taxed with taunts of Tonypandy, Churchill replied plaintively, "I have always been in sympathy with the miners."

In the immediate aftermath of Churchill's decision to send troops to South Wales, he acquired an unfortunate reputation for reckless intervention in situations where cooler heads might have prevailed. In early January 1911 he confirmed his critics' suspicions of his trigger-happy tendencies in an incident which became known as the Siege of Sidney Street. The battle began at 4am on 3 January 1911 when armed detectives arrived at No. 100 Sidney Street, off the Mile End Road, looking for a criminal gang of Latvians who three weeks before had been surprised by police trying to tunnel into a jeweller's shop in Houndsditch. In the subsequent affray the Latvians killed two policemen before making their escape. They had been tracked down to Sidney Street and Churchill gave the police permission to send for a heavily armed platoon of Scots Guards from the Tower of London to attend the incident. He then could not resist attending the unfolding drama himself, accompanied by Edward Marsh. It is not clear whether Churchill attempted to assume overall command of the operation, but it is certain that when the house in which the Latvians were holed up caught fire Churchill instructed the fire brigade attending the incident to let it burn down. Inside, two charred bodies were found. Many photographs of the gun battle were taken, including those of Churchill clearly relishing being under fire. He later gave evidence at the inquest. In the Commons Arthur Balfour pointedly inquired: "I understand what the photographer was doing, but what was the Right Honourable gentleman doing?"

Churchill's restless attentions were now ranging far beyond the coal mines of the Rhonda and the mean streets of Stepney. At the beginning of July 1911, Kaiser Wilhelm announced that he had despatched a German gunboat, the *Panther*, to the Moroccan port of Agadir. His motives raised immediate concern in France and Britain. The French because they were about to declare Morocco a protectorate; the British because for over one hundred years they had enjoyed a virtual monopoly of gunboat diplomacy. The dispute with the Kaiser was speedily settled with his recognition of France as the predominant power in the North African littoral, but the Agadir incident had a dramatic effect on Churchill's geopolitical outlook. The man who in 1908 soothed voters with the assurance that they had nothing to fear from Germany was now convinced that they had everything to fear. The starting pistol in the race to Armageddon had been fired.

3

FIRST LORD OF THE
ADMIRALTY

In October 1911, Churchill was appointed First Lord of the Admiralty. In the Cabinet pecking order the move represented a small downwards repositioning, but one which was more than offset by the challenge of commanding the floating forces of Empire, the provision of a handsome official residence in Admiralty House at the head of Whitehall, and use of the 4,000-ton Admiralty yacht *Enchantress* in which Churchill spent some eight months in the Mediterranean and home waters before the outbreak of the First World War. With the exception of Irish Home Rule, the Admiralty was to occupy the greater part of Churchill's attention in the years leading up to 1914 and was to refocus him from a champion of social reform to a doughty advocate of the Royal Navy as a bulwark against German ambitions.

At the heart of this transformation was the menacing bulk of the 1906 battlecruiser *Dreadnought* and her offspring, the target of Churchill and Lloyd George's attacks in the former's first days at the Board of Trade. The scales had fallen from Churchill's eyes in 1909, when the threat posed by Germany's rival battlecruiser programme became apparent. Growing tension with Germany had revived the prospect of war, a possibility which Churchill had airily dismissed only a few years earlier. This change was all too evident to Churchill's close friend Violet Asquith when she and her father, the Prime Minister, were Churchill's guests on the *Enchantress*:

> Winston on glorious form though slightly over-concentrated on instruments of destruction. Blasting and shattering are now his idées fixes. As we leaned side by side against the taffrail, gliding past the lovely, smiling coastline of the Adriatic, bathed in sun, I remarked: 'How perfect!' he startled me by his reply: 'Yes – range perfect – visibility perfect – If we had got some six-inch guns on board how easily we could bombard ...' etc etc – and details followed showing how effectively we could lay waste the landscape and blow the nestling towns sky-high. He was enthralled by the technologies of naval warfare and his sense of its results in human terms was for the time being in abeyance.

The half-mad genius behind Churchill's enthusiasm for a new kind of naval warfare was the retired Admiral Sir John "Jackie" Fisher, the dynamic, diminutive moderniser of the Royal Navy in the early 1900s who had been appointed First Sea Lord in 1904 and resigned six years later. A close friend of Churchill and the driving force behind the development and design of *Dreadnought*, Fisher was also a fierce proponent of the torpedo and the pre-emptive strike. When he was created Baron Fisher, he adopted the motto "Fear God and dread nought" in a reference to his beloved battlecruiser. For all his swagger, Fisher had never fought in a major fleet action, and his flamboyance and the stirring sight of *Dreadnought*'s battlecruiser successors cleaving majestically through a heavy seaway masked a fragility which was to be cruelly exposed at Jutland in 1916. The British battlecruisers were bigger and more heavily armed than their German counterparts but carried thinner protective armour and inferior magazine protection, potentially serious design flaws. Nevertheless, the battlecruiser represented the "nuclear option" of its time. Churchill declared that its success or failure in a critical engagement in the North Sea could decide the outcome of a war between Britain and Germany in an afternoon.

Churchill's friendship with Fisher proved ultimately to be a mixed blessing. Their correspondence with each other, in which Fisher produced a steady stream of guidance and information, is laced with an affection alien to today's politicians and senior commanders. They also provide the context in which Churchill's time as First Lord can be evaluated. Within a month of his appointment, Churchill had, with one exception, replaced the entire Board of Admiralty. He created a Naval War Staff similar to the Army's General Staff. With Fisher's encouragement, he appointed Sir John Jellicoe over the heads of a number of senior Admirals to be Second in Command of the Grand Fleet to ensure that he would automatically succeed to the supreme command before the end of 1913. The clear-sighted but overly cautious Jellicoe was not wholly in thrall to the spell cast by *Dreadnought*, warning the Admiralty in October 1914, several weeks after the outbreak of World War, that "It is quite within the bounds of possibility that half of our battle fleet might be disabled by underwater [submarine] attacks before the guns opened fire at all, if a false move is made."

Although *Dreadnought* had been developed and built in record time before Churchill became First Lord, he presided over the introduction in December 1914 of arguably the first fast battleship, *Queen Elizabeth*, carrying a main armament of eight 15in guns in four twin-gun turrets, the foundation of a fast division of battleships to succeed the battlecruisers. The oil-fired *Elizabeth* marked another crucial development, leading to Churchill's signature of the Anglo-Persian Oil Convention ensuring sufficient supplies in time of war. He also followed Fisher's advice by devoting time to submarines and naval aircraft. Churchill had been a keen aviator in the years before 1914, although he never qualified to fly solo. He foresaw the role that aircraft could play in warfare and in 1912 established the Royal Naval Air Service (RNAS) which was to play a significant part in air operations in 1914 during the opening weeks of the First World War.

On 26 July 1914, Churchill agreed with the First Sea Lord, Prince Louis Battenberg[10] that the Grand Fleet, assembled for review at Portland, was to be ordered not to disperse because of the prevailing international tension. The timing was well-judged. A general mobilisation of the Army might at this stage have provoked immediate retaliatory action from Germany while the state of naval readiness, demonstrably less threatening, ensured control of the seas around Britain. Three days later, Britain's warships sailed to their stations in the North Sea while telegrams were simultaneously despatched to stations around the world. Anticipating objections, Churchill chose not to inform the Cabinet of these moves but secured the agreement of the Prime Minister. On the brink of war Churchill was, in the words of the acutely perceptive Violet Asquith, filled with "glowing zest ... For three years he had devoted all his powers to preparing the Navy to meet the challenge of this hour, and he knew that he had done it well. The hour had come. He hailed it with a cheer ... he was alive to things which others did not see. His powers of concentration on one aim to the exclusion of all else was at once his weakness and his strength."

Since 1906 the Royal Navy and the German *Kriegsmarine* had been engaged in an arms race in which the British had maintained a slim but significant advantage. In the summer of 1914, the Royal Navy's order of battle included 20 Dreadnought-class battleships and nine Dreadnought-type battlecruisers, the latter warships of the same displacement as the original Dreadnought but faster and less heavily armoured. The *Kriegsmarine*, by comparison, had 13 Dreadnought-class ships and five battlecruisers. What concerned Churchill was the overall quality of the Royal Navy's leadership. If there was to be a decisive fleet action in the North Sea, would

---

10. Battenberg, a competent First Sea Lord of the Admiralty, was forced to resign in October 1914 because of the overwhelmingly anti-German sentiment in Britain and was succeeded by Admiral Fisher.

a successor to Admiral Nelson emerge? Churchill was not so sure. On the eve of war her reflected that there was "a frightful dearth of first class men in the [admiral's] lists". At the end of the Great War he observed, "We had competent administrators, brilliant experts of every description, unequalled navigators, good disciplinarians, fine sea officers, brave and devoted hearts; but at the outset of the conflict we had more captains of ships than captains of war."

One of the unforeseen but unavoidable consequences of Fisher's reforms had been to minimise the self-reliance of commanders, which had been such a feature of Nelson's day, by drawing the Navy's ships into ever larger fleets. This was exacerbated by the threat posed by the torpedo, which necessitated the deployment of screens of cruisers and torpedo-boat destroyers around the high-value targets represented by the capital ships. The strict maintenance of these lines of battle discouraged independence of thought among junior and middle-ranking commanders. As Jellicoe had observed, the risks involved were simply too great. Added to this was the vast increase in the range and striking power of the Navy's main armament. The rate of fire became an obsession in the Admiralty. In the coming war it was about to be tested almost to the point of destruction.

When war broke out in August 1914, the Royal Navy and the British public were thirsting for action. Admiral David Beatty, the gunboat captain who had tossed a bottle of champagne to Churchill in Egypt in 1898 and now commanded the Royal Navy's battlecruiser squadron, exulted, "For thirty years I have waited for this day!" The unchallenged ferrying of six divisions of the British Expeditionary Force (BEF) across the Channel to France was a singularly successful operation but unheralded by the public and the press. This and the virtual war-long naval blockade of German's North Sea ports, and the maintenance of international trade routes, were unspectacular but crucial contributions to Allied victory. However, they lacked the "Nelson touch" and did not dominate the headlines in the early years of the war. It can be safely assumed that Churchill was of the Beatty school of thought, or rather action, but the opening naval exchanges of the war produced mixed results. On 22 September 1914, the obsolescent cruisers *Aboukir*, *Cressy* and *Hogue*, which were patrolling off the Dutch coast, were coolly sunk, one by one, by the U-boat *U-19*. Each of the cruisers was hit by a single torpedo. Some 2,500 sailors went into the water, of whom 300 were rescued by a Dutch trawler. Twenty young midshipmen lost their lives in the action and were dubbed by the press as "Winston's babies", an implied criticism of the First Lord. A Royal Navy submarine officer reflected, "The North Sea is no place for big ships. I only hope the person responsible for putting them there gets hung."

The German High Seas Fleet did not oblige the flamboyant Beatty. Most of its ships withdrew to harbour. The losses the High Seas Fleet sustained in the action off Heligoland Bight on 28 August, when Beatty's battlecruisers sank three light cruisers and a destroyer, reinforced the German High Command's reluctance to risk a fleet action in the North Sea. On the European mainland the opening days of August 1914 briefly promised a war of movement as the German drive on Paris was halted and then turned back at the Battle of the Marne in early September, after which both sides extended their operations northwards, each trying to work round the other's flanks in what was later dubbed "The Race to the Sea". All the while the German High Command, fearing a British intervention, was casting anxious looks over its shoulder to the Belgian port of Antwerp. Churchill also had his eyes on the city. In the late summer of 1914, as was his wont, he was operating at sea and on the land. From a British perspective the objective of The Race to the Sea was the securing of the Channel ports and the supply lines to the BEF. Antwerp was by no means at the head of the British list of such ports, but it controlled the Scheldt estuary and had played a part in our military history since the days of Marlborough's continental forays. Now it housed the Belgian government, which had retreated there from Brussels. German occupation of Antwerp would signal the end of Belgian resistance to the German invasion.

On the night of 2 October Churchill was summoned to a meeting at a house in Carlton Gardens, where he found the Secretary of State for War Lord Kitchener, whose home it was, the Foreign Secretary Edward Grey and Battenberg. He was informed that the Belgian government was on the point of evacuating Antwerp, whereupon Churchill volunteered to investigate the situation on the spot and deliver reinforcements, including the barely trained men of the British Naval Division, effectively Churchill's private army. He arrived at 3pm on the following afternoon in one of the armoured Rolls-Royces which he had deployed in the RNAS operations in Belgium. A whirl of activity accompanied his arrival. He urged the Belgian monarch, King Albert, to fight on for ten days to enable the British to consolidate their defensive line between Lille and the sea, a measure which lasted only five days. It nevertheless saved the bulk of the Belgian Army, which was successfully extricated rather than annihilated.

This was the improvised adventurism in which Churchill revelled. His precise status was ambiguous, his clothes, a cape and a yachting cap, absurd. He set up his headquarters in a smart hotel; employed Admiral Sir Henry Oliver, Chief of Naval Intelligence, as his secretary; lay in bed in the mornings dictating numerous telegrams for the Admiralty to despatch; and spent the afternoons touring Antwerp's outer defences in his armoured Rolls-Royce. His nights were given over to conferences. It was a rehearsal for the hectic days he was to spend in France in the early summer of 1940.

During all this frenetic activity Churchill ensured that he was not deprived of his creature comforts. After visiting some Royal Marines, he wrote: "Twenty minutes in a motor car and we were back in the warmth and light of one of the best hotels in Europe, with its perfectly appointed tables and attentive servants all proceeding as usual." He was so taken with the role he had assumed, a mixture of Richard Hannay, Bulldog Drummond and Richmal Crompton's William, that he suggested to Asquith that he might, with the appropriate military rank, assume command of the British defenders of Antwerp. Kitchener, who annotated the telegram, thought that the rank of Lieutenant-General might be appropriate. The suggestion reduced the Cabinet to fits of laughter. Violet Asquith was shaken by Churchill's "sense of proportion (or rather lack of it)... His desire to exchange the Admiralty, in which for years he has invested all his treasures and which was now faced with its first test and greatest opportunity, for the command of a mere major-general [*sic*], one of many, in the field seemed to me to be hardly adult." Her father, Prime Minister Herbert Asquith, simply sent Churchill a message saying that the government could not spare him at the Admiralty.

On 7 October Churchill was replaced by General Sir Henry Rawlinson[11] and returned to London, where his daughter Sarah had just been born. Shortly afterwards Antwerp fell to the Germans. The RNAS, which had been operating from Ostend, relocated its headquarters to Dunkirk, which was to become its single largest operational base for most of the war. Its location, strategically placed on the left flank of the Allied line and at the end of one of its cross-Channel arteries, encouraged the RNAS to diversify its operations into every aspect of aerial activity, from maritime patrolling to strategic bombing. This was encouraged by the relative freedom which the Admiralty allowed its successive commanders and Churchill's vigorous efforts to find an offensive role for the Navy, of which the RNAS was a small but highly distinctive part, appealing irresistibly to the First Lord's buccaneering instincts.

The opening weeks of fighting had given the false impression of a war of movement. But in September 1914, as each side tried to outflank each other in the Race to the Sea, the first trenches – initially mere scrapes in the ground - began to appear. Within weeks the stalemate they had produced during the fighting on the River Aisne in September 1914 spread down the 500-mile battle line from the North Sea to the Swiss frontier. The front had

---

11. Rawlinson was later commander of the British Fourth Army during the Battle of the Somme and after the First World War was appointed C-in-C, India. He died in post in 1925.

horribly congealed and was to stay that way until the spring of
1918. Senior commanders and politicians cast around for ways
to break the deadlock. The French Commander-in-Chief on the
Western Front, General Joseph Joffre, devised a plan to strike at
Germany's vulnerable supply and communications lines running
into its extended front; Joffre's British opposite number, Field
Marshal Sir John French, urged a drive on the Belgian coast;
Admiral Fisher, restored in 1914 by Churchill as First Sea Lord,
argued for an attack on Germany from the Baltic; Lloyd George
suggested an offensive into Austria launched from the Adriatic;
Kitchener proposed to open up another front in Palestine aimed
at the Ottoman Empire, which had joined the war on the side
of the Central Powers, Germany, Austria-Hungary and Bulgaria,
in October 1914. But it was Churchill who secured backing for
his plan, which was to seize the Dardanelles, the international
waterway connecting the Sea of Marmara with the Aegean and
Mediterranean and giving access to the Black Sea via the Bosporus.
Churchill argued that the seizure of the Dardanelles would
safeguard the Suez Canal and relieve pressure on the Russians
by opening up a supply and communications route. A lodgement
on the Gallipoli peninsula, on the northern side of the Straits
would also provide a platform for a drive on Istanbul, forcing the
Germans to withdraw troops from the Western Front.

Churchill's reasoning opened up a rift in the British High
Command between so-called "Westerners", those who
believed that the defeat of Germany could only be achieved
by the destruction of its armies on the Western Front, and
the "Easterners," who, like Churchill, believed in an indirect
approach to victory by first defeating the Ottoman Empire
and then striking at the Central Powers through the Balkans.
Churchill would propose a not dissimilar strategy for the defeat
of the Axis to the Americans in 1942-43. He had devised his
Dardanelles plan, presented to the War Council in mid-January
1915 and principally a naval operation, with Admiral Carden,
commander of the Mediterranean Fleet. The Straits would be
cleared of mines, British warships would bombard and subdue

the forts guarding the Dardanelles, and only a small force would have to be landed to secure them. Naval Intelligence considered that "it may generally be considered that the defences [in the Dardanelles] are too dispersed and not strong enough at the critical point." Churchill and the British High Command had a low opinion of the fighting qualities of the Turkish soldier. Kitchener believed that the systematic destruction of the forts by naval gunnery "will exert great moral effect on the Turk". When confronted with this early example of "shock and awe", "Johnny Turk" would think again and meekly throw in the towel. What the British did not take into account was that the Turks were fighting on their own soil and had been well schooled by German military advisers. The commander of the Turkish troops holding the Gallipoli peninsula, General Liman von Sanders, had arrived in Istanbul at the head of a military mission in 1913.

The British had also blundered by showing their hand on 4 November 1914, before hostilities with Turkey had begun in earnest, when Royal Navy warships bombarded the entrance to the Dardanelles. On 13 December the submarine *B11* sank a Turkish patrol vessel on the Asian side of the Straits. The Turks immediately began strengthening their defences, and by March 1915 had sown hundreds of mines in the Straits and had also sited torpedo tubes at their narrowest point. By the end of April, there were six Turkish divisions in the theatre. Nevertheless, Churchill's plan, presented with his usual forcefulness, seemed clear-cut and compelling. It would cost the British, their Allies and the Turks many thousands of lives and Churchill his post as First Lord of the Admiralty.

When he was confronted by the Third Sea Lord, Admiral Sir Frederick Tudor, who asked him what he would do if the forcing of the Dardanelles could not be accomplished by ships alone, Churchill breezily reassured his colleague that the operation would go ahead exactly as planned. However, Churchill was less confident when discussing the Dardanelles with Commodore Roger Keyes, appointed the Naval Chief of Staff for the operation. Keyes noted that Churchill's confidence failed to mask his nervousness about the imminent attack on the Dardanelles as this was "the biggest coup he [Churchill] had ever played for."

The big coup also precipitated a catastrophic falling out with the reappointed Fisher, with whom Churchill had previously been the best of friends. Now they were, in the words of military historian Basil Liddell Hart, like "two scorpions fighting in a bottle". In a clash of superegos something had to give. Fisher had always blown hot and cold over the Dardanelles. Churchill, in his determination to seek an alternative to "chewing barbed wire in Flanders", was the fiercest proponent of a purely naval attack. At the end of January, Kitchener had been obliged to physically prevent Fisher from walking out of a Defence Committee meeting to discuss the operation. Thereafter, the First Sea Lord sank into an ominous silence on the subject. His reappointment as First Sea Lord had proved a two-edged sword. At first, he had galvanised the Admiralty, but at 74 his age was overtaking him. He unfailingly arrived for work at an impossibly early hour but by four in the afternoon was sometimes found soundly asleep at his desk.

At the end of February, the British and their French allies took the naval route in an attempt to silence the Turkish guns. However, the Turks deployed many concealed and mobile batteries which made life very difficult for the Allied minesweepers – most of which were converted trawlers – and prevented the larger ships, notably the battleship *Queen Elizabeth*, from dealing with the forts guarding the Straits. The War Cabinet then decided to hastily assemble a large landing force – eventually 75,000-strong – to mount a full-scale amphibious assault on the Turkish artillery positions. It was concentrated on the Greek island of Lemnos under the command of General Sir Ian Hamilton, Churchill's old colleague in the Boer War. By the end of February there were three wholly unco-ordinated plans under way: Churchill's "ships alone" policy; the joint Army-Navy operation originally planned; and a much bigger amphibious landing with the major part being shouldered by ground forces.

On 18 March it was decided to give the "ships alone" policy one more chance. No fewer than 16 Allied battleships, most of them obsolete pre-*Dreadnought* types, were committed. In the early afternoon, disaster ensued. The French battleship *Bouvet* struck a mine and sank. It was to be a good day for the mines and guns and a bad day for the battleships. *Irresistible* and *Ocean* went to the bottom. The French *Suffren* and *Charlemagne* were crippled by artillery fire and the Royal Navy's battlecruiser *Inflexible*, which had played a significant role in the Navy's victory over a German naval squadron off the Falkland Islands in November 1914, was so badly damaged by the shore batteries that it had to be towed to Malta for extensive repairs. Meanwhile, disagreement between Churchill and Fisher had descended into open warfare. On 2 April Fisher wrote to Churchill, "You are just simply eaten up with the Dardanelles and can't think of anything else! Damn the Dardanelles! They'll be our grave!"

On 25 April Hamilton's expeditionary force landed on the rocky coastline of the Gallipoli peninsula. The Turks were taken by surprise, but Hamilton's timid generalship allowed them to rush up reinforcements and confine his men to the landing areas. The British element in the expeditionary force and the Australian and New Zealand Army Corps (ANZAC) were to be pinned down for almost a year. Trench warfare ensued in conditions far worse than in France. The British and the Anzacs held no secure rear, only beaches exposed to Turkish artillery. Everything – even water – had to be landed at night. Disease, particularly dysentery, took a terrible toll. Two more landings at the beginning of August offered a fleeting chance of a breakout from the beachheads, but the opportunity was frittered away. The troops were evacuated in December without a man being lost during the withdrawal. The Dardanelles disaster led to Churchill's resignation and the end of the Liberal government, but before we consider these events we should address another intervention by Churchill in the course of the First World War which had lasting consequences and was of crucial importance in 1940.

By the autumn of 1914, barbed wire and machine guns had brought about a stalemate on the Western Front. In October of that year the British official war correspondent, Colonel Ernest Swinton, approached the General Headquarters (GHQ) with a proposal to use the pre-war Holt agricultural tractor as a means of overcoming barbed wire and broken ground. GHQ was not interested but Swinton's scheme found an enthusiastic backer in Winston Churchill. The armoured cars employed by the RNAS in Belgium had enjoyed some success but had been hampered by trenches which the Germans had dug across the roads. The Admiralty's work on a solution to this problem coincided with Swinton's proposal and led in February 1915 to the establishment of an Admiralty Landships Committee.

In Volume I of *The World Crisis*, Churchill paints a vivid but misleading picture of the subsequent development of what was to emerge a year later as the tank. Churchill wrote, "The first design of the Tank, made at my request ... in September 1914 carried a bridge in front, which, on arriving at a trench, it dropped passed over and automatically raised behind it." In fact, Churchill was referring to a machine designed to haul heavy howitzers which was in no way a precursor of an armoured fighting vehicle. Nor was it a "caterpillar tractor", as Churchill states in Vol. II of *The World Crisis*, but had eight-foot driving wheels which made it look like an elongated version of the tractor used in road building. The development by the Admiralty of its prototype looked for a time like grinding into a dead end, as the giant wire-crushing rollers prevented the vehicle from tackling an incline. With Churchill's encouragement it morphed into a "landship", running on giant 40-foot wheels to carry infantry forward, a tempting target for enemy artillery. By the spring of 1915, the persistent Swinton had succeeded in swinging development back along the lines of the caterpillar tractor, the fundamental design feature of the tank to this day, which was to be employed in interdicting the enemy's machine guns and artillery.

In spite of the impracticality of the initial designs for the tank and Churchill's hazy notion of its potential usefulness in combat, there can be no doubt that without his infectious enthusiasm the whole concept might have been killed off by indifference. After several false starts, the first viable armoured fighting vehicle, for security reasons codenamed a "tank", as in "water tank" and dubbed "Big Willie", successfully underwent trials at Hatfield Park in Hertfordshire at the beginning of 1916, meeting the War Office requirements of crossing a trench ten feet wide and climbing a vertical obstacle four-and-a-half feet high. Not everyone in the British High Command was convinced by the new weapon. Kitchener dismissed "Big Willie" as "a pretty mechanical toy", but Sir Douglas Haig, commander of the British Expeditionary Force from December 1915, was keen for the speediest possible use of the new machines.

The tanks were first employed in significant numbers on 15 September 1916 during the Battle of the Somme but were thrown forward in uncoordinated fashion. Churchill had always insisted that they should be given their baptism of fire in greater numbers in concentrated shock action, a tactic which would pay dividends when tanks were successfully employed en masse in November 1917 at Cambrai. By then Churchill had resigned from the Admiralty, served briefly on the Western Front and after his return been appointed Minister of Munitions. His early enthusiasm for the tank had dimmed and he resisted strenuous efforts to enlist his support from the proponents of armoured warfare. He chose not to intervene when the War Office cut its programme for the building of tanks in 1918 from 4,000 to 1,350.

Churchill's reluctance to intervene was in large part the result of the collapse of his strategy at the Dardanelles. The simmering feud with Fisher had exploded into full-blown volcanic eruption on 14 May 1915, following what Churchill later described as a "sulphurous" meeting of the War Council, established in November 1914 to direct the overall conduct of the conflict, at which Fisher claimed, not wholly truthfully, that he had been against the Dardanelles expedition from the outset. At another War Council meeting on the following day, Churchill noted that "Hamilton's army had been definitely brought to a standstill on the Gallipoli Peninsula, was suspended there in circumstances of peril, was difficult to reinforce, and still more difficult to withdraw. The Fleet had relapsed into passivity." Fisher had ordered the withdrawal of Queen *Elizabeth*, a frank admission of failure which obliged the naval commander on the spot, Admiral Sir John de Robeck, to invent a story that the battleship was going to Malta for repairs.

Another brewing scandal, the shortage of shells on the Western Front, piled more pressure on the Liberal government.

On 15 May, while walking back to the Admiralty from a meeting at the Foreign Office, Churchill was intercepted by an agitated Private Secretary who informed him that the volatile Fisher had resigned as First Sea Lord, his eighth resignation in the last six-and-a-half months. His letter of resignation stated, "I find it increasingly difficult to adjust myself to the increasingly daily requirements of the Dardanelles to meet your [Churchill's] views – as you truly said yesterday – I am in the position of continually vetoing your proposals." In the letter, Fisher had announced that he planned to go to Scotland, but after a frantic search the First Sea Lord was found in a modest room at the Charing Cross Hotel – he was notoriously mean – handily not far from the Admiralty and Downing Street. The latter was the more anxious to locate Fisher, prompted by the crisis at the Admiralty and the scandal of the shell shortage that had been amplified by coverage in national newspapers. For the moment, Churchill believed that the row with Fisher was a storm in a teacup.

Summoned to Downing Street by the Prime Minister, Fisher appeared "mellow and friendly" but still insistent that he would not work with Churchill. The First Lord set about finding a successor to Fisher, alighting on another septuagenarian, Sir Arthur Wilson. He then set off, accompanied by Clementine, to pay a surprise visit to Asquith, who was staying in a house on the Thames at Sutton Courtenay with Churchill's predecessor at the Admiralty Sir Richard McKenna and his wife, and Prince Paul of Serbia. Here Churchill offered his resignation, which Asquith declined, with the proviso that he would have to first consult Bonar Law, the Conservative leader and shortly to become a member in the new wartime Coalition Government.[12] He then asked the Churchills to

---

12. The Coalition Government was formed in December 1916 under David Lloyd George after the disastrous losses suffered by the British Army in the first 29 months of the war, particularly on the Somme. It continued in power after November 1918, although it became increasingly reliant on Conservative support.

dine with him. Asquith's daughter Violet, whom he had packed off while he talked with the First Lord, found Churchill "standing at the bottom of the lawn on the river's brink looking like Napoleon at St Helena". Both Churchill and Clementine were low and distressed.

Churchill was now in an exposed position. Unlike Asquith, he had always harboured a liking for odd political groupings and was not inimical to a wartime coalition with the Tories. Back in London, however, Lloyd George told him bluntly that his days at the Admiralty were over. He was deeply unpopular with the Conservatives and heartily disliked by many in the Liberal Party. At a pinch he might be bought off with the Colonial Office.

Before he had time to consider this demotion, Churchill was plunged into a fresh crisis at the Admiralty. Naval Intelligence had concluded that the *Kriegsmarine* was about to launch a full-scale sortie into the North Sea. Churchill threw himself into action and, unhampered by the quarrelsome Fisher, ordered the Grand Fleet to set sail while at the same time submitting an acceptance of his removal as First Lord with a hint that he would be prepared to serve in another capacity "in the field". This was a bridge too far for many MPs. A typical reaction came from Sir Alfred Emmott, Churchill's fellow member for Oldham in the Parliament of 1900, who wrote to Asquith warning on 20 May, "I do implore you for the sake of the Dominions not to put Churchill [in the Colonial Office] … The effect on the Dominions would be lamentable and possibly disastrous. He has neither the temperament nor manners to fit him for the post."

Two days earlier the *Kriegsmarine* had returned to port. The moment of danger had passed for the Grand Fleet but not for Churchill. He continued to bombard Asquith with letters, as did Clementine, who came close to insulting the Prime Minister by telling him, "Winston may in your eyes and in those with whom he has to work have faults, but he has the supreme quality which I venture to say very few of your present or future Cabinet possess, the power, the imagination, the deadliness to fight Germany." On 21 May, Churchill wrote a six-page letter to Asquith pleading his indispensability to the campaign in the Dardanelles. On the same day Asquith replied, "You must take it as settled that you are not to remain at the Admiralty." Churchill's reply was characteristic: "All right, I accept your decision. I shall not look back." After he was ousted from the Admiralty, Churchill was given the sinecure post of Chancellor of the Duchy of Lancaster, retaining a nominal post in Cabinet and the War Council. However, in November 1915 the War Council was reconfigured and Churchill was dropped. On 11 November he wrote to Asquith, expressing regret that he would no longer take part in in the Council's deliberations. However, he had no intention of remaining in well-paid inactivity: "I am an officer, and I place myself unreservedly at the disposal of the military authorities, observing that my regiment is in France ... Time will vindicate my administration of the Admiralty, and assign me my due share of the vast series of preparations and operations with which I have secured us the complete command of the sea."

4

A GOOD AND SINCERE SOLDIER

The dominant image of World War I is that of the trenches, the interminable, seemingly static strip of murdered nature on the Western Front, stretching some 475 miles from the North Sea to the Swiss border. Even today, the words have a horrible ring to them, and in the years following 1918, set the men who had seen or served in that unique environment apart from those who had not. Such service left its mark. Something of the same shadow passes over the faces of German veterans of the Second World War when they talk of the Eastern Front. They need not tell you of the horror they witnessed. You can see it in their eyes.

By the end of 1915, the front line occupied by the British Expeditionary Force (BEF) ran south for approximately 70 miles, from north of the city of Ypres to the River Somme, and east, from Albert to the English Channel, for some 60 miles. Until March 1916 the BEF's General Headquarters (GHQ) were at St Omer, 40 miles east of Boulogne. On 18 November, Major Churchill was greeted on the quayside at Boulogne by the driver of a limousine despatched by his C-in-C, Sir John French, with whom he dined that night. French, peppery and sometimes inclined to panic, was on the way out. He was replaced a month later by General Sir Douglas Haig, a cool personality, virtually inarticulate in meetings, but a wily political infighter with the ear of King George V.

At GHQ on the evening of the 18th, French had offered Churchill the choice of remaining at St Omer as an aide-de-camp or assuming command of a brigade. Churchill, itching for action, chose the latter but with the request that he serve as a regimental officer in the line before being appointed to the rank of brigadier. Two days later he was attached as supernumerary to the 2nd Battalion of the Grenadier Guards, headquartered near Neuve Chapelle, to familiarise himself with trench warfare, an abrupt change from the hot water, clean linen and champagne of St Omer. Sixteen years had passed since Churchill had experienced field soldiering in South Africa, but he nevertheless presented a characteristically brave face about his new role, writing reassuringly to Clementine on 18 November: "I am sure that I am going to be entirely happy out here and at peace. I must try to win my way as a good and sincere soldier. But do not suppose I shall run any foolish risks or do anything which is not obviously required."

His battalion commander, Colonel George Jeffreys, gave Churchill a less than friendly welcome, telling him, "I think I ought to tell you that we were not at all consulted in the matter of your coming to join us." Jeffreys' adjutant added, "I am afraid we have had to cut your kit rather... We have found a servant for you, who is carrying a spare pair of socks and your shaving gear." On the 21st, Churchill wrote to Clementine requesting the immediate despatch of the following items:

> 1. Warm brown leather waistcoat 2. A pair of trench wading boots, brown leather bottoms and waterproof canvas tops coming right up to the thigh 3. A periscope (most important) 4. A sheepskin sleeping bag; that will either carry kit or let me sleep in it. Bertram [a servant] will advise you on all these. In addition please send me 2 pairs of khaki trousers, I pair of my brown button boots, three small face towels. Voilà tout.

Churchill added that the little brown pillow he had taken to France was "a boon and a pet" and observed that with the fading of the light the artillery fire was dying was dying away to be replaced by machine gun and rifle exchanges. He concluded, "I am writing from a dugout a few hundred yards behind the trench where the Colonel and adjutant are... I am so glad to be free of worry and vexation." Two days later Churchill turned his attention to the inner man, requesting "Sardines, chocolate, potted meats" to supplement his rations. On the 27th he asked for "2 bottles of my old brandy and a bottle of peach brandy". A month later he wrote, "... the sort of things I want you to send me are these - large slabs of corned beef: Stilton cheeses: cream: hams: sardines – dried fruits; you might also try a big beef steak pie; but not tinned grouse or fancy tinned things."

Churchill may have got his Stilton and sardines but he never got a brigade. French's successor, Douglas Haig, was scrupulously correct in his dealings with Churchill but the promotion to brigadier never materialised, a source of constant resentment amounting to near obsession with the former First Lord. Initially, Churchill spent much of his time kicking his heels at St Omer. On 19 December he said goodbye to French, picnicking with him in a country cottage before the Field Marshal returned to England to assume command of the British home forces. In these idle weeks Churchill cemented new relationships which were to last a lifetime. The first was with the ebullient Canadian Sir Max Aitken, honorary colonel in the Canadian Army, entrepreneur, newspaperman and founder of the Canadian War Memorial Fund which promoted war artists and photographers. Aitken had established an unofficial Canadian War Office near St Omer, where he was able to cosset and flatter Churchill, much to the subsequent disapproval of Clementine, who was keenly aware of her husband's occasional weakness for mountebanks and bounders, of which Aitken was certainly one.

Churchill forged another new friendship with the 30-year-old Edward Spears,[13] born to Anglo-Jewish parents in France and a captain with the Royal Irish Hussars. Spears was an exotic creature in the British Army, publishing in 1906 an English

---

13. In 1918 Spears changed his surname from Spiers to Spears.

translation of a French general's book, *Lessons of the Russo-Japanese War*, and later working at the War Office to develop an Anglo-French codebook. In August 1914, he found his niche on the Western Front as a fluently bilingual liaison officer with the Allied High Command. In 1915 he was made a Chevalier de la Légion d'honneur and awarded the Military Cross. In December 1915, while attached to the French Tenth Army in front of Arras, he was assigned to accompany Churchill on a tour of the French front. Churchill was captivated by the young officer who, like himself, was a spellbinding conversationalist but shrewdly able to hold himself in check while his senior companion pontificated.

On 5 December, while with Spears at Arras, Churchill was presented with a French grey-blue Adrian steel helmet, three million of which had been made by Christmas 1915. Throughout his long life, Churchill favoured mildly eccentric items of headgear which set him apart from the crowd, but the Adrian provided barely adequate protection in the trenches. The British had tested the helmet and concluded that the metal of which it was made was of poor quality and might stop three shrapnel balls out of four. Nevertheless, a 1916 photograph survives of Churchill, now a colonel commanding 6th Royal Scots Fusiliers, sporting his Adrian alongside his second-in-command, Major Sir Archibald Sinclair. Both men are striking sombre martial poses and, tightly buttoned up in their trenchcoats, resemble bronze statues frozen on the parade ground. One item of regimental headgear, the Glengarry cap, did not find favour with Churchill. Trying it on in front of a mirror, Churchill chuckled, swore and promptly discarded it.

Churchill also used some of his initial time at the front to good effect by writing and despatching to GHQ a grandiose paper entitled "Variants on the Offensive", suggesting a number of innovations to break the deadlock which by now had gripped the Western Front. One section, "Attack by Armour", advocated the employment of caterpillar-tracked "landships", which he indicated were already being developed in England, combined with infantry advancing behind armoured shields. Haig read the paper in December 1915 and took note of it during his assumption of command in France, despatching a Royal Engineers officer at GHQ, Major Hugh Elles, to observe the trials of the second prototype, nicknamed "Big Willie", at Hatfield Park. The armoured vehicle's specifications required "Big Willie" to cross a trench 2.4 metres (8 feet) wide and climb a parapet 1.4 metres (4ft 6in) high. To meet these requirements, the rhomboidal "Big Willie" was designed with tracks running round the top of its hull, a low centre of gravity and armed with two naval 6pdr guns installed in sponsons (half turrets) on each side of the hull. "Big Willie" passed its trials with flying colours, although it was dismissed by Lord Kitchener, Secretary of State for War, as "a pretty mechanical toy". Haig begged to differ and urged the speediest possible use of the weapon, now code-named "tank" because without its guns it looked like a water carrier. Appropriately renamed "Mother", the Mark I tank was soon to be tested in battle on 15 September 1916 at the battle of Flers Courcelette.

By then, Churchill's time in the trenches was over, but not before he had been exposed to conditions on the front line. On 5 January 1916, he arrived at Meteren, five miles short of the Belgian frontier, and ten miles from the front line, to take command of the 6th (Service) Battalion, Royal Scots Fusiliers, with the rank of colonel and bringing with him a bath and boiler, strictly a breach of military etiquette but an acknowledgement of an essential adjunct to his life at home and abroad until the end of his life. The bath was little more than an enlarged soap dish, but it was subsequently continually borrowed by Churchill's fellow-officers.

Churchill and his small staff were billeted in the village of Moolenacker for just under three weeks. The battalion's orders were to hold 1,000 yards of the front line at the centre of which was the village of Ploegsteert, famously dubbed "Plugstreet" by the British troops. As battalion commander, Churchill was initially based either at a hospice in Moolenacker run by the Sisters of Zion or at the nearby Laurence Farm, which was closer to the front line and thus the battalion's advanced headquarters.

The Fusiliers had suffered heavy casualties at the Battle of Loos at the end of September in 1915 and subsequently had a grim time in the Ypres salient. Morale was low, and Churchill wrote to Clementine, in oddly contradictory terms, the next day: "This regiment is pathetic. The young officers are all small middle class Scotsmen – very brave and willing and intelligent; but of course all quite new to soldiering. All the seniors and all the professionals have fallen. I have spent the morning watching each company in turn drill and handle their arms. They are very good. The mess is also well managed – much better than with the Grenadiers. The regiment is full of life and strength and I believe that I shall be a help to them." Churchill's second-in-command was Major Sir Archibald Sinclair, a Life Guard and future member of Churchill's wartime government. Churchill had wanted Edward Spears to step into this role, but Spears, a staff officer liaison man to his fingertips, would have been quite unsuitable for the role.

Churchill's arrival was greeted with some suspicion by the officers and men of the Royal Scots. One of the junior officers, Captain A.D. Gibb, reflected in his 1924 memoir, *With Winston Churchill at the Front*: "Everybody liked the old CO, and nobody could see why any prominent outsider should come in and usurp his place so easily. Why could not Churchill have gone to the Argylls[14] if he must have a Scottish regiment!" The immediate arrival of senior staff officers from Divisional Headquarters, the despised "red tabs", did little to endear Churchill to his new command.

At 1430hrs on the day of his arrival Churchill convened all his officers in Orderly Room No.1 of the Battalion HQ, an unkempt farmhouse. After the officers had said their farewells to the departing colonel, Churchill sank into a chair and observed the individuals under his command intently as they stepped up one by one, saluted and stood to attention. There was no small talk and

---

14. The Argyll and Sutherland Highlanders

Gibb prayed fervently that this prolonged ordeal would come to an end as swiftly as possible.

Things did not improve the next day at a second meeting in which Churchill "declared war" on the lice which infested the front-line trenches and billets. Nevertheless, within two weeks the battalion had smartened up considerably and had begun to warm to their new colonel. Gibb later recalled: "All the company commanders were invited to dine in the HQ mess and there learnt a little of the charm and courtesy of the man as distinct from the Colonel. No doubt he sought to win us, but for that he is only to be admired, and his capacity for coaxing and charming the best out of even the most boorish is a gift which I have never ceased to wonder at."

In a letter written a week later to Clementine, Churchill observed of his new command: "Yesterday I spent seeing all the officers and NCOs, company by company, and explaining to them how I wish things to be done. It was odd to see these politicians of a year ago – Glasgow grocers, fitters, miners – All Trade Unionists probably, who I have harangued in bygone days in the St Andrews Hall – now transformed into Sergeants and corporals stiffened by discipline and hardened by war into a fine set of warriors. In the morning Archie [Sinclair] practised bomb-throwing. It is a job to be approached gingerly. You pull out the safety pin and as long as you hold the bomb in your hand nothing happens... As soon as you have thrown it, you bob down behind the parapet,[15] until the explosion has occurred... Everyone has to learn. It is perfectly simple and safe as long as you do it right."

Churchill encouraged the men to sing on the march and was notably relaxed when dealing with them on parade, asking one old lag in the rear rank, "What is your age?" The reply was "41 sir," prompting the observation, "41? An excellent age. It is my own."

---

15. In Flanders, where the water table was high, the trench was some three feet deep topped by an eight-foot wall of sandbags to provide cover against snipers.

Initially, company parades were rendered shambolic by Churchill's insistence on barking out cavalry orders.

Nevertheless, his relations with the rank and file in his regiment were marked by his sympathetic attitude and genuine warmth, unclouded by the condescension displayed by many regular officers. With fellow officers, he was remarkably frank about incidents in his earlier career, happy to discuss events at Antwerp in 1914, arguing his case over the disaster in the Dardanelles in the following year and recalling debating duels in the House of Commons. Nevertheless, he remained somewhat bitter when the subject of Prime Minister Asquith came up, an opinion shared by many of his colleagues at the front. He was happy to entertain his audience with tales of the explosive Admiral Fisher, a "ferocious brute" but the type of warrior Britain needed to win the war. He was less complimentary about Lord Kitchener, not the relentless military machine of the public imagination but nevertheless "a very nice old cup of tea".

On the Western Front, as a rule of thumb, an infantryman would spend about a week a month in the forward fire and support trenches and one week in the reserve lines. The rest of the time he spent behind the line. On 27 January, Churchill led his battalion into the trenches in front of the Belgian border at Plugstreet. This marked the beginning of his real Great War soldiering, which was interrupted on 6 March by the two weeks' leave he requested in England to attend to his parliamentary duties in Westminster. At this point in the war, the Western Front was relatively quiet, although the chance of sudden and random death in the front line was ever-present. Mortar shells lobbed across no man's land were a constant threat, as was sniper fire. Neither seemed to cause Churchill much concern. On one occasion, Gibb recalled, he encountered Churchill in the front line shortly after his colonel had ordered a heavy bombardment of the enemy trenches. Churchill immediately suggested they view the German response from the firestep[16] in the fire trench: "As we stood

---

16. A ledge on the forward side of the trench used by sentries and by all troops to repel an enemy attack.

up on the firestep we felt the wind and swish of several whizzbangs [German shells] flying past our heads which, as it always did, horrified me. Then I heard Winston say in a dreamy far-away voice: 'Do you like war?' The only thing to do was to pretend not to hear him. At that moment I profoundly hated war. But at that and every moment I believe Winston Churchill revelled in it. There was no such thing as fear in him." Churchill could be found in the front line at least three times a day, the last at about 1am in the morning. In wet weather he was invariably encased in waterproofs topped with his light-blue helmet. He was particularly obsessed with what he considered to be the correct laying of sandbags, prompting Gibb to muse that in another life he must have been apprenticed to a bricklayer or master mason, an insightful observation when one considers Churchill's later enthusiasm for the laying of bricks.

During his time at Plugstreet, Churchill entertained a string of distinguished visitors. One of the earliest was Lord Curzon, Viceroy of India from 1899 to 1905, who arrived on a freezing cold February day and was led down the duckboards to the front line. Another of Churchill's guests was the distinguished barrister F.E. Smith, later Lord Birkenhead, then serving as a Lieutenant-Colonel with the Indian Corps. Unfortunately, Smith arrived without the necessary pass and was arrested, occasioning an embarrassing intervention by Haig. Brigadier-General Jack Seely, commander of the Canadian Cavalry Brigade and the only Member of Parliament to serve on the Western Front throughout the war, was another guest at Plugstreet, playing the piano at a battalion concert and surprising the sardonic Gibb that here was a senior officer from whose society it was possible to derive some slight pleasure.

It was fortunate, perhaps, that Churchill's brief time at the front did not coincide with the bloodbaths which characterised British strategy in the spring and summer of 1916. The Somme offensive, which began in June of that year, had emerged as a plan at the Chantilly conference in December 1915. It was anticipated that a combination of "wearing-out" operations and major offensives would lead to a German collapse on the Western Front, but the German offensive at Verdun, launched in February 1916, eliminated the wearing-out aspect of the strategy and reduced the offensive potential of the French Army. Much now rested on the shoulders of the British Fourth Army while a wrestling match over its precise objectives on the Somme broke out between Haig and Fourth Army's commander, General Sir Henry Rawlinson.

In the spring of 1916, Churchill's soldiering was being played out at a more relaxed pace than the build-up on the Somme. Gibb provides us with a glimpse of his colonel in relaxed and mildly chaotic mood on a sunny day in the courtyard at Laurence Farm: "The Colonel sat tilted on a rickety chair reading his pocket Shakespeare and beating time to the gramophone which was being assiduously fed by one of the servants. The Adjutant was cursing and tearing his hair at a table in the open, over wind and weather reports and intelligence reports. The sergeant-major was preening himself in the sun. The other officers were lying about reading or sleeping ... Democracy and domesticity! There was something to be learned from the picture."

Churchill had returned from his leave to France on 13 March, torn between pursuing his military career and returning to his life in politics. At the end of April, Haig dangled the possibility of a brigade, but Churchill was no longer tempted by the prospect of promotion. However, his dilemma was soon to be resolved by routine Army paper shuffling. The depleted 6th and 7th Battalions, Royal Scots Fusiliers were to be amalgamated under the command of the colonel of the 7th, who was Churchill's senior. Colonel Churchill was off the hook. There was a well-lubricated lunch party and a farewell photograph for which Churchill donned his Glengarry bonnet. Churchill and Gibb travelled by train back to the new headquarters in Béthune, sustained by a large hamper of food and drink plundered from the battalion mess. Gibb produced a bottle of whisky, prompting Churchill to observe: "Whatever else they may say to me, my dear Gibb, at least nobody can say I have ever failed to display a meet and proper appreciation of the virtues of alcohol." Churchill's last night with the battalion was convivially spent at a restaurant, where the Colonel was the focus of both the soldiers' attention and that of the local demoiselles. On 7 May, he crossed the Channel back to Blighty. Gibb had the last word:

I am firmly convinced that no more popular officer ever commanded troops. As a soldier he was hard-working, persevering and thorough. The expected fireworks never came off. He was out to work at tiresome but indispensable detail and to make his unit efficient in ... the very highest possible degree. I say nothing of his tactical and strategic ability – these were not tested in our time, but I cannot conceive that exceptionally creative and fertile brain failing in any sphere of human activity to which it was applied. And moreover he loved soldiering; it lay very near ... his heart and I think he could have been a very great soldier... No man was ever kinder to his subordinates and no commanding officer I have ever encountered was half so kind.

On his return from France, Churchill fully expected to return to the Cabinet. In the meantime he precipitately threw himself back into politics. Any debate in the Commons which concerned the general conduct of the war demanded his attention. His experience in the front line had impressed on him the marked distinction between those serving in the trenches and the staff officers, the hated "red tabs", safe in the rear areas. Much of what he said on this and other subjects was true, but its effect was vitiated by the frequency with which he spoke. In addition, he remained extremely defensive about his record as First Lord of the Admiralty. It would seem that everything was fine up to his departure. Thereafter everything had swiftly gone downhill. It was quite easy to derail him in full flow in the Commons by shouting "What about the Dardanelles?" He rapidly became equally unpopular with Conservatives and Liberals alike.

Churchill's hopes of reinstatement were raised by an invitation from Lord Curzon to attend the first meeting of the newly formed Air Board, but nothing followed. The death of Lord Kitchener in the summer of 1916, drowned while en route to Russia on board the cruiser HMS *Hampshire*, created a vacancy as Secretary of State for War, which was filled by Lloyd George who moved over from the Ministry of Munitions. At Munitions, Lloyd George was succeeded by Edwin Montagu, whose recent marriage to Venetia Stanley, Asquith's inamorata, proved no barrier to holding office. Churchill was plunged into deep gloom and even contemplated a return to France. Rather than risking German "whizzbangs" he consoled himself with remunerative newspaper articles penned for the *Sunday Pictorial*, owned by Harold Harmsworth, Lord Rothermere. As well as rewarding him handsomely for his journalism, Harmsworth commissioned William Orpen to paint a portrait of Churchill, which hung in its subject's London drawing room until his death.

Churchill emerged from the Cromer Commission of Enquiry on the Dardanelles disaster with his reputation, if not intact, by no means holed beneath the waterline. He would have to wait until Asquith was succeeded as Prime Minister by Lloyd George before he was appointed to a ministerial position. There was no doubt that Lloyd George wanted Churchill back, citing his "his fertile mind, his undoubted courage, his untiring industry, and his through study of the art of war". Whether he wanted him back in his small War Cabinet, the successor to the War Council established in December 1916, was another matter. Here Lloyd George would have to ensure that Churchill's "more erratic impulses" were kept under control and a close watch maintained on his judgement to prevent him plunging into ill-considered action. At the moment, however, Churchill remained damaged goods, particularly to the Conservatives on whom Lloyd George depended. Moreover, Lloyd George wanted to be Prime Minister more than the saviour of Churchill's stalled career.

Churchill rowed his way back with a powerful speech delivered in the Commons on 10 May 1917, a significant date in his long career. It dealt with the U-boat menace in the First Battle of the Atlantic and the imminent arrival of the Americans on the Western Front: "Master the U-boat attack. Bring over the American millions. And meanwhile maintain an active defensive on the Western Front, so as to economise French and British lives, and so as to train, increase and perfect our armies and our methods for a decisive effort in a later year." On 18 July 1917 Churchill became Minister of Munitions, with Cabinet rank but outside Lloyd George's War Cabinet. It was hardly a heavyweight appointment but significant, nonetheless. Not only was Lloyd George aware of how formidable an opponent Churchill could be, he also appreciated that in contrast to many of his colleagues the new Minister of Munitions was a proactive, stimulating and optimistic presence, a boon rather than a burden to be supported. As Churchill had told Captain Gibb in 1915, war was a game that had to be played with a "smiling face". Conservative MPs reacted with alarm at the announcement of Churchill's appointment, but his time at the Ministry was subsequently judged a success. He slimmed down its complex bureaucracy and increased the pay of skilled engineers, but was impatient with would-be strikers. He dealt with this problem by persuading the Prime Minister to threaten them with conscription, a fate which most were happy to avoid in the spring of 1918.

A marked feature of Churchill's spell as Minister of Munitions was the amount of time he spent in France rather than at the Ministry. France, where he always felt at home, was where the action was, and inevitably Churchill had to be there. This was particularly evident in the spring of 1918 when the Germans launched what they hoped would be a crushing blow on the Western Front. As the German Quartermaster-General Erich Ludendorff put it: "The situation in Russia and Italy makes it possible to deliver a blow on the Western Front... Our general situation requires that we should strike at the earliest possible moment before the Americans can throw strong forces in."

The German High Command hoped to drive a wedge between the British and the French, the former casting anxious eyes over their shoulders to their communications with the Channel ports, the latter fixated on the defence of Paris. The offensive, spearheaded by storm troops, a new military phenomenon, began in thick fog on 21 March. The British Commander-in-Chief, Haig, had correctly anticipated the German strategy but had deployed most of his reserves in northern France, risking the security of Fifth Army – against which the main German blow was aimed on the River Somme – in order to insure against a less probable risk to the Channnel ports. Churchill was in France on his fifth trip in six months when the offensive was launched, visiting the headquarters of his old formation, the 9th Scottish Division. Churchill woke up to the sound of the hurricane German preliminary bombardment and was eager to stay to watch the ensuing battle. Wiser counsels prevailed and the combative Minister was hastily evacuated. Two days later he was back in London, where he briefed Lloyd George, the Chief of the Imperial General Staff, General Sir Henry Wilson, and Sir Maurice Hankey, head of the Cabinet Secretariat, in his flat in Ecclestone Square. Churchill was in a high state of excitement, at last back at the centre of events.

Within days he had returned to France at the request of the Prime Minister. Lloyd George wanted Churchill to meet Marshal Ferdinand Foch, the bristling spirit of all-out attack, who was shortly to be appointed the Allied Supreme Commander. Citing military protocol, General Wilson contrived to head Churchill off meeting Foch and steer him towards the 76-year-old Georges Clemenceau, dubbed "Le Tigre" by the French, and for the second time Prime Minister of France. Clemenceau was as ferocious a fire-eater as Churchill and was only too happy to whisk him on a tour of Allied commanders, including Haig and Foch, all the while conversing with his new companion in his uniquely fractured English. At Beauvais, they were put in the picture by Foch, who told them that the German offensive was rapidly running out of steam. Churchill was thrilled by Foch's supreme confidence. He recalled: "The worst was over. Such was the irresistible impression made upon every mind by his astonishing demonstration, during which every muscle and fibre of the General's being had seemed to vibrate with excitement and passion of a great actor on the stage." Silence fell before Clemenceau stepped forward to embrace Foch. Later they were joined by Haig and General Sir Henry Rawlinson, commander of Fourth Army, two less explosive attendees, who promised a stiffening of the sagging British line with French reinforcements. Clemenceau and Churchill then set off into the battle zone before Churchill, grasping the folly of exposing Clemenceau to mortal danger, brought a halt to their expedition.

Churchill had estimated that the war would last until 1919 but by mid-July 1918 the Germans had been fought to a halt before being thrown back by a series of Allied counterblows. On 11 August, Ludendorff tendered his resignation to the Kaiser, who refused it but nevertheless observed, "I see that we must strike a balance. We have nearly reached the limit of our powers of resistance. The war must be ended." Churchill was adamant that peace negotiations with Germany should not begin until it could be manifestly demonstrated that the enemy had been defeated and that the militarism which had led to war had been eradicated. As the end of the conflict grew nearer, the paradoxically conflicting sides to his nature became increasingly evident. He deplored the wasteful loss of life on the Somme and at Passchendaele but was in favour of the use of poison gas and was incensed when the Red Cross sought French help in attempting to outlaw it. He clashed with Lloyd George over the fate of the Kaiser at the end of the war. The Prime Minister wanted him hanged while Churchill urged that he should be spared, possibly on humanitarian grounds, a legacy of his time as Home Secretary, but also because of his exaggerated respect for European royalty and the divine right of kings.

At 11am on 11 November 1918, the day the Armistice was signed, Churchill was at the window of his office gazing down towards Trafalgar Square. Accompanied by Clementine, he drove to Downing Street where he offered his congratulations to the Prime Minister, with whom he had earlier clashed angrily over his role in any future government. Now all was smiles and Lloyd George asked him to return that evening for dinner with Birkenhead and General Wilson, an indication of the depth of feeling which existed between the two outstanding Prime Ministers of the first half of the 20th century. The dinner was to be an all-male occasion.

Clementine was left at home to celebrate war's ending with her children but without her husband.

In the longer perspective of world history, perhaps the most interesting period of Churchill's political and military career in the years 1914 to 1918, and immediately thereafter, was not his stewardship of the Royal Navy, nor his time in the trenches, nor his work at the Ministry of Munitions, but his reaction to the October Revolution of 1917 in which the Bolsheviks seized power in Russia and Vladimir Ilich Lenin became the leader of the new government. On 3 March 1918, Russian delegates signed a peace treaty with Germany, giving up Poland, Lithuania, the Ukraine, the Baltic provinces and Transcaucasia, releasing German troops for the spring offensive on the Western Front. For the next three years, Russia was to be torn apart by civil war between the "Red" armies of the Bolsheviks and the "White" forces of their opponents.

Russia's former allies in the First World War were drawn into what became known as the War of Intervention, a confused conflict in which the principal aim of its Western and Japanese[17] participants was the recovery of their investments, military and otherwise, in Imperial Russia rather than the overthrow of the Bolshevik regime, an impossible task given the size of Russia and the relatively meagre resources which they had committed to the task. Not so Winston Churchill, energised as always by conflict and sublimely unconscious of the war-weariness of the British by this stage. Lloyd George wanted to repair relations with Russia while Churchill was convinced that Bolshevism was a menace to the world. He threw himself into a harebrained scheme to support the Tsarist Admiral Alexander Kolchak's White Russian government, in Omsk on the South Siberian Plain, with two British battalions from Hong Kong and seize control of the Trans-Siberian railway. In addition, there were some British troops commanded by General Sir Edmund Ironside (later Chief of the Imperial

---

17. The Japanese had a particular territorial interest in the northern half of the offshore island of Sakhalin, which they retained until 1925.

General Staff, CIGS) in the ports of Archangel and Murmansk, respectively on the White and Barents Seas, and more in Southern Russia attached to the armies led by the White Russian General Anton Denikin. A chaotic situation was further complicated by the passage from Vladivostok to Prague of 70,000 men of the Czech Legion nominally under the command of Kolchak.

The evacuation of the Czech Legion in September 1920 brought an end to all but the Japanese intervention in Russia. For Churchill, the episode had stirred memories of Antwerp and, less happily, the Dardanelles. He had completely overestimated the West's ability to snuff out the Bolshevik menace, relying in large part on the opinion of Marshal Foch, who considered that "There is no great difficulty and there need be no serious fighting" in ousting the new Russian regime, advice which persuaded the US President Woodrow Wilson to add an American detachment to the Allied force. Churchill remained unrepentant. In *The Aftermath*, the last volume of *The World Crisis*, published at the end of the 1920s, he wrote of "not a wounded Russia only, but a poisoned Russia, an infected Russia, a plague-bearing Russia; a Russia of armed hordes smiting not only with bayonet and with cannon, but accompanied and preceded by swarms of typhus-bearing vermin which slew the bodies of men and political doctrines which destroyed the health and even the soul of nations."

Churchill's adventurism soured his relations with Lloyd George, who later blocked his chances of becoming Chancellor of the Exchequer, and earned him the undying hatred of the Labour Party, which had never forgotten Tonypandy.

5

A BRILLIANT, WAYWARD CHILD

The Great War had seen the rapid development of three weapons – warplanes, tanks and submarines – which were to have a decisive effect on the course of the Second World War. In the inter-war years, Churchill's political interventions also played a significant part, but not always a positive one, in their subsequent deployment in time of war.

In 1915 the Landships Committee established by Churchill when he was First Lord of the Admiralty marked a crucial point in the development of the tank. In the years 1918-1921, when Churchill combined the posts of War and Air Minister, his influence on the development of air power was equally dramatic, if less positive. With the arrival of peace in November 1918, there was a rapid dismantling of the air fleets amassed during four years of war. In October 1918 the inventory of the Royal Air Force, which succeeded the Royal Flying Corps in April 1918, boasted 22,171 aircraft in service and in store and 291,175 personnel plus nearly 350, 000 men and women in the aviation industry, which, as the war drew to a close, was delivering just under 2,700 machines a month. However, by the beginning of January 1920, 26,000 officers, 21,600 cadets and 227,230 non-commissioned ranks had left the Royal Air Force, whose strength had dwindled from a wartime peak of 188 operational squadrons to 33 in March 1920, with eight of these still in the process of formation. When Churchill became Colonial Secretary in 1921, *The Times* noted of his spell at the Air Ministry: "He leaves the body of British flying well nigh at that last gasp when a military funeral would be all that would be left for it."

In the War Office there was also disappointment for all those advocates of the role of armour in future conflicts. After 1918 the Army, starved of funds, disbanded most of its tank formations and was left with five battalions, and a wartime order for 6,000 Mark C medium tanks was downgraded to only 50 vehicles. After Churchill became Chancellor of the Exchequer in 1924, the Army Estimates were steadily pared back, and advocates of the armoured idea like J.F.C. Fuller and Basil Liddell Hart were studiously ignored. By the end of the 1920s the Experimental Armoured Force (later renamed the Armoured Force) had been disbanded. It was not until 1931 that a tank brigade was formed on a provisional basis. In November 1927 Churchill offered to support Liddell Hart in his proposals for the mechanisation of the Army and the abolition of horsed cavalry formations but was forced to back down in the face of strong opposition from the military establishment.

As Chancellor from 1924 to 1929, Churchill did not spare the Royal Navy, prompting a threat of resignation from the entire Board of the Admiralty and an intervention backing them from the Prime Minister Stanley Baldwin. The Navy fought off the cuts but nevertheless suffered long-term consequences. Warren Fisher, Permanent Under-Secretary of the Treasury, later wrote of the cuts to the armed forces:

We converted ourselves to military impotence. To have disarmed so drastically after the war was not unnatural, though possibly not wise. But the government of 1924 to 1926 had no excuse for further reducing our armed forces to a skeleton, as by then it was known that the Weimar Republic was in the process of reconstructing a disguised army on a truly formidable scale. This British government's tragic action formed unfortunately a model for subsequent governments.

Churchill also failed to grasp the potential threat posed by the submarine in the 1930s. He remained firmly of the "battleship school" of naval theory. He later admitted that he had "too readily accepted when out of office the Admiralty view of the extent to which the submarine had been mastered" and had not sufficiently measured the "dangers to, or the consequent deterrent upon, British warships from air attacks". He would have cause to regret this at critical moments in the Second Battle of the Atlantic, the longest single struggle of the Second World War, and the loss in 1941 of the *Prince of Wales* and *Repulse* off the coast of Malaya in 1941, sent to the bottom by Japanese torpedo bombers.

Throughout his career Churchill's drive and assertive personality inspired affection and misgivings in equal measure. In March 1915, the month after he had given the go-ahead for the campaign in the Dardanelles, Asquith had written to a friend, "Isn't it a pity that Winston hasn't a better sense of proportion, and also a larger endowment of the instinct of loyalty. He will never get to the top in English politics, with all his wonderful gifts; to speak with the tongue of men and angels, and to spend laborious days and nights in administration, is no good if a man does not inspire trust." Thirteen years later, in 1928, Churchill's principal rival in the Cabinets of the 1920s, Neville Chamberlain, wrote in a private letter expressing his mixed feelings about this force of Nature: "One doesn't often come across a real man of genius or, perhaps, appreciate him when one does. Winston is such a man ..." He went on: "There is too deep a difference between our natures for me to feel at home with him or to regard him with affection. He is a brilliant, wayward child who compels admiration but who wears out his guardians with the constant strain he puts upon them." A political opponent, Arthur Ponsonby, the Labour son of Queen Victoria's private secretary, wrote of Churchill: "He is so far and away the most talented man in political life besides being charming and a 'gentleman' (a rarish thing these days). But this does not prevent me from feeling politically that he is a great danger, largely because of his love of crises and faulty judgement. He once said to me years ago, 'I like things to happen and if they don't happen I like to make them happen.'"

At this stage in his life, with all is vicissitudes, Churchill had nevertheless reached a peak of personal contentment, at the centre of which was the family home at Chartwell in Kent which he had bought for £5,000 in 1922. Clementine's original opinion of the house, in a rural setting with fine views of Kentish valleys and the distant hills of the South Downs, was favourable: " ... I feel that we shall live there a great deal and be very, very happy." However, the house, dating back to the 16th century, was in a dilapidated condition and she feared, correctly as it turned out, that its restoration would prove expensive and lengthy. Much of the initial work, at a cost of some £20,000, was undertaken by Philip Tilden, a fashionable young architect who had previously worked on Philip Sassoon's house in Port Lympne. The landscaping, including a lake and much brickwork, shows the influence of Chartwell's owner and bears comparison with Hyde Park, the family home of his future wartime ally Franklin Delano Roosevelt. Thanks to two generous financial rescue missions by supporters of Churchill, in the late 1930s and mid-1940s, the house was to stay in his hands until his death.

A frequent visitor to Chartwell was F.A. Lindemann, who held the chair of Experimental Philosophy at Oxford University and was affectionately known to Churchill as "the Prof". Born in Baden-Baden to a wealthy Alsatian father and an Anglo-American mother, Lindemann had known Churchill since the early 1920s. A lucid but often wrong-headed exponent of wide-ranging scientific theory, Lindemann became an indispensable aide to Churchill, although the two men were not natural bedfellows. Lindemann had a crankish diet consisting mainly of eggs and, with the exception of an occasional carefully measured glass of brandy, was a non-drinker. Nevertheless, Churchill valued his unconditional loyalty and the succinct advice he gave his friend. Lindemann was extremely popular at Chartwell, where the quarrelsome side of his character was seldom on display. In 1935, Churchill secured Lindemann a place on the Air Ministry's scientific committee to consider the question of air defence. Here,

Lindemann clashed so violently with its chairman, Sir Henry Tizard, that the committee had to be wound up and reconstituted without "the Prof". In the long run Tizzard, the man largely responsible for the establishment of Britain's pre-war radar defence system, proved the better scientist, but Lindemann nevertheless retained his favoured position, for better or worse, as Churchill's scientific adviser.

In 1921 Churchill became Colonial Secretary. In this position he was faced with two immediate problems: relations with the Irish Free State, established in January 1921 with Dominion status similar to that of Canada, and a settlement with the Arabs in the Middle East. Navigating these potentially hazardous political waters brought him into contact with two remarkable men, Michael Collins and T.E. Lawrence, Lawrence of Arabia. During his time at the War Office, Churchill had played an important role in the recruitment and deployment in Ireland of the "Black and Tans", a paramilitary formation not unlike the post-war German *Freikorps*, composed of veterans of the Great War who were tasked with fighting terror with terror. The predictable result was the rapid disintegration of British rule in Ireland. Churchill, instinctively aggressive when challenged, dug in his heels, in spite of pleas for moderation from Clementine, who wrote to him from the South of France with remarkable candour: "It always makes me unhappy and disappointed when I see you inclined to take for granted that the rough iron fisted 'hunnish' way will prevail."

Churchill remained a hard-liner when it came to Ireland, although he had been a Home Ruler before 1914. However, he remained fearful that it was impossible to bring about any reconciliation within the constraints of Imperial policy. Any severance of Ireland's links with the Crown was unacceptable to him. The defeat of Republican terrorism had to come first, but victory in the battle seemed remarkably elusive. In *The Aftermath*, Churchill confessed: "The choice was by now clearly open: crush them [the Irish rebels] with iron and unstinted force, or try to give them what they want. These were the only alternatives, and though each had ardent advocates, most people were unprepared for either. Here indeed was the Irish spectre, horrid and inexorable."

Lloyd George then attempted to break the logjam. On 22 June 1921 King George V made a speech in the Stormont Parliament in Ulster, established in Ulster in 1920, which signalled a movement towards a truce in Ireland. It took effect in July 1921 and was followed by a meeting between British politicians, headed by Lord Birkenhead (the former F.E. Smith) and Irish delegates in London at the beginning of October. Among the Irish contingent was the 30-year-old Michael Collins, the "Big Fella", a superb exponent of guerilla warfare and a gifted negotiator. Churchill attended in his role as Colonial Secretary. Churchill got on extremely well with Collins, a famously "hunted man" whose elusiveness in the days of the Black and Tans reminded him of his own adventures during the Boer War. He invited Collins to his flat in Sussex Square and showed him the 1899 proclamation issued in Pretoria, putting £25 on his head, and comparing it with the £5,000 reward for Collins issued some 20 years later. In his biography of Churchill, Roy Jenkins suggested, albeit fancifully, that such was the brief bond between the two men that, had Collins lived, he might have become a valued member of the "Other Club",[18] but it was not to be. The Irish Treaty was duly signed in December 1921, acknowledging the separation of Ireland between the northern province of Ulster and the Irish Free State. Collins was a victim of the Irish Civil War that broke out between the supporters and opponents of the Treaty, which demanded an oath of allegiance to the British Crown. He was assassinated by anti-Treaty forces on 22 August 1922.

Churchill met T.E. Lawrence at the Cairo Conference at the beginning of March 1921. On the agenda were the lands beyond the Suez Canal between the Mediterranean and the Persian Gulf, in

---

18. The Other Club was a dining society founded in 1911 by Churchill and F.E. Smith which met in the Savoy Hotel. Churchill never let anything, even the London Blitz of 1940-41, interfere with his attendance at its meetings. Members included David Lloyd George, Sir Alfred Munnings, Robert Boothby and Oswald Mosley, the latter resigning in 1935.

particular Iraq, then known as Mesopotamia. The end of the First World War had seen the dismemberment of the Ottoman Empire. A huge area had been carved up into separate states, three of which – Mesopotamia, Transjordan and Palestine – were assigned by a League of Nations[19] mandate to British control. At the Cairo Conference, agreement was reached that the British ground forces in Mesopotamia would be largely withdrawn and replaced by a system of "air control" exercised by RAF bombers and fighters.[20] In these negotiations Churchill was closely advised by Lawrence, for whom he developed an intense admiration. Churchill and Lawrence had devised a plan for Transjordan and Mesopotamia before the conference began. They agreed that the Hashemite Prince Feisal, with whom Lawrence had worked during the capture in 1917 of Aqaba and later at the Paris Peace Conference, would become the king of a new country, Iraq, created out of Mesopotamia. His brother, Prince Abdullah, would rule a country created from Palestine west of the River Jordan which became Transjordan and is now Jordan. The quixotically patched-up creation of Iraq, split between Shi'ite, Sunni and Kurdish territories, was to store up problems which reverberate today. At the end of the conference Churchill was famously photographed perched on top of a camel beside Lawrence and Gertrude Bell, the distinguished Arabist and only woman attending the negotiations.

One post-war problem simmering away in the Middle East erupted in 1922 in the so-called Chanak incident. The Treaty of

---

19. The post-war international organisation formed after the First World War on the principles of national self-determination and democracy, which did not survive the upheavals of the 1930s.

20. Air control, the policing by the Royal Air Force of remote parts of the British Empire and those territories which had fallen under British control as a result of League of Nations mandate, was effectively the RAF's raison d'être in the financially straitened years following the First World War. It provided the service with a heightened profile and aircrew with operational experience. See *The Bombers* (1987) by Robin Cross.

Sèvres, a subsidiary of the Treaty of Versailles, had been signed with the Turks ceding territory in Asia Minor to the Greeks. Mustapha Kemal, the ruler of modern Turkey, drove out the Greeks, in the process isolating the British garrison at Chanak, in a neutral zone on the Dardanelles, and threatening access to the Black Sea. Churchill, his memories of the Gallipoli venture still raw, was roused to his bellicose worst, a sentiment not shared by the British people or the governments of the Dominions, who declined to plunge into another conflict with the Turks. Their reluctance was understandable as Churchill had failed to inform them of Prime Minister Lloyd George's commitment to the Greeks before he despatched the telegrams seeking Dominion support in action taken against the Turks. Fortunately, the Turks defused the crisis by agreeing not to attack the British zone. Five weeks later, the Lloyd George Coalition expired, a drama in which Churchill played no part as he had been stricken with appendicitis.

In the General Election which followed, Churchill was to lose his seat at Dundee. He ran a notably bad-tempered election campaign from a nursing home in London's Dorset Square, lashing out at all-comers including Bolshevik "baboons", the new Conservative Prime Minister Bonar Law, and his old friend Beaverbrook. In a press release he thundered against the press baron: "In the last years he has boxed the entire political compass from extreme Tory to extreme Radical according to caprice, and an insatiable appetite for excitement and intrigue has carried him hither and thither. His transAtlantic [sic] methods have been equally harmful to British politics and to British journalism. It is high time that it became the subject of proper publicity."

These metropolitan fulminations cut no ice with the good folk of Dundee, then a severely depressed area. Churchill's campaign was further damaged by the appearance at the hustings of a clearly inebriated Birkenhead. Clementine, escorted by the faithful Spears and wearing a string of pearls, fared no better and was spat upon by female members of the audience she attracted. Spears recalled, "Clemmie's bearing was magnificent – like an aristocrat going to the guillotine in a tumbril." Churchill, looking far from well, arrived in Dundee on 11 November, Armistice Day, balked at climbing the stairs leading out of the railway station and had to take the lift. Seated on the platform and bedecked with his war medals, he addressed an audience of 3,000 at the Caird Hall for an hour and a half, during which he was frequently heckled. A meeting in the city's Drill Hall lasted barely 45 minutes and ended in disorder. At a genteel gathering of 300 women in the well-to-do suburb of Broughton Ferry, he committed the cardinal error of attacking D.C. Thomson, the local news magnate and publisher in the 1930s of the comic magazines *Beano* and *Dandy*. Churchill castigated Thomson as a "man with a bee in his bonnet". Thomson's newspapers replied in kind.

Churchill came third, behind the Prohibitionist Edwin Scrymgeour, a candidate he fought on no fewer than four occasions in his Parliamentary career and whom he described as "quaint and hen-dim", and E.D. Morel, who took the second Dundee seat. Churchill was now the man in the tumbril but characteristically remained generous in defeat. In London, however, he reflected that he was left "without an office, without a seat, without a party and without an appendix". There was some consolation in his Companionship of Honour, conferred at the end of November, two days before he and Clementine left for five and a half months in the South of France. Here he recovered his health, completed the first volume of *The World Crisis*, which was serialized in the following February, and applied himself to Volume II. He made three brief trips back to England, principally to supervise the ongoing works at Chartwell.

In December 1923, Churchill was defeated in a by-election at Leicester West. In February 1924 he contested a seat in Westminster after the death of the incumbent MP, J.S. Nicholson. He fought a vigorous campaign as an Independent and Anti-Socialist, riding around the West End of London in a coach and four with a trumpeter on the box, a stunt dreamt up by a new acolyte, Brendan Bracken, a thrusting, exuberant Irishman. This time Churchill lost narrowly but the contest had propelled him towards the

Conservative cause, a journey on which he had been travelling for several years. In 1920 *The Times* had noted: "He [Churchill] has latterly become more Conservative, less from conviction than from the hardening of his political arteries. His Liberal velléités have dried up, the generous impulses of his youth throb more slowly, and apart from some intellectual gristle his only connections with Liberalism are personal." He rejoined the Conservatives after winning the seat at Epping in October 1924 in an election called by the short-lived Labour government of Ramsay MacDonald. Later renamed Woodford, it was the seat Churchill held for the rest of his life.

An intriguing political mystery coincided with the polling at Epping. The Foreign Office had released a letter, purportedly written by Grigory Zinoviev, president of the Communist International, to British Communists, urging them to launch a Bolshevik revolution in their home country. In the summer the Labour government had recognised the Soviet Union and signed a trade agreement with it. The Zinoviev letter, long recognised as a fake either concocted by the British Secret Service (MI5) or possibly Russian monarchists in Berlin, had no effect on the General Election, which was lost by Labour. On 2 November, writing in the *Weekly Dispatch*, Churchill commented:

From the earliest moment of its birth the Russian Bolshevist Government has declared its intention of using all the power of the Russian Empire to promote a world revolution. Their agents have penetrated into every country. Everywhere they have endeavoured to bring into being the 'germ cells' from which the cancer of Communism should grow. Great assemblies have been held in Russia of conspirators and revolutionaries of every race under the sun for the purpose of concerting world revolution. From the beginning, Britain, the British Empire and, above all, India have been openly proclaimed as the first and chief objectives...There was, therefore, nothing new and nothing particularly violent in the letter of Zinoviev ... to the British Communists.

In November 1924 Churchill unexpectedly became Chancellor of the Exchequer, the post having been turned down by Neville Chamberlain. He immediately showered the Prime Minister Stanley Baldwin, Cabinet colleagues and departmental heads with a barrage of memoranda and letters, all of them bearing his personal stamp and many of them dictated, a skill which he had quickly mastered and employed throughout the rest of his political and literary career. His time as Chancellor, in particular his decision in 1925 to return to the Gold Standard,[21] is now regarded as a qualified disaster, although at the time he had few critics. Among them, however, was J.M. Keynes whose *Evening Standard* articles, later published in the book *The Economic Consequences of Mr Churchill*, hit their target. Keynes wrote of Churchill's policies, "the whole object is to link rigidly the City and Wall Street. The movement of gold or short credits either way between London and New York, which is only a ripple for them, will be an Atlantic roller for us."

In May 1926, Britain was plunged into a General Strike which the Trades Union Congress (TUC) called after the failure to resolve a bitter dispute between the miners and the coal-owners. Baldwin despatched Churchill to manage a government-funded newspaper operating from the offices of the *Morning Post*, the *British Gazette*, but was careful not to give his combative Chancellor an entirely free hand while simultaneously removing him from the day-to-day management of the dispute. Judging from the *Gazette*'s editorial line, this was just as well. Churchill could never resist a fight and his message to the Trades Union Congress (TUC), which he castigated as "the enemy", was inflammatory: "I do not agree that the TUC have as much right as the Government to publish their side of the case and to exhort their followers to continue action.

---

21. The Gold Standard was a monetary system in which the standard economic unit of account was based on a fixed quantity of gold. It was the basis of the international monetary system from the 1870s to the early 1920s and from the late 1920s to 1932 and subsequently from 1944 to 1971.

It is a very much more difficult task to feed the nation than to wreck it." The General Strike was called off after nine days but the dispute between the miners and the coal-owners rumbled on until November, when the miners reluctantly went back to work.

It is interesting to note that in the summer of 1925 Churchill had been in favour of curbing the worst inclinations of the intransigent coal-owners by the appointment of a Royal Commission on the future of the coal industry and the payment of a temporary subsidy. When considering his many generous interventions to help the working class, one is often left with the feeling that they were characterised by a de haut en bas attitude, rather than any identification with the plight of those he was helping. However, when the crisis engulfed the nation in the General Strike, Churchill's characteristic reaction to being challenged was to go on to the attack, on this occasion against the TUC. When faced with a show-down, Churchill's overmastering urge was always to come to grips with the enemy, demonstrated dangerously at Antwerp in 1914 and later heroically in 1940. However, this was not invariably the best course of action. During the General Strike many of his Cabinet colleagues thought Churchill's behaviour verged on the reckless, prompting one of them to observe that the Chancellor thought that he was Napoleon. Churchill himself was aware of these character traits and would often defuse the tension they caused with self-deprecating humour. Two months after the General Strike was over, he was able to disarm his audience in a House of Commons debate when challenged by a Labour MP to pit parliamentary legitimacy against industrial grievances. Churchill's reply was at first orotund: "I have no wish to make threats which would disturb the House and cause bad blood." Then, after a pregnant pause: "But this I must say. Make your minds perfectly clear that if ever you let loose again a General Strike, we will loose upon you ... another *British Gazette*." He sat down amid gales of laughter.

In the summer of 1929, the Baldwin government fell and was replaced by a Labour administration with no overall majority but dependent for its survival on the goodwill of the Liberal Party. The

Conservatives lost 150 seats and became for the first time a smaller Parliamentary party than Labour. Churchill held his Epping seat with a reduced majority. Tom Jones, the Deputy Secretary of the Cabinet, has left a colourful snapshot of him on election night:

> At one desk [in Downing Street with Baldwin] sat Winston ... doing lists in red ink, sipping whisky and soda and growing redder and redder, rising and going out to glare at the [ticker tape] machine himself, hunching his shoulders, bowing his head like a bull about to charge. As Labour gain after Labour gain was announced, Winston became more and more flushed with anger, left his seat and confronted the machine in the passage; with his shoulders hunched he glared at the figures, tore the sheets and behaved as though if any more Labour gains came along he would smash the whole apparatus. His ejaculations to the surrounding staff were quite unprintable.

Churchill's loss of office was by no means an unmitigated disaster. As the election approached, it was clear that his time as Chancellor was coming to an end and moving him to another Cabinet post would have been an effective demotion. Remarkably, while still serving as Chancellor his writing career had continued apace. The fifth volume of *The World Crisis*, *The Aftermath*, covering the period from the Armistice in November 1918 to the Chanak incident in September 1922, had been published in March 1929, shortly before Churchill's fifth budget. No sooner had he finished work on *The Aftermath* than Churchill began writing, in the late summer of 1928, the autobiographical *My Early Life*, a short self-deprecating masterpiece free of the official documents which clog *The World Crisis* and his later multi-volume work *The Second World War*.

On 3 August 1929, Churchill sailed from Southampton on the *Empress of Australia* on a three-month trip to Canada and the United States. In Canada the Canadian Pacific Railway provided him with a special saloon car, a "wonderful habitation" according to its appreciative occupant, who wrote to Clementine,

"I have been wonderfully received in Canada. Never in my whole life have I been welcomed with so much genuine interest and admiration as throughout this vast country ..." After three weeks in Canada, Churchill spent the same amount of time in California, telephoning Clementine from San Francisco, hobnobbing with Charlie Chaplin in Hollywood and staying with newspaper baron William Randolph Hearst at his colossal folie de grandeur at San Simeon, a palace subsequently immortalised by Orson Welles as Xanadu in *Citizen Kane*.

Churchill's giddy progress through the abundant hospitality of America's West Coast was about to be interrupted by events on the East Coast of the continent. Before he had set sail for America, Churchill had been advised by Sir Harry McGowan, the chairman of Imperial Chemical Industries (ICI), to plunge heavily on the stock market in anticipation of the growth of his literary income. After touring battlefields of the American Civil War, he arrived in New York on 24 October, days before the Wall Street Crash. The onset of the Great Depression can be dated precisely. Since 1921 the American stock market had prospered as never before, and in the 18 months before the Crash had enjoyed a runaway boom. On 29 October 1929, the boom ended; share prices fell even faster than they had risen, and thousands of speculators faced ruin. The US financial collapse soon overwhelmed Europe. America's loans to Europe had already stopped; now America's purchases from Europe ground to a halt. World trade was more than halved within two years and unemployment soared, particularly in the most industrialised countries, notably Germany.

Churchill had speculated over-ambitiously in the months preceding the Crash, which brought him personal losses approaching $750,000. From being a potential source of wealth, writing became a means of survival, a treadmill rather than a balloon ride over the rainbow. Writing proved the Churchill family's salvation, but it was a close-run thing. Chartwell's interior was shrouded in dust sheets with the exception of Churchill's study and the family took refuge in a cottage originally meant to be a butler's residence, an expedient which Churchill's daughter Mary found extremely "cosy". Nevertheless, Churchill maintained a lavish lifestyle, renting for much of 1930 a house in London's Eaton Square. It was not until 1932 that he bought a relatively modest flat near Westminster Cathedral in Morpeth Square.

Churchill aimed to restore a measure of financial stability with a 40-lecture tour of the United States, which began in December 1931 with a talk in Worcester, Massachusetts, entitled "Pathway of the English-Speaking People". Disaster struck on the evening of 13 December on New York's Fifth Avenue when Churchill was on the way to join the financier Bernard Baruch and some friends. Crossing the road from Central Park and forgetting that in America traffic drove on the right, he was struck by an automobile. Although not life-threatening, his injuries were serious: head wounds, cracked ribs and heavy bruising. Churchill was taken to Lennox Hill Hospital where he remained for eight days before he and Clementine travelled by ship to Nassau where they stayed for three weeks. Clementine wrote to Randolph that her husband was very downcast on account of the three heavy blows he had recently suffered: the loss of money in the Wall Street Crash; the loss of position in the Cabinet; and his injuries in the accident in New York.

Superficial appearances to the contrary, Churchill, a diehard Free Trader, had always been an uneasy fit in the Baldwin's Protectionist Cabinets. The issue which more than any other isolated him from his colleagues was the status of India. After the First World War there had been a great deal of discussion about gradual Indian progress towards self-government without there being any significant change at any level to British rule on the subcontinent. Churchill's profoundly romantic Imperialism was viscerally opposed to the conclusion in 1930 of Lord Irwin (later Lord Halifax), Viceroy of India, that Dominion status for India was implicit in the 1919 Government of India Act, which had provided for a commission to review the question. In an angry article in the *Daily Mail*, Churchill fired a broadside against the so-called Irwin Declaration: "Against the perpetration of such a crime as the immediate granting of Dominion status it is necessary without delay to marshal the sober and resolute forces of the British Empire, and thus preserve the life and welfare of all the people of Hindustan."

In January 1931, Irwin released Mahatma Gandhi, leader of the Indian National Congress, from his imprisonment for defying the British-imposed Salt Tax. Churchill responded by resigning from the Shadow Cabinet. The dhoti-clad Gandhi was regarded with particular animus by Churchill. A month later, while addressing the Council of the West Essex Unionist Association, he declared that it was "alarming and also nauseating to see Mr Gandhi, a seditious Middle Temple lawyer, now posing as a fakir of a type well known in the East, striding half-naked up the steps of the Vice-Regal palace, while he is still organising and conducting a defiant campaign of civil disobedience, to parley on equal terms with the representative of the King-Emperor." In the same speech Churchill risked digging his own political grave, averring that he would not join any government "about whose Indian policy I was not reassured". These outbursts kept Churchill out of any consideration for office from 1931 to 1935, endearing him to the Conservative Right but alienating younger progressive Conservatives. Nevertheless, he assumed that with the passing of the Government of India Act in 1935, which gave India the title of Dominion status but not the reality, he might return to the Cabinet. But no offer came from the men whom he had so recently publicly castigated as political pygmies.

Churchill's intermittent bouts of misjudgement, which had so troubled Asquith, also placed him on the wrong side of Britain's government, establishment and the majority of its people during the Abdication crisis of 1936. In spite of the pleading of his wife and friends, his romantic and loyalist instincts placed him, at almost the last minute, behind King Edward VIII; too late to save the King but in plenty of time to further damage his own reputation. The twice-divorced Mrs Simpson was clearly unacceptable to the British Royal Family, the Government, the Labour and Liberal Parties and the Prime Ministers of the Dominions. There was every reason why the King could "not have his popsie", a question that

Churchill had vainly raised with Baldwin at the height of the crisis. On 7 December 1936, when Churchill pleaded for delay in the matter in the House of Commons, he was shouted down.

Churchill's political antennae had let him down him nine years before, in the 1920s, when he met Benito Mussolini, and arguably later in the early 1930s when he decided against an opportunity to meet Adolf Hitler. He met Mussolini on a three-week Mediterranean holiday in 1927, five years after the former Socialist and self-styled Fascist dictator had been asked to form a government by the Italian King Victor Emmanuel III. Mussolini's bombastic, nationalistic fervour appealed to Churchill who later told journalists, "Anyone could see that he [Mussolini] thought of nothing else but the lasting good, as he understood it, of the Italian people and that no lesser interest was of the slightest importance to him." He later wrote to Clementine, praising Mussolini as "one of the most wonderful men of our time". In a 1933 speech Churchill was moved to describe the Italian dictator as "the greatest law-giver among living men", claiming that "with the Fascist regime Mussolini has established a centre of orientation from which countries which are engaged in a hand to hand struggle with socialism must be guided." In an article written for *Colliers Magazine* as late as 1937, Churchill described Socialism and Nazism as godless creeds while professing admiration for Mussolini the nationalist with his "extraordinary qualities of statesmanship, his magnificent courage and audacity, energy, his resolute will, his sure grasp of the possible". This in part explains Churchill's almost complete silence over the Italian invasion and conquest of Abyssinia in 1935-6.

Churchill's blind spot to the Italian subjugation of Abyssinia also played a part in his failure to address the accession to power in Spain of General Francisco Franco, whose Nationalist cause was crucially dependent on the military aid it received from Germany and Italy. In times of peace the military establishments of the major powers are seldom reluctant to test their latest weaponry in combat conditions. This battle-proving can be achieved by proxy, and in the mid-1930s the Spanish Civil War provided a convenient arena for an exercise which marked a significant staging post on the way to world war. In July 1936, the garrisons in twelve cities in Spain and five in Spanish Morocco revolted against Manuel Azana's Leftist coalition government. Their commander, General Francisco Franco, had within a week appealed to Germany for help in ferrying colonial troops from Morocco to the Spanish city of Seville. The Germans responded with 20 Ju52 transports, artillery and ammunition, the first instalment in a flood of state-of-the-art weaponry which became the bedrock of the so-called Kondor Legion, a key element in Franco's forces. The Italians also sent men and machines in bulk to Franco's Nationalists while the Soviet Union came to the aid of the Republican government.

On the face of it, one might have expected Churchill to grasp the danger posed by a Nationalist/Fascist victory in Spain achieved with considerable German and Italian help. However, his deeply held anti-Socialist instincts and suspicion of the influence of the Communist Party on the Republicans overrode any inclination he may have entertained to urge an intervention in Spain to check the support given to Franco by the Germans and Italians. It was not until March 1938, when the fate of the Republican government had been effectively sealed, that he pointed out the dangers of a Nazi-backed victory in Spain. This paradox underlay Churchill's growing obsession with the threat posed by Germany in the mid-to-late 1930s which distorted his focus on events on the global periphery, not least in the Far East, where he continued to discount the danger posed by Japan. In this he was not alone, and the reckoning was not to come until 15 February 1942 with the fall of Singapore to General Tomoyuki Yamashita's 25th Army, the single greatest disaster inflicted on Britain's Imperial Army.

The meeting that never was with Adolf Hitler can be dated to September 1932 when Germany was riven by political turmoil and disintegrating democracy. The summer had witnessed a savage escalation of political violence which brought Germany to the edge of civil war. In July, in the run-up to the fourth of no fewer than five elections that year, there were 86 politically motivated murders as Communist and Nazi militias fought it out on the streets. This election also saw a Nazi propaganda innovation: a combination of films about Hitler and the distribution of 50,000 gramophone records of him making an "Appeal to the Nation". The Nazis had exploited the serious unemployment in Germany, then running at over four million, to devastating effect, winning 230 seats in the German Reichstag, a chamber with 480 members, representing 37 per cent of the popular vote. Churchill's son Randolph was covering these events as a journalist with the *Sunday Graphic* and was eager for his father to meet the new star in the German political firmament. Churchill père was in Germany at the time, principally to inspect the battlefield at Blenheim, scene of his ancestor John Churchill's 1704 triumph, after which he stayed for a week at the Regina Hotel in Munich, from the early 1920s the stamping ground of the nascent National Socialist German Workers' Party (NSDAP), the Nazis.

At the Regina Hotel, Churchill was assiduously cultivated by a man who had a hot line to Hitler. Ernst "Putzi" Hanfstaengl was a Harvard graduate and an art dealer with dual German-American nationality who had known Hitler since 1922 and had become his foreign press chief. The cultured Hanfstaengl, one of the more louche members of Hitler's bizarre entourage, had a snobbish disdain for the Führer's social shortcomings but nevertheless considered his boss "a virtuoso on the keyboard of the human psyche". In this he was correct. Riding the irresistible emotional surge of a mass meeting, Hitler had no equal. Churchill and Hanfstaengl got on well with each other and "Putzi" was invited to dinner. Churchill recalled:

... he went to the piano and played and sang many tunes and songs in such remarkable style that we all enjoyed ourselves immensely. He seemed to know all the English tunes that I liked ... He was a great entertainer, and at that time ... a favourite of the Führer. He said I ought to meet him, and that nothing would be easier to arrange. Herr Hitler came every day to the hotel about 5 o' clock and would be very glad indeed to see me. I had no national prejudices against

Hitler at this time. I knew little of his doctrine or record and nothing of his character. I admire men who stand up for their country in defeat, even though I was on the other side. He had a perfect right to be a patriotic German if he chose.

According to his own account of the evening, Churchill then asked Hanfstaengl[22] why Hitler was so violently opposed to the Jews, a question which killed the prospects of a meeting with Hitler stone dead. The two men never met, although between 1936 and 1938, during Joachim von Ribbentrop's time as German ambassador in London, the possibility of such an encounter was dangled before Churchill and each time was declined. Would the future wartime Prime Minister have proved as susceptible to Hitler's bogus charm as had a past Prime Minister, Lloyd George, been in 1936?[23] It is hard to imagine Hitler in 1937 pulling the wool over Churchill's eyes, as Mussolini had succeeded in doing ten years before.

There was a curious postscript to Ribbentrop's ambassadorship. On 11 March 1938, the ambassador and his wife were given a farewell luncheon by Prime Minister Neville Chamberlain at Downing Street, in diplomatic circles an unusual event. Also present among the 16-strong party were the Churchills. To add to the surreal atmosphere attending the occasion, the Foreign Office Permanent Under-Secretary Sir Alexander Cadogan received during the course of the meal a message informing him of the German movement into Austria, the *Anschluss*, incorporating it into the Greater Reich. When Chamberlain was informed of this embarrassing concatenation of events, he became extremely keen to bring the meal to a decorous conclusion. However, the Ribbentrops contrived to hang about for another half an hour, during which Frau Ribbentrop took the opportunity to suggest to

---

22. Hanfstaengl had the good sense to emigrate to the United States before the outbreak of war, where he became a useful source of information to American intelligence.
23. In September 1936 Lloyd George visited Germany and hailed Hitler's "marvellous transformation in the spirit of the people".

Churchill that he should not be so beastly to the Germans. This was the last time Churchill was to lunch in Downing Street until the outbreak of the Second World War. It was also Ribbentrop's final moment as the guest of the British Prime Minister. He was to be hanged in Nuremberg on 16 October 1946, 14 months after Churchill himself had ceased to be Prime Minister.

In the years following the First World War, Churchill was firmly of the belief that Germany should be allowed to enjoy the prosperity to which it was entitled by the undeniable ability of its people and also because before 1914 it had been an important purchaser of British goods and services. However, in March 1933, in the House of Commons, he made an observation which rapidly became notorious, "Thank God for the French Army." Adolf Hitler, a politician who five years earlier had seemed bound for obscurity, had on 30 January 1933 become Chancellor of Germany. British public opinion was in the main undisturbed by this ominous development and tended to be more hostile to the French than the Germans. A year later *The Times* declared, "In the years that are coming there is more reason to fear for Germany than to fear Germany." In his book *The Gathering Storm*, Churchill dated his recognition of the threat posed by Hitler and Nazi Germany to 1931. In the summer of 1928 he had played a leading role in persuading the government led by Stanley Baldwin to re-commit to the "Ten Year Rule", which ordained that defence planning should proceed on the basis that no major conflict was likely within the coming ten years. By the spring of 1936, however, when Hitler had marched troops back into the Rhineland, territory demilitarised by the Treaty of Versailles, Churchill told the House of Commons: "We cannot look back with much pleasure on our foreign policy in the last five years. They have been disastrous years ... We have seen the most depressing and alarming changes in the outlook of mankind which have ever taken place in so short a period. Five years ago we all felt safe; five years ago we were all looking forward to peace."

Nevertheless, in those febrile times Churchill's convictions were not always set in stone. In the autumn of 1937 his alarm about the danger posed by Nazi Germany had temporarily subsided to the extent that he could write: "Three of four years ago I was myself a loud alarmist ... In spite of the risks which wait on prophecy, I declare my belief that a major war is not imminent, and I still believe that there is a good chance of no major war taking place in our lifetime." Hitler was about to prove him wrong. The union of Germany with Austria (*Anschluss*) had been set out in 1920 by the infant Nazi Party, and on the first page of Hitler's semi-autobiographical *Mein Kampf* (published in 1923) there was a declaration that Austria must be reunited with the German motherland not for economic reasons but because "one blood demands one Reich." *Anschluss* had been achieved in March 1938. The triumphant reception which German troops had received in Vienna had immeasurably strengthened Hitler's hand.

The German takeover of Austria exposed Czechoslovakia horribly, a state created after the First World War from the ruins of the Austro-Hungarian empire. The Czechs, Slavs whom Hitler had held in contempt since his pre-1914 days in Vienna, offered a greater prize than Austria. However, any move against them was fraught with danger. A Franco-Czech treaty bound the French to support the Czechs in the event of any aggression and, since the British were allied with the French, armed conflict with Germany risked lighting the touchpaper for a European conflict. Looming ominously in the background was the Soviet Union, which also had treaty obligations to the Czechs and had indicated its willingness to help the French. But the Red Army had no direct access to Czech territory. Poland, deeply hostile to the Soviets, and pro-German Romania, blocked its passage westward.

Hitler pressed ahead. The web of alliances between the Czechs and his enemies to the east forced his hand. Moreover, Czechoslovakia's thriving industrial base, including the Skoda armaments factories, and its abundant raw materials, made it a tempting target. The three million ethnic Germans living in the Sudetenland, on Czechoslovakia's western border with Germany, gave Hitler a ready-made pretext to demand that they be brought home to the Reich. War seemed likely, a prospect that in equal measure alarmed many ordinary

Germans and Hitler's High Command, which was not prepared to contemplate a war with France and Britain.

Hitler faced down his generals, who backed off. Any lingering hopes that they might avoid disaster by mounting a coup against Hitler were then shattered by Neville Chamberlain. Tragically for the Czechs, Chamberlain believed that he could deal with Hitler. Somewhere in this extraordinary creature, he thought, there must lurk a man of reason, and that this entity could be coaxed, blinking, into the sunlight, if only Chamberlain could convince him that he could get his way by negotiating rather than going to war. Chamberlain, who had never flown before, now embarked on the first example of shuttle diplomacy. On 15 September he flew to meet Hitler at Berchtesgaden, then a week later at Bad Godesburg. It availed the British Prime Minister nothing; Hitler only increased his demands, before suddenly backing down. The British and French pressed the Czechs into ceding the Sudetenland. Mussolini then stepped in, appealing to Hitler to postpone a mobilisation and accept a negotiated settlement along the lines proposed by the British. This was the last thing that Hitler wanted, but he reluctantly agreed. At the end of September, a four-power conference was held in Munich. Attending were the Germans, Italians, British and French but not the Czechs. They were to have no say in the dismemberment of their country.

Chamberlain was given a hero's welcome when he flew back from Munich, brandishing a tattered piece of paper signed by Adolf Hitler. Hitler later said that Chamberlain was such a nice old gentleman that it would have been impolite not to sign it, but the truth was staring everyone in the face. Peace had been secured, albeit temporarily and only at the price of tossing the Czechs under the oncoming Nazi train. Churchill had been heavily involved in the unfolding crisis, meeting with Halifax, the Foreign Secretary, four times between the end of August and 22 September and with Halifax and Chamberlain twice in September. The meetings were frank and courteous, during which Churchill indicated that he was prepared to make concessions to the Sudeten Germans by granting them a measure of autonomy. However, he was insistent that if

Nazi Germany set foot in Czechoslovakia war would follow and that this would require close collaboration with the Soviet Union. Chamberlain would necessarily have to take the Soviets into his confidence. Churchill's strictures were politely ignored.

On 29 September, when Chamberlain was away in Munich, a meeting of the Focus Group, an early version of an informal "think tank", was held in the Savoy Hotel. Among those present were Churchill, the Labour Leader Clement Attlee, Archibald Sinclair and Anthony Eden, who had resigned from the government in February 1938, citing his differences with Chamberlain over the appeasement of Germany. Harold Nicolson, also present, recalled that it was proposed that Churchill, backed by Attlee, Eden and Sinclair, should send a telegram to Chamberlain imploring him not to betray the Czechs. Eden was unwilling to do this, as it would be interpreted as a vendetta against Chamberlain. Attlee also declined as this course of action would need to be first approved by the Labour Party. The meeting subsided into gloom before its participants, with the exception of Harold Nicolson, moved on to dinner at the Other Club, where they were joined by Colin Coote, then a journalist on *The Times* and later editor of the *Daily Telegraph*, and two serving Ministers Duff Cooper and Walter Elliot. Coote later recalled that Churchill was in a towering rage: "One could always tell when he was deeply moved, because a minor defect to his palate gave an echoing timbre to his voice. On this occasion it was not an echo but a supersonic boom. How, he asked, could honourable men with wide experience and fine records in the Great War condone a policy so cowardly? It was sordid, squalid, sub-human and suicidal."

The "squalid" Munich agreement was debated in the House of Commons over four days during the following week. Churchill timed his speech for the third day, declaring that "we have sustained a total and unmitigated defeat, and France has suffered even more than we have." Chamberlain's exertions had not only failed to snatch the tempting meal from the table but they had also enabled Hitler to eat his fill course by course, a sally which prompted a rumble of dissent from the government benches. Churchill continued: "All is over. Silent, mournful, abandoned, broken, Czechoslovakia recedes into the darkness. She has suffered in every respect from her association with Western democracies and with the League of Nations, of which she has always been an obedient servant." In his next volley against the government, Churchill accurately predicted the death of Czechoslovakia as an independent nation, observing, "We have passed an awful milestone in our history, when the whole equilibrium of Europe has been deranged." The Western democracies had been weighed in the balance and found wanting. Churchill then fired another shaft which missed its mark. He claimed that Britain and France could have successfully gone to war against Germany in 1938, a moment in which the French military machine of Churchill's imagining would have prevailed over the German foe. This delusion, fostered by his brief time in the trenches in the First World War and still lingering in early May 1940, was dispelled after the debacle of Dunkirk. More accurate was his warning that the Prime Minister's desire to establish improved relations with the German government, as opposed to the German people, was doomed to failure.

Much of the ammunition fired by Churchill in his running battle with the government had been supplied by Desmond Morton, whom he had known since the Great War when Morton, who was then one of Haig's ADCs, was responsible for looking after the Minister of Munitions during his visits to the Front. When Churchill later became Secretary of State for War he found a place for Morton in Military Intelligence where he remained until 1940. On his own initiative, or possibly with the successive approval of Stanley Baldwin, Ramsay MacDonald and Neville Chamberlain – Morton's preferred explanation – he acted as conduit for the passing to Churchill of information, not always accurate but nevertheless alarming, about the German military programme, particularly that relating to aircraft production.

Another invaluable source of information was Ralph Wigram, the much-admired head of the Central Department in the Foreign Office. Wigram was an immensely strong-willed character who at the age of 36 had been struck down by and recovered from polio. Before the illness he had been an accomplished athlete, but his recovery left him physically impaired. A junior official,

Valentine Lawford, recalled the handicaps Wigram subsequently strove to master: "head down and to one side, forelock hanging perpendicular, white knuckles pressed heavily on a stick for support – as if it were his stick and head and hand alone, with a laborious manifold motion, dragging first his back, then his thigh, then his foot along the echoing corridor behind them."

In November 1934, Wigram prepared a memorandum detailing the extent of German rearmament. He argued that an increasingly arrogant Germany was readying itself to wage an aggressive war and was building airfields which would enable it to strike both West and East. He correctly predicted that once the shackles which had bound the German nation since the signing of the Treaty of Versailles had been cast aside, Germany would turn its attention to the absorption of Austria and the penetration of Central Europe. To counter this, he urged the closest co-operation between the British and French governments to arraign Germany before the League of Nations. Assessing the accelerating rate of German armaments production, he predicted that by 1938 it would be too late for the British and French to act. Wigram died, possibly his own hand, in December 1936.

On 28 November the House of Commons debated the German air programme. Churchill had been provided with a sheaf of statistics prepared by Morton and Wigram. The Cabinet had met three times before the debate to discuss the expansion of the British aviation programme, which was strongly opposed by Chamberlain who had convinced himself that the information coming out of Germany did not justify any such action. It had been agreed that the expansion should be cut back by over 50 per cent. In the debate Churchill launched a stinging attack on the government: "To urge preparation of defence is not to assert the imminence of war. On the contrary, if war was imminent preparations for defence would be too late." Churchill warned that Germany already possessed a powerful and well-equipped army, but the imminent threat lay in German rearmament in the air. He then pointed to a major popular fear of the time, one that had been stated in November 1932 by no less a figure than former Prime Minister Stanley Baldwin, that "the bomber will always get through." Churchill added for good measure: "It is no exaggeration to suppose that a week or ten days intensive bombing upon London would leave thirty or forty thousand people dead or maimed, a civilian population in grave panic and millions driven out into open country. The flying peril is not one from which one can fly. It is necessary to face it from where we stand. We cannot possibly retreat." This powerful argument was echoed four years later by J.B.S. Haldane in his book *ARP*, the acronym for Air Raid Precautions:

> They [Hitler and Mussolini] would be prepared to lose half their air force to lay London in ruins. We may therefore expect an attack by successive waves of several hundred aeroplanes which would drop their bombs almost simultaneously. A bombing aeroplane can carry a load which varies from half a ton upwards. But we may take one and a half tons as an average. Thus a squadron [sic] of 270 planes could drop 400 tons of bombs, or nearly double the weight dropped on Britain during the whole of the last war, in half a minute. This would probably kill about 8,000 people and wound some 15,000. And this would be repeated several times a day, provided the enemy were willing to stand the heavy losses of aeroplanes involved. In fact, the knock-out blow might kill some 50,000 to 100,000 Londoners.

The irony contained within these apocalyptic predictions is that the most ardent disciples of the elusive knock-out blow were the senior officers in RAF Bomber Command, who from 1942 tried repeatedly to deliver it at great cost to its aircrew and to the German civilians they killed and, in the anodyne words of Professor Lindemann, "dehoused". There is an added irony in the fact that several of the RAF officers whom Churchill met on his visit to Mesopotamia in 1922 were the architects of Bomber Command's area bombing policy in the Second World War, notably Squadron Leader Arthur Harris, who became AOC-in-C

Bomber Command in 1942, Flight Lieutenant R.H.M. S. Saundby, Harris's wartime deputy, and Flight Lieutenant R.A.B. Cochrane, later AOC No. 5 Bomber Group.

In September 1936, Churchill had visited France and was taken by General Maurice Gamelin, the Commander-in-Chief of the French Army, to watch the annual manoeuvres. It was on this trip that Churchill met the politician Paul Reynaud, then a backbench Deputy representing a Paris district, for the first time. During his visit Churchill made a major speech in the Théâtre des Ambassadeurs defending democracy and civilisation, contrasting both with the creeds of the Communist Leon Trotsky and the Nazi Josef Goebbels. He was always happier lambasting the internationalist ambitions of Communism and Nazism than railing against the nationalism of leaders like Mussolini.

At the beginning of August 1939, Churchill was reunited with his old friend Edward Spears, now the Conservative Member of Parliament for Carlisle. Spears had been invited to lunch at Chartwell to discuss his book *Prelude to Victory*, an account of the Western Front in 1917 with a foreword by Churchill, which was on the point of publication. At lunch Churchill observed that his guest had written a book on one war when another one loomed large on the horizon. Spears did not allow this gloomy reflection to blight an agreeable social occasion. He recalled, "There is never a dull moment in the Churchill household, where wit and intelligent discussion of people and affairs combine with a background of peculiar charm into an expression of the best English civilisation in our time can produce."

After lunch Churchill raised the question of a visit to the Maginot Line in France which he had asked Spears to arrange for him. They were to be the guests of General Alphonse Georges, deputy to General Maurice Gamelin. Churchill was eager to meet Georges and interrogate him about the likelihood of a German drive into France through the Belfort Gap from the direction of Basel, violating Swiss neutrality. A few days later Spears was in France and was dismayed to find the country bitterly divided, its ageing military leadership demoralised, and the haute bourgeoisie among whom Spears customarily moved disinclined, after the German occupation of Czechoslovakia in March 1939, to be drawn into the murky waters of the politics of Central and Eastern Europe.

A few days later, on 14 August, he was joined in Paris by Churchill, and the two men lunched with General Georges at a restaurant in the Bois de Boulogne. Georges was an interesting character. He had been severely injured in the assassination of the King of Yugoslavia in Marseilles in October 1934, and permanently wore a glove on one of his hands. He had been advised to avoid flying but compensated for this by driving a Cadillac limousine at high speed. He was notably Right-wing in his political convictions and for this reason had been passed over for the highest command in favour of Gamelin. In an empty restaurant, as Parisians were on their summer holidays, Spears, Churchill, Georges and the general's aide de camp sat in a shady corner eating strawberries soaked in white wine. Georges agreed with Churchill that war with Germany was imminent, adding for good measure that it was the Germans rather than the British and French who had gained most from the Munich agreement. Hitler, he maintained, had always been bluffing. Moreover, the German acquisition of the Skoda armaments factories in Czechoslovakia and the Czech tank fleet presented a clear threat to France.

Churchill was principally preoccupied with the French Maginot Line, the fixed and fortified defensive system on the Franco-German border, behind which manoeuvre armies could, in theory, form and deploy. He was exercised by the fact that the line came to an end near Montmédy in north-eastern France and was thereafter prolonged by field works facing the forests and hills of the Ardennes. Spears vividly recalled this element of the exchange, noting Churchill's "pursed mouth, his look centred on the fruit on the table as if he were crystal-gazing. His face had ceased smiling, and the shake of his head was ominous when he observed that he hoped that these field works were strong, that it would be very unwise to think that the Ardennes were impassable to strong forces."

The next day Churchill and Spears were taken on a tour of the Maginot Line with its underground railways, subterranean concrete bunkers, communications tunnels, and cupola-mounted artillery and observation posts. Much of France's pre-war defence budget had been absorbed by the Line, the expression in steel and concrete of the trench systems of World War I. Its lack of depth, caused by the cost overrun of the ambitious project, was a factor that worried Churchill. Moreover, the apparent security offered by the Line, however illusory, had led to a complacency and inertia which infected every level of the French Army. Regaining the surface, Churchill and Spears gazed across a countryside disfigured by acres of dragon's teeth tank obstacles before driving to Strasbourg and a ceremonial lunch laid on by General Frère, the military governor and a grand mutilé of the First World War who was later to die of maltreatment in a German concentration camp. Throughout his visit Churchill had been struck by the prevailing air of calm aloofness which hung like a cloud over the garrisons of the Maginot Line, where the lack of any physical activity was all too evident. Churchill's impression was confirmed by General Edouard Ruby, Chief of Staff of the French Second Army, who was struck by the fact that on the Line "every exercise was considered as a vexation, all work as a fatigue. After several months of stagnation, nobody believes in the war any more."

On the 16th the two Englishmen met the French Army's Commander-in-Chief, General Maurice Gamelin, whom Spears had known since 1914 when he was a colonel on the staff of General Joseph Joffre, then the French Army's C-in-C. The youthful-looking staff officer remembered by Spears had become an urbane, well-upholstered commander, accustomed to the affable but dignified handling of important visitors. Months later he was to meet Churchill in less agreeable circumstances. On the next day Churchill and Spears were back in Paris. Spears had been struck by Churchill's seemingly boundless energy. Waking at first light, he had called his companion into his bedroom for an intense discussion before polishing off an entire chicken for breakfast, simultaneously summarising their discussions with Georges and

Gamelin with an incisiveness that the impressionable Spears found little short of awe-inspiring. Less inspiring for Spears was the apprehension of war which was now enveloping France. As he drove to meet friends in the south-west, he encountered a mood of resignation but little or no defiance. The French were prepared to defend their homeland but were not willing to go to war for Poland. Spears' gloom was deepened by the announcement on 22 August of the Nazi-Soviet non-aggression pact. He got no further than Perigueux, where he heard a radio announcement that the British Parliament had been recalled for 24 August. Troops were mobilising and men and horses were clattering through the darkened streets. The next day Spears drove back to Dieppe to catch the night-boat for England.

6

DEBACLE IN FRANCE

By the summer of 1939, two very different newspapers, the *Daily Telegraph* and the *Daily Mirror*, were calling for Churchill to be brought into Neville Chamberlain's Cabinet. However, his personal following in the House of Commons was tiny, the result of his unrepentant views on India and his miscalculation over the abdication of the King. He had squeaked past a vote of no confidence in his own constituency. Anthony Eden and his large group of supporters kept their distance, justifiably fearing contamination by association. However, the national mood was shifting. Chamberlain's policy of appeasement had clearly failed, and he wrote in his diary, "Churchill's chances [of office] improve as war becomes possible, and vice versa." Churchill's natural belligerence was now seen by many as an asset.

On the outbreak of war, Churchill returned to office as First Lord of the Admiralty, immediately ordering that his 1915 map be restored to the wall. His fortunes as First Lord were decidedly mixed. On 14 October a German submarine, *U-47*, penetrated the defences of Britain's most important northern naval base at Scapa Flow and sank the battleship *Royal Oak*. In November the German battlecruisers *Scharnhorst* and *Gneisenau* sank the armed merchantman *Rawalpindi* in the North Atlantic before evading Allied forces and returning to base. The score was evened in December when the German pocket battleship *Admiral Graf Spee* was bottled up by the Royal Navy in Montevideo harbour, in neutral Uruguay, and scuttled on the orders of its commander Captain Hans Langsdorf.

In April, the fate of the Allied campaign in Norway was decided by German dominance in the air, a factor to which Churchill had repeatedly drawn attention in the 1930s. Three days into the campaign Churchill gave one of his least impressive performances in the House of Commons, delivering an interim report on the fighting. Harold Nicolson considered that the First Lord " ... indulges in vague oratory coupled with tired jibes. I have seldom seen him to less advantage ... It is a feeble, tired speech and it leaves the House in a mood of great anxiety." The Allies withdrew from Norway at the beginning of May. Significantly, Churchill escaped censure for the dismal planning and execution of the Norway campaign. Nevertheless, naval losses during the campaign had been heavy, swelling a medium-sized military failure into a major political crisis at home.

Germany was now poised to sweep into Belgium and France. Chamberlain's lacklustre days as Prime Minister seemed numbered, but it was far from clear who would succeed him. In a public opinion poll taken in early April, before the unfolding of defeat in Norway, Anthony Eden was the favourite, closely followed by Churchill, then Halifax and, trailing in last, Lloyd George. In Whitehall mistrust of the mercurial Churchill lingered. Sir James Grigg, Permanent Secretary at the War Office, fretted that it was imperative that Chamberlain got a grip before Churchill arrived to "bugger up the whole war".

The debate on Norway in the House of Commons took place over two days on Tuesday the 7th and Wednesday the 8th of May. On the 7th, the Conservative MP Leo Amery delivered a fatally disabling blow to the wavering Prime Minister by evoking the spirit of Oliver Cromwell when dismissing the Long Parliament: "You have sat too long here for any good you have been doing. Depart, I say, and let us have done with you. In the name of God, go." On the following day, Lloyd George rose from his political grave to urge the Prime Minister "to give an example of sacrifice because there is nothing which can contribute more to victory in this war than that he should sacrifice the seals of office."

Churchill deftly completed the demolition job with panache. Nicolson noted that the First Lord faced a tricky task: "On the one hand he has to defend the Services; on the other, he has to be loyal to the Prime Minister. One felt that it would be impossible for him to do this after the debate without losing some of his own prestige, but he manages with extraordinary force of personality to do both these things with absolute loyalty and apparent sincerity, while demonstrating by his brilliance that he really has nothing to do with this confused and timid gang."

Only 486 members out of a House of 615 cast their votes, registering a Conservative majority of 81, in less dramatic circumstances a sustainable result but not one in which Britain's very future was at stake. On 10 May, Hitler invaded the Low Countries. Halifax had already excluded himself from the leadership contest because of his seat in the House of Lords, a decision he conveyed to Chamberlain on the morning of Thursday 9 May. That evening, the proprietor of the *Daily Telegraph*, Lord Camrose, was at Downing Street. He later noted his exchange with Chamberlain, who "had considered the question as to whom he should ask the King to send for, and had discussed the matter with Halifax and Winston [Churchill]. He was informed that the feeling in the Labour Party had swung against Halifax; but, in any case, the latter had said that he would prefer not to be sent for as he felt his position would be too difficult and troublesome for him. He (Neville) would therefore advise the King to send for Winston."

Churchill succeeded Neville Chamberlain as Prime Minister on Friday 10 May 1940 and formed a National Government, assuming the additional responsibility of Minister of Defence. This newly created post, with its wide-ranging but deliberately vague powers, gave him a largely free hand to shape military strategy without bringing him into direct conflict with his service heads, a factor which had limited Prime Minister Lloyd George's freedom of manoeuvre in the First World War. That evening Churchill, Attlee and Arthur Greenwood, Deputy Leader of the Labour Party, met in the Admiralty to discuss the shape of the National Government. Almost 40 years after he had been elected to Parliament, Churchill had achieved a lifetime ambition. At the age of 65 he was Prime Minister, taking over in the gravest of national crises. He had not been the choice of the King; his appointment was viewed with alarm by many in the Whitehall establishment; and he was not the choice of the Conservative Party in the House of Commons. In these distinctly unfavourable circumstances, soon to worsen, he nevertheless became the champion of an embattled nation.

In the spring of 1940, British and French forces were deployed in three army groups behind the French frontier: 103 French divisions and 9 comprising the British Expeditionary Force (BEF). In a Joint Declaration the French and British had agreed, on 28 March, that they would not make a separate peace agreement with Germany. The Franco-British Supreme War Council, extravagantly named in light of events in the coming six weeks, had anticipated that the main German thrust would be directed through the Low Countries as it had been in 1914, and indeed this had been the original German intention. But the plan had been changed in February 1940. The invasion of the Low Countries was retained, but the point of maximum pressure, the *Schwerpunkt*, was now to be applied in the south, through the heavily wooded Ardennes, which the Allies had considered impenetrable by armour. The complex French defensive barrier, the Maginot Line, running for 385 miles from the Franco-Belgian border at Longwy to the Swiss border at Metz, had been outflanked.

Between 13 and 15 May, Luftwaffe bombers, dive-bombers and fighters flew 1,215 sorties in a rolling series of attacks along a three-mile stretch of the River Meuse around Sedan, destroying the French Ninth Army, mauling Second Army and punching a 50-mile hole in the French line. At 1900 hrs on the 14th, Churchill received a message from the French premier Paul Reynaud stating that the Germans had crossed the Meuse and requesting ten more RAF fighter squadrons to hold the line. Eventually, ten more squadrons were added to the order of battle of the RAF's Advanced Air Striking Force operating in France. However, only four were despatched across the Channel, the other six flying from Fighter Command airfields in southern England.

At 0730 hrs on 15 May a stressed Reynaud telephoned Churchill to tell him "we have been defeated." Churchill attempted to rally his counterpart, reminding him that in 1918 the Ludendorff offensive had run out of steam after 40 days of heavy fighting, but Reynaud continued to insist that the Battle of France was already lost. At this stage in the campaign, Churchill's opinion of the fighting qualities of the French Army were still coloured by his own experiences in the First World War and the memory of the Miracle of the Marne and of Verdun. Now the leaders and men of the French Army were of an inferior calibre. Momentarily, Churchill reflected that in that war the Allies had survived similar setbacks but, as he confessed later, he had not yet grasped the speed and savagery of the aerial and armoured blows delivered by the *Wehrmacht* on the Meuse. By the morning of the 16th the German penetration had reached 60 miles, compelling Churchill to fly to France for a meeting with its top political and military leaders. He flew in one of three Government Flamingo passenger aircraft, accompanied by General Sir John Dill, recently appointed Vice-Chief of the Imperial General Staff, General Sir Hastings Ismay, Churchill's Chief of Staff in the Prime Minister's role as Minister of Defence, and Air Marshal Joubert de la Ferté, Deputy Chief of the Air Staff. As the Flamingo climbed into a bank of rain-cloud, the three men agreed that there had been many breakthroughs in 1914-1918 but they had all been stopped, often by counter-attacks launched from the flanks of the salient punched into the Allied line.

When they arrived at Le Bourget airport, Churchill and his companions realised that the situation was grave. The French officer assigned to meet them informed Ismay that the Germans were expected in Paris within a week. A flabbergasted Ismay noted that driving through the streets of Paris, "... the people seemed listless and resigned, and they gave no sign of the passionate defiance that had inspired the cry 'Ils ne passeront pas' in the previous struggle... There were no cheers for Churchill." By 5.30pm, the British party were in a magnificently appointed room at the Quai d' Orsay, home of the French Foreign Ministry. Waiting for them were General Maurice Gamelin, the French C-in-C, Edouard Daladier, the French Minister **of War, and the** dapper and diminutive Paul Reynaud. All three men **were** a picture of dejection.

Reynaud normally had the swagger and **drive which** often animates small men and was the closest politician **the French had** to Churchill, having long understood the threat posed by **Hitler.** Something of a political outsider, his stance was compromised by the views of his mistress Hélène de Portes, who supported the significant French defeatist political faction which now looked to an accommodation with the Germany.[24] Daladier, pillar of the centrist Radical Party and dubbed the "Bull of Vaucluse", was the quintessential French political insider. He had been Reynaud's immediate predecessor as Prime Minister, and in 1938 was one of the men who had signed the Munich agreement. Thereafter he was obliged to rely for his survival on the Right-wing elements of his government. Injured in a horse-riding accident in March 1940, he had become increasingly reliant on alcohol. The bull's horns, it seemed, were more like those of a snail.

Gamelin gave the British visitors a brief tour d'horizon, using an easel-mounted map which displayed a small, sinister bulge at Sedan. Amiens and Arras, Gamelin explained, were threatened by advancing German armoured divisions which might swing north to the coast or west to take Paris. The C-in-C talked, uninterrupted, for five minutes and was followed by an ominous silence, during which Churchill wandered over to the window. In the courtyard below, elderly *fonctionnaires* were feeding bonfires with barrowloads of documents as smoke swirled up to the sky. Churchill tore himself from the dismal scene to ask Gamelin, in his "indifferent" French, about the positioning of his strategic

---

24. De Portes never gave her side of the story as she was killed in a road accident in July 1940 while being driven by Reynaud, who survived the crash.

reserve, "la masse de manoeuvre". Turning to the Prime Minister with a shrug and a shake of the head, Gamelin replied that there was none ("Aucune"). Churchill was briefly rendered speechless by this revelation. Later he admitted that Gamelin's confession was one of the greatest surprises of his life and spoke volumes about the dismal lack of communication between the French and British High Commands. Churchill returned to the window to absorb this bombshell while Gamelin was pressed about attacking the flanks of the German penetration before concluding, with another Gallic shrug of the shoulders, that a counter-attack was impossible because of "inferiority of numbers, inferiority of equipment, inferiority of method".

Churchill later observed, "There was no argument; there was no need of argument. And where were we British anyway, having regard to our tiny contribution ... This was the last I saw of General Gamelin. He was a patriotic, well-meaning man and skilled in his profession, and no doubt he has his own tale to tell." In fact, Gamelin's memoirs, published in 1946, are singularly unhelpful on this vexed question. That evening Churchill and Ismay were driven to Reynaud's apartment, which they found in darkness. Eventually, Reynaud emerged from his bedroom in his dressing gown. Daladier was summoned and Churchill confirmed that agreement had been reached with the British Cabinet over the fighter squadrons. Daladier remained silent, rising from his chair to shake the Prime Minister's hand.

On 22 May, Churchill was back in Paris, again accompanied by Ismay and Dill. Personalities in France had now changed but not the dire plight of the French Army. Gamelin had been replaced as Supreme Allied Commander by the 73-year-old Maxime Weygand who had been Marshal Foch's Chief of Staff in World War I. Weygand had never commanded troops in battle but had a reputation for fitness and vigour. He was that very French phenomenon, a "political" general of extremely conservative views, small of stature and with a foxy face which reminded one observer of an "aged jockey". The Vice-President of the Supreme War Council, and Reynaud's Deputy Premier, was Marshal Philippe Pétain, the 84-year-old hero of Verdun and recently France's Ambassador in Madrid. However, in the spring of 1940 the Marshal's bearing was less than heroic. In the words of General Sir Edward Spears, Churchill's First World War colleague and from 25 May his personal representative to Reynaud: "Pétain still held himself erect but was now so very much older and in plain clothes which emphasized the break with the past ... but he seemed dead, in the sense that a figure that gives no impression of being alive can be said to be dead ... when occasionally I looked towards him he seemed to have not heard what was being said."

In the political game of musical chairs that bedevilled French politics in the early summer of 1940, Reynaud had assumed the role of Minister of National Defence and War from Daladier, who had become Foreign Minister. It was now clear that the German advance had turned north towards the sea. Churchill drove with Reynaud to the chateau at Vincennes, on the outskirts of the capital, home of the Grand Quartier Générale (GQG) headquarters of the French Army, arriving at noon.

Churchill initially found the atmosphere at Vincennes one of unrelieved gloom: "... in the garden some of those figures I had seen around Gamelin ... were pacing moodily around. It is the ancien régime remarked the ADC." Weygand, however, made a better impression, in Churchill's view "looking like a man of fifty". Nevertheless, his strategy differed little from that of his predecessor, namely a southward withdrawal to the line of the River Somme. Nevertheless, Ismay felt a glimmer of optimism imparted by the new French C-in-C: "He gave the appearance of being a fighter – resolute, decisive and amazingly active, in spite of his wizened face and advanced years. He might have been made of india rubber. One dared to hope that the Allied armies would now have the leadership that had hitherto seemed lacking." Before he left, Churchill, in a forlorn attempt at flattery, told Weygand, "There is only one fault in you: you are too young!"

Weygand, however, had proved less than decisive. On the 21st he had flown to inspect the French First Army Group to the north of the bulge in the Allied line, but his aircraft had to make a forced landing at Calais. There followed a muddled four-hour conference at Ypres attended by King Leopold of Belgium, Admiral Sir Roger Keyes, attached to the Belgian king but with no military standing at the meeting, and General Hervé Billotte, commander of First Army Group. The commander of the BEF, Lord Gort, arrived too late for the meeting but conferred briefly with Billotte, who was mortally injured in a road accident later that evening. Gort, bluff, bulldoggish and uncommunicative, was a much-decorated veteran of the First World War. He was patronised by his polished French counterparts, who considered that at best he would make a good colonel. He was now about to demonstrate a shrewder appreciation of the developing disaster than anyone else on the ground. On the morning of the 20th Churchill had despatched the CIGS Field Marshal Sir Edmund Ironside to France to order Gort to attack south to link up with the French at Amiens, a potentially catastrophic movement as the city was in German hands by midday. Following the Vincennes meeting on the 22nd, Churchill issued another directive urging action north of the swelling salient. However, by the morning of the 23rd it was clear to Gort, who had received no orders from Weygand for four days, that the projected counter-blow was mere wishful thinking.

On his despatch, to France in September 1939, Gort had been instructed to take his orders from General Joseph Georges, Allied commander of the North East Front and one of the few effective leaders in the French Army, but if any order imperilled the BEF he would be at liberty to appeal to the British government before executing it. In spite of his mounting misgivings about the reliability of his French allies during the eight months of the Phoney War, Gort, a dutiful Guards officer, had busied himself with the day-to-day training and administration of the BEF. At this moment of extreme peril for the Expeditionary Force, he appealed to the British War Minister Anthony Eden, who on the 23rd replied, "Should, however, situation on your communications make this [the Weygand Plan] at any time impossible you should inform us so that we can inform the French and make naval and air arrangements to assist you should you have to withdraw on the northern coast."

This exchange opened the way for the evacuation of the British Expeditionary Force from Dunkirk from 26 May, an operation made easier by Adolf Hitler. On 24 May, Hitler had visited the headquarters of General Gerd von Rundstedt, commander of the German Army Group A, to discuss the vulnerability of his flank and the fact that on the 21st, in the Arras sector, General Erwin Rommel's Seventh Panzer Division had been mauled by the Matilda tanks of the British Army's First Tank Brigade. Rundstedt was concerned that in the marshy Flanders terrain, which both he and Hitler knew well from the First World War, the Matildas and British artillery might inflict another. severe reverse on German armour. In turn this might compromise the German plans for the second phase of the Battle of France, the defeat of the French forces south of the Somme. The German armour was halted for two days.

On the 31st, Gort handed over his command to Major-General Harold Alexander, commanding 1st Division, and returned to England. Churchill meanwhile was travelling in the opposite direction, on his third trip to France and another meeting with the Supreme War Council. Accompanying him in Paris were Clement Attlee, his Deputy Prime Minister, Generals Dill and Ismay and the bilingual General Spears who, in Churchill's words, "could say things to the high French personnel with an ease and force which I have never seen equalled". Churchill, Attlee, Ismay and the British Ambassador were received by Reynaud in his room at the French War Office in the Rue Saint-Dominique. Also present was Pétain, senile and shuffling, Weygand, Admiral Jean François Darlan, C-in-C of the French Navy, Roland de Margerie, the head of Reynaud's private office, and Paul Baudouin, secretary to the War Cabinet, a sly defeatist who was already urging Weygand to make a separate peace with the Germans.

The campaign in Norway was the first item on the agenda. The French quickly accepted Churchill's proposal of an evacuation from the Norwegian port of Narvik before the discussion moved on to the disintegrating front in northern France. At this point it seemed to Churchill that the British and French High Commands were wholly ignorant of what was happening on their ally's front. The French expressed astonishment when the Prime Minister informed them that 165,000 men, of whom 15,000 were French, had been taken off the beaches at Dunkirk and then immediately voiced their concern about the marked British numerical preponderance. Churchill sought to reassure them by insisting that the evacuation would proceed on equal terms, "Bras dessus bras dessus" (arm in arm) while the British formed a rearguard. The discussion then moved on to the likelihood of Italy's entry into the war, the importance of keeping Spain out of the war and of maximising aid from the United States. By then Churchill was in full flow, striving to rally his sceptical but captive audience with the insistence that "we had only to carry on the fight to conquer ... If Germany defeated either ally or both, she would give no mercy; we should be reduced to the status of vassals and slaves for ever." The normally reserved Attlee then weighed in, asserting, "The British people now realise the danger with which they are now faced, and know that in the event of a German victory everything they have built up will be destroyed. The Germans kill not only men but ideas. Our people are resolved as never before in their history."

The meeting ended but was followed by informal exchanges in which Churchill's stern resolve was not echoed by the French. Spears acted as interpreter for Churchill while Pétain, detached and sombre, seemed serenely unruffled by the ongoing rush of military setbacks engulfing the two allies. Churchill noted that one of the French party observed offhandedly that the succession of reverses might in certain circumstances require a modification of Reynaud's war policy. Spears was then emboldened to ask Pétain if this would include the blockading and bombing of French ports already in German hands, to which there was no reply. Churchill later observed, "I was glad to have that said. I sang my usual song; we would fight on whatever happened or whoever fell out."

On 10 June, Italy declared war on Britain and France in a shameless scramble for the spoils of war. The next day Churchill secured another meeting with the Supreme War Council, this time convened at Briare near Orléans, as the Germans were within 50 miles of Paris and the French government was moving to Tours. Early in the afternoon the faithful Flamingo, with its escort of 12 Hurricanes, took off from Hendon. With Churchill were Anthony Eden, Dill and Ismay. Avoiding Luftwaffe fighters with a wide sweep over the Channel, they arrived at a sleepy provincial airfield to be met by a grim-faced French colonel who proved unresponsive to Churchill's smiling greeting, like someone meeting poor relations at a funeral. Spears recalled that the British party then drove a few miles "to a hideous house [the Chateau du Muguet] the sort of building the nouveau riche French bourgeoisie delight in, a villa expanded by a successful business in groceries or indifferent champagne into a large monstrosity of red-lobster-coloured brick and stone the hue of unripe Camembert. This was Weygand's abode where the Prime Minister was to sleep." Here they found Reynaud, Pétain, Weygand, and General Vuillemin, Chief of the French Air Staff and another defeatist, and the tall and awkward General Charles de Gaulle, formerly commander of the French Fourth Armoured Division and since 6 June Under-Secretary of State for War and National Defence. De Gaulle remained calm and phlegmatic but, according to Spears who was also present at the meeting, his companions sat "with set white faces, their eyes on the table. They looked for all the world like prisoners hauled up from some deep dungeon to hear an inevitable verdict." Spears, however, was immediately impressed by de Gaulle, whose "heavily hooded eyes were very shrewd, when about to speak, he oscillated his head his head slightly, like a pendulum, while searching for words... It was easy to imagine that head on a ruff, that secret face at Catherine de Medici's Council Chamber." A hint of the statesman to come, alternately magnificent and infuriating.

In the tense talks which followed that evening there were no reproaches or recriminations. Nevertheless, neither the British nor the French had a clear picture of the constantly shifting front line or of precise German intentions. As the chateau possessed only a single telephone line, housed in a downstairs lavatory, the confusion was compounded. Churchill urged the French to defend Paris, arguing that drawing the Germans into an inferno of house-to-house fighting would absorb much of their hitting power. He reminded Pétain of the night he had spent with the Marshal in his train in the German spring offensive of 1918 during the collapse of the British Fifth Army and how Pétain had restored the situation. Churchill also reminded Pétain of the words of the then French Prime Minister Georges Clemenceau, "I will fight in front of Paris, in Paris, and behind Paris." Pétain murmured that in those perilous times he had a strategic reserve of some 60 divisions and now there was none. The reduction of Paris to rubble would not turn the tide.

Weygand then attempted a summary of the military situation, as far as he knew it, and asked Churchill to commit the entire strength of RAF Fighter Command to the battle in France. This, he said, was the decisive moment. Churchill, mindful of the Cabinet's previous sanctioning of only 10 squadrons committed to the front in France, pointed out that the decisive moment would come when Hitler threw the full strength of the Luftwaffe against Britain. If Britain was to prevail, it was essential to keep command of the air by retaining Fighter Command on home soil. Returning to an earlier theme, the Prime Minister then called for a maximum last-ditch effort by the French ground forces to bring the Germans to a halt. He was told that the Germans' total air supremacy in the theatre, refugee-clogged roads, and the collapse of the French government and military command and control systems, rendered this impossible.

The strain between the two allies then broke through the surface. General Weygand let slip the word "armistice", prompting Reynaud to snap that this was a matter for politicians. Churchill observed that in the event of France's agony being brought to an end, the British would not stand in her way but would continue to fight on "for ever and ever and ever". Showing his frustration, he declared that if Hitler launched an invasion, the advice of his "technical experts" was that the British should drown as many of the invaders as possible on their way over and knock the others on the head as they stumbled ashore. With a weary smile, Weygand conceded that, in the event of an invasion, the English Channel provided Churchill with an excellent anti-tank ditch.

Churchill remained characteristically pugnacious, suggesting a series of desperate measures, including the despatch of British bombers to airfields in the South of France to raid the Italian cities of Turin and Milan. Reynaud, by now near the end of his tether – he was to resign within a week – tentatively agreed to this but the plan, such as it was, proved stillborn. Shortly afterwards, Ismay received a telephone message from Air Chief Marshal Sir Arthur Barratt, commander of the British Advanced Air Striking Force in France, that the airfields in the South of France where the bombers were to be based had been blockaded by the French Army and the local population, who had parked cars, carts and lorries on the runways. In the small hours, sitting over brandy and coffee, Reynaud told Churchill that, following a discussion with Pétain, Weygand had drafted a document proposing an armistice. However, he had been too ashamed to present it to the French Prime Minister. This was the last straw for Churchill, who reflected that Weygand was the man who had demanded the delivery of Fighter Command into the hands of the French after he had decided that all was lost. The British Prime Minister went "unhappily to bed in that disordered chateau".

The conference resumed the next morning. De Gaulle had left for the front and was replaced by Admiral Jean François Darlan, C-in-C of the French Navy, red-faced and nautical, his hands thrust deep into his monkey jacket. Reynaud begged for more fighters, Weygand for more bombers. Churchill informed them that their requests would be considered by the Cabinet on his return to London but repeated his warning that it would be a crucial blunder to strip the United Kingdom of its fighter defence. He then made three points: again he raised the question of the defence of Paris, arguing that this would enable the French and British to launch a counter-offensive on the lower reaches of the Seine; he urged attacks on the enemy's communications systems; and he held out the hope of the United States joining the war. His argument fell on deaf ears. Weygand said that he no longer had sufficient forces for an operation on the Lower Seine, adding that since 1939 the Germans had built 5,000 more tanks, an absurdly exaggerated figure which was supported by Reynaud, who sighed with raised shoulders and open hands, palms upwards, that France's only hope lay with the industrial resources of the United States.

Churchill's reply was solemn, measured and delivered twice for emphasis. If there was a fundamental change in the situation, the French should inform the British government at once before coming to a final decision. Talks would then follow at a location chosen by the French. The meeting was over. Before he left, Churchill took aside Admiral Darlan to seek his assurance that he would never let the *Kriegsmarine* get its hands on his command. Darlan solemnly promised that he would never do so. In the last resort he would send the fleet to Canada. Churchill and his party flew back to England through cloudy skies, depriving the Flamingo of its fighter escort. Approaching the French coast, the sky cleared and the Prime Minister could see Le Havre ablaze 8,000ft below.

The next day, the 13th, Churchill flew back to France, this time to Tours, in response to another telephone call from Reynaud. the Flamingo landing in a thunderstorm on a bomb-pitted airfield. Churchill, Ismay, the Foreign Secretary Halifax, Churchill's Minister of Aircraft Production, Lord Beaverbrook, and Sir Alexander Cadogan, the Permanent Secretary at the Foreign Office, then drove to the prefecture in Tours, where they were not expected. Characteristically, Churchill immediately sallied forth to order lunch. At the Grand Hotel, a miserable meal was made almost unendurable by the appearance of the insinuating Baudouin, oozing oily defeatism. The British party, which now included Spears and the British Ambassador in Paris, returned to the prefecture. Here they were greeted by Georges Mandel, the French Minister of the Interior. Mandel was eating joints of roast chicken while simultaneously fielding and making telephone calls, an energetic figure in the sea of gloom enveloping the French.

Churchill eyed Mandel's meal fondly. The fowl and the Minister of the Interior were swiftly removed and the final session of the

Supreme War Council got underway in mid-afternoon. Churchill and his colleagues were confronted with Reynaud and Baudouin, the first a forlorn figure, the latter, for most of the time a silent but a sinister presence who stared fixedly at the French premier throughout the subsequent exchanges. Reynaud began by announcing that the situation of the French Army was now desperate. He requested that the French be released from the Joint Declaration of March 1940. To Spears he appeared little more than a ventriloquist's dummy, animated, perhaps, by the hidden hand of Madame de Portes, who had tried vainly to burst into the room where the conference was being held. Inside the room, confusion arose when the devious Baudouin intervened to insist that Churchill's response to Reynaud's announcement, "Je comprends" (I understand) - made before it was translated – was a specific agreement to the French armistice rather than a frank acknowledgement of the dilemma facing Reynaud, now buried up to his neck under the disintegrating shards of French military and political machinery. On the interpretation of such nuances do world-changing events sometimes depend.

Churchill then suggested that he and his colleagues should withdraw to consider their position. For the next half an hour, they paced around a dreary courtyard dripping with recent rain, until Beaverbrook broke the spell by telling Churchill that he should once again insist that an immediate telegraph should be sent to Roosevelt and that no further commitments be made until the President answered: "We are doing no good here. In fact listening to these declarations of Reynaud's only does harm. Let's go back home." Back in the Prefecture, de Gaulle appeared and commandeered Cadogan's armchair. Churchill told Reynaud that he would be returning to England that evening to contact the US President with a joint Franco-British appeal. It was as if a weight had been lifted from Reynaud's shoulders. No separate peace would be negotiated until Roosevelt had spoken. Then he and Churchill would meet again to decide the way forward. If the United States entered the war, victory was assured, Churchill added: "It will be a war of continents fought across the oceans, and the enslaved nations will be freed one by one as they were in the last war." Before leaving, Churchill had one more request. Some 400 German aircrew, most of whom had been shot down and taken prisoner by the French, should be taken into British custody. Reynaud willingly agreed to this, but no action was subsequently taken by the French. The men of the Luftwaffe were soon able to fly against Britain. The conference broke up just before six o' clock. Outside the Prefecture, Spears encountered de Gaulle, who had played no active part in the discussions, but now told Churchill's representative that Baudouin was telling everyone who would listen, particularly journalists, that the Prime Minister completely understood the French position, enabling Reynaud to make a separate peace. Was this true, enquired de Gaulle, as this would give the defeatists all the ammunition they needed. Spears attempted to reassure de Gaulle, explaining the meaning which Churchill intended to convey with the use of "je comprends." This failed to convince de Gaulle, who observed that Baudouin "is putting it about that France is now released from her engagement to England. It is unfortunate."

On the 14th de Gaulle flew to London where he met members of the French Economic Mission, the British government's diplomatic adviser Sir Robert Vansittart and Desmond Morton. It was clear by now that there was to be no decisive intervention by Roosevelt, prompting a final British throw to keep France, or at least the French Navy, the troops in North Africa and possibly a redoubt in Brittany, in the war. The next day, at a luncheon at the Carlton Club, attended among others by Halifax, Vansittart and the French Ambassador, the idea was floated of an amalgamation in an indissoluble union of the British and French states. Initially Churchill, who was not at the Carlton Club meeting, was inclined to dismiss the idea, but on the 16th the War Cabinet fell in behind it. The subsequent 300-word document, covering common citizenship, a combined War Cabinet and armed forces and a vague nod towards a single polyglot parliament, was conveyed to Reynaud by none other than de Gaulle, subsequently the stern sword-bearer of French sovereignty, who immediately returned to Bordeaux.

The desperate proposal, one of the intriguing might-have-beens of world history, was not welcomed by Reynaud's colleagues; Pétain likened it to "being chained to a corpse". The British War Cabinet had clearly underestimated the grip that the defeatist faction had now gained on the French state. On the evening of 16 June, Reynaud resigned, the proposal having been dismissed out of hand by the French Cabinet. Pétain, now Prime Minister, then set about forming a government of capitulation. One of the first appointments, as Foreign Minister, was Baudouin. A final meeting between Churchill and Reynaud, scheduled for the 17th off the coast of Brittany, was cancelled while Churchill sat fuming in a train at Waterloo station. In the early evening the same day, Spears and de Gaulle arrived at the airfield in Bordeaux, where Spears was confronted with an extraordinary scene: "The aerodrome was filled with more flying machines than I had ever seen in one place before or since, packed wing to wing as far as one could see. It was evident that every machine capable of taking to the air had been collected, presumably in readiness to fly to Morocco. It was shocking to see them offering such a fabulous target. Since when had they left their armies? Why were they not taking off for Africa? How long had they been collected there like a great herd of flying sheep?... So this was the French counterpart to the RAF at Dunkirk, I thought bitterly."

After an agonising delay, de Gaulle and Spears clambered on board an aircraft and were soon cruising over the sea back to Britain. Below, Spears spotted a huge ship, *Champlain*, keeling over and spilling hundreds of men, many of them British troops, into the water. Eventually, the aircraft touched down briefly in Jersey. De Gaulle asked for coffee and, taking a sip, declared that the beverage was in fact tea. Spears later recalled that it must have been the General's first encounter with that tepid liquid which, in England in those days, passed for either one or the other beverage. De Gaulle's wartime martyrdom had begun.

Churchill was emerging from his own baptism of fire, bloody, unbowed and not without cost, as his wife reminded him in a letter on 27 June:

... one of the men in your entourage (a devoted friend) has been to me and told me that there is a danger of your being generally disliked by your colleagues and subordinates because of your rough, sarcastic and overbearing manner – It seems that your Private Secretaries have agreed to behave like schoolboys and take what's coming to them and then escape out of your presence shrugging their shoulders – Higher up, if any idea is suggested (say at a conference) you are supposed to be so contemptuous that presently no ideas, good or bad, will be forthcoming. I was astonished and upset because in all these years I have been accustomed to all those who have worked with and under you, loving you – I said this and I was told 'No doubt it's the strain.' My darling Winston – I must confess I have noticed a deterioration in your manners; and you are not so kind as you used to be ... with this terrific power you must combine urbanity, kindness and if possible Olympic [*sic*] calm... You won't get the best results by irascibility and rudeness... Please forgive your loving, devoted and watchful Clemmie.

7

AMERICAN FRIENDS

Franklin Delano Roosevelt took office as President of the United States on 4 March 1933 on the day that Japanese troops marched into the Chinese provincial capital of Jehol. On the next day Adolf Hitler was confirmed as Chancellor of Germany. Roosevelt was quick to grasp the threat posed by the ruthless expansionist policies of Germany, Japan and Italy. But deep-seated isolationist and pacifist opinion at home left him with scant room to manoeuvre, while the domestic demands of the "new deal for the American people" he had promised when he had sworn the oath of office dominated the presidential agenda.

In the election year of 1936, Roosevelt pursued a "hands off" policy during the Spanish Civil War while General Francisco Franco's Nationalists received substantial military assistance from Germany and Italy. By 1937, Roosevelt was deeply troubled not only by events in Europe but also by Japanese aggression in the Far East. Shanghai had been heavily bombed and Nanking pillaged. Roosevelt remained committed to peace but cast around for ways to bring international pressure to bear on Germany, Italy and Japan. In October 1937, in a speech delivered in Chicago where isolationist sentiment was at its strongest, Roosevelt warned that "an epidemic of world lawlessness" was on the march. He said, "Where an epidemic of physical disease starts to spread, the community approves and joins in a quarantine of the patients in order to protect the health of the community against the spread of the disease." The "quarantine speech" was interpreted as a new initiative in American foreign policy, the abandonment of isolationism and a direct warning to Japan. In truth Roosevelt's intentions remained ambiguous. When an aide asked him what precisely he meant by the quarantine speech, he replied, "I can't give you any clue to it. You will have to invent one." When on 12 December 1937 Japanese warplanes sank an American gunship, the USS *Panay*, Roosevelt was quick to accept Japan's apologies and an indemnity.

War in Europe seemed increasingly inevitable, but the United States remained determinedly neutral. Roosevelt's willingness to aid Europe's democracies was severely limited by the Neutrality Acts of 1935 to 1939, which prevented the United States from becoming embroiled in foreign conflicts. Nevertheless, the US government gave the British and the French the go-ahead to place large orders for aircraft with American manufacturers, an initiative which kickstarted a massive industrial expansion. However, an attempt by Roosevelt to modify the Neutrality Acts failed to make it through Congress. Events then took a hand. By mid-June 1940, Adolf Hitler was master of Western Europe. The British Expeditionary Force had been bundled out of the Continent. The expectation was that Hitler's next move would be a cross-Channel invasion of England. Anticipating this, Prime Minister Winston Churchill had appealed to Roosevelt for the loan to Britain of up to 50 elderly US Navy destroyers. Keenly aware of the political problems such a transfer might cause, Roosevelt's reply was notably guarded. He was seeking his third term and was unsure that he could get the measure through Congress.

However, the mood music was beginning to change. On 22 June 1940 Congress passed a National Defense Tax Bill and a month later voted $37 billion – more than the entire American cost of World War I – to produce a "two-ocean" navy and a massive expansion of the army and air force. Roosevelt was then nominated for an unprecedented third term. Isolationists charged that the President was dragging the nation into war. However, support for the British, now engaged in the opening phase of the Battle of Britain, was growing. In the following July, Churchill made another appeal for support, cabling Roosevelt, "Mr President, with great respect I must tell you that in the long history of the world this is a thing to do NOW." Roosevelt evaded Republican obstruction in Congress with an executive order, and agreement on the destroyer transfer was reached on 2 September, at the price of granting the Americans a 99-year lease on a number of naval and air bases in the British West Indies and Bermuda. Military preparations had now moved to the top of the political agenda in the United States. In September 1940, as the Battle of Britain reached its climax, Congress passed the Selective Training and Service Act to draft men between the ages of 21 and 36. At first the US Army was short of everything except bodies, but slowly the powerful production gears of the US economy began to mesh. Roosevelt was re-elected in November. When Congress met in January 1941 the President appealed to it to support the nations that were fighting in defence of what he called the Four Freedoms: freedom of speech, freedom of religion, freedom from want and freedom from fear.

In 1941 what had started as a European war became a world war. This was a turning point at which the British, facing national ruin in the early summer of 1940, emerged as victors five years later alongside the United States. Yet the Americans were still not at war. However, at the same time as Roosevelt spoke in defence of the four freedoms which were the bedrock of democracy, an extraordinary individual arrived in Britain as the President's personal emissary. Harry Hopkins was later characterised by Churchill as a man who sometimes played "a decisive part in the whole movement of the war". A Left-leaning welfare administrator of impeccable probity who had known Roosevelt since the late 1920s, he had risen to the post of Secretary of Commerce by 1938, had played a significant role in Roosevelt's election for a third term, and was said to have presidential ambitions himself. Hopkins' poor health – he had stomach cancer - cut short his political ambitions and he had to settle for the role of Roosevelt's éminence grise with no official position, living in the White House, where he married his third wife in 1943. In his new role, Hopkins remained the tireless advocate of single issues, and around 1940 had switched from the defeat of domestic poverty to the defeat of Adolf Hitler, to the exclusion of all else.

Hopkins arrived in Downing Street in the second week of January 1941. Churchill spent some three hours alone with him at lunch and then over port and brandy. He was immediately impressed with Hopkins' drive and intellectual grip. Roosevelt's emissary informed the Prime Minister, "The President is determined that we shall win the war together. Make no mistake about it. He has sent me here to tell you that at all costs and by all means he will carry you through, no matter what happens to him – there is nothing that he will not do so far as he has human power." Churchill, who was now straining every sinew to draw Roosevelt into declaring war on the Axis (Germany, Italy and later Japan), grasped from the outset Hopkins' fixity of purpose: "There he sat, slim, frail, ill but absolutely glowing with refined comprehension of the Cause. It was to be the defeat, ruin and slaughter of Hitler... In the history of the United States few brighter flames have burned."

Churchill was immediately taken with the 50-year-old Hopkins. He was not cut out to be a confidant of the Prime Minister. He came from humble origins in Sioux City, Iowa, was a passionate New Dealer and possessed a mordant sense of humour. This last undoubtedly appealed to the Prime Minister. Perhaps it was the very real sense of Hopkins as an outsider but one with the ear of the President that fired Churchill's imagination. Hopkins was immediately added to Churchill's guest list for a weekend stay at Ditchley Park in Oxfordshire, the home of Ronald Tree, Conservative MP for Market Harborough. There Hopkins hobnobbed with the colourful social set with whom Churchill felt most at home, including Venetia Montagu, once the object of Asquith's chaste affections, and the Marquesa de Casa Maurry, who, as Mrs Dudley Ward, had been at one time the mistress of King Edward VIII. Hopkins then accompanied the Prime Minister to Scapa Flow in Scotland to inspect the Fleet. Next, Churchill's party travelled to Glasgow, a vital shipbuilding and munitions hub.

At the North British Hotel Hopkins brought tears to the Prime Minister's eyes when, in a speech at the end of dinner, he quoted the Book of Ruth on the future of Anglo-American relations: "Whither thou goest, I will go; and where thou lodgest, I will lodge; thy people shall be my people and thy God my God."

Churchill's sightseeing tour also took in Dover where Hopkins watched the firing of the massive 14-inch Channel artillery pieces "Winnie" and "Pooh", retrieved from the reserves of the battleship *King George V* and fired by men of the Royal Marines Siege Regiments stationed at "Hellfire Corner". Hopkins' whistle-stop itinerary ended with a tour of Portsmouth and Southampton, both of which were heavily bomb-damaged. By now, Churchill and Hopkins had become bosom companions, and the Prime Minister's charm offensive had been wholly successful. Hopkins informed Roosevelt that Churchill "was the directing force behind the strategy and conduct of the war in all its essentials. He has an amazing hold on the British people of all classes and groups." The Prime Minister also had a hold on Hopkins and Hopkins on him, which later enabled the American to tease his new friend when the conversation flagged or when it continued interminably.

This established an indirect personal link between Prime Minister and President, who had only met each other once before in a fleeting encounter in 1918, when the latter was Assistant Secretary to the Navy. Hopkins' visit preceded a series of significant meetings with Americans whose support was vital to the Anglo-American war effort. Among them were Wendell Wilkie, the pro-British Republican candidate in the 1940 Presidential election, and Gilbert Winant, who had succeeded the unlamented Joseph Kennedy as the US Ambassador to the Court of St James in March 1941. A man of few but telling words with an arresting physical likeness to Abraham Lincoln, Winant became a frequent weekend guest of the Prime Minister.

March 1941 was a crucial moment in the forging of Anglo-American relations. Roosevelt's Four Freedoms were fine, resounding words, but what the British needed above all else was a supply of arms on easier terms than those of "cash and carry", which they could no longer afford to pay. Roosevelt's answer was the Lend-Lease Act passed by Congress in March 1941. The Act allowed the British to borrow war supplies from the United States against the promise of later repayments. By the end of the month, Congress had voted Lend-Lease the sum of seven billion dollars, the first instalment in a programme, later extended to the Soviet Union after the attack by the Japanese on Pearl Harbor, to arm and feed the Allies, which would eventually total over 50 billion dollars.

At the end of July, the indefatigable Hopkins was off to the Soviet Union, to meet Stalin. He had flown in a British-manned but American-built bomber, an early indication of the shifting geopolitical forces which would thenceforth influence the direction of the war. Hopkins was back from the Soviet Union in time to join Roosevelt and Churchill at their meeting in Placentia Bay, Newfoundland, in August 1941. The event had been brokered by Hopkins on a sunny late-July afternoon in Downing Street. Churchill sailed on 4 August in the battleship *Prince of Wales*, which in the previous May had played a vital part in the sinking of the German battleship *Bismarck*. He was joined aboard *Prince of Wales* by Hopkins, exhausted by his trip to the Soviet Union. For Churchill, however, the top-secret voyage presented him with a brief interlude during which he could enjoy some relief from the unrelenting military and political pressure he had been under since May 1940. Nevertheless, the journey was not without some initial upsets. The handsome quarters which the Prime Minister had been given above the battleship's propellers vibrated unbearably as the battleship ploughed through heavy seas, obliging Churchill to move to the captain's cabin.

On the second day of the crossing the sea was so rough that Admiral Sir Dudley Pound, the First Sea Lord and a member of the Prime Minister's party, decided to drop *Prince of Wales*' destroyer escort and continue alone, zigzagging at high speed and maintaining radio silence to avoid interception by U-boats. Churchill amused himself by reading C.S. Forrester's *Captain Hornblower R.N.*, lent to him by Oliver Lyttelton, Minister of State in Cairo. When he was able to break radio silence, the Prime

Minister sent Lyttelton a message, "I find Hornblower admirable," causing considerable confusion in the Middle East signals set-up which assumed that "Hornblower" was the code-name for an operation of which they were unaware. When not engrossed in the Hornblower saga, Churchill exercised by exploring the battleship's lower decks and the bridge. In the evenings he enjoyed watching the film *Lady Hamilton*, starring Vivien Leigh and Laurence Olivier, one of his favourites, which he saw at least five times. In his diary, another of his companions on the voyage, Cadogan, noted: "Film *Lady Hamilton* after dinner... PM still deeply moved. At the close he addressed the company: 'Gentlemen, I thought this film would interest you, showing great events similar to those in which you have been taking part.'"

Roosevelt had also maintained the secrecy of the rendezvous in Newfoundland by going on a fishing trip to Maine before boarding a US Navy cruiser to make his way to Placentia Bay. He was accompanied by General Marshall, the US Army's Chief of Staff, Admirals King and Stark and Sumner Welles of the State Department, a wealthy and sophisticated career diplomat. As Churchill had with him two of his three Chiefs of Staff, the meeting at Placentia Bay provided the first opportunity for senior members of the British and American High Commands to get to know one another. More important was the personal chemistry between Prime Minister and President. Both were prima donnas, but at this stage in the war Churchill was more in need of Roosevelt than the President was of him.

On 9 August Churchill went aboard the cruiser *Augusta* to meet the President, who was supported[25] by his son Elliott while the National Anthems were played. Churchill wore one of the many eccentric uniforms he customarily affected, on this occasion that of an Elder Brother of Trinity House, while Roosevelt wore

---

25. Roosevelt's infirmity, the result of polio contracted in the summer of 1921, left him unable to walk unaided. This was to all intents and purposes artfully concealed from the American public.

elegantly expensive civilian clothes and when in relaxed mode wafted a cigarette holder, a shade effete, perhaps, but more stylish than Churchill's spit-sodden cigar. The next day Roosevelt repaid the compliment, boarding *Prince of Wales* and joining Churchill in a sunlit religious service on the quarterdeck while the Stars and Stripes and the Union Jack hung side by side from the pulpit. The senior British and American military, naval and air commanders stood in a body behind the Prime Minister and the President, lustily singing hymns selected by the Prime Minister: "For Those in Peril on the Sea, "Onward Christian Soldiers" and "O God, Our Help in Ages Past", the last having been chanted at the funeral of John Hampden, cousin of Oliver Cromwell and doughty opponent of arbitrary rule. Nearly half of those present at this moving demonstration of fellow feeling, if not military alliance, were to die on 10 December 1941 when *Prince of Wales* was sunk off the east coast of Malaya by Japanese aircraft.

The talks which followed were not as striking as the well-orchestrated preliminaries. The Prime Minister and the President agreed that the defeat of Nazi Germany should be the foremost priority on their agenda and issued the Atlantic Charter, a joint declaration of shared principles and war aims which emerged after much heated haggling. Churchill was particularly unhappy with Point Three, which guaranteed "the right of all peoples to choose the form of government under which they will live". Initially, Churchill had assumed that this referred to the European nations subjected to Nazi rule but quickly grasped that this applied to the governance of India and the rest of the British Empire. By the same token, Roosevelt, remembering the fate of the League of Nations, was equally reluctant to countenance a revival of that ill-fated body implied in Point Eight.

Nevertheless, the final declaration embodied the spirit of Roosevelt's Four Freedoms and sowed the seeds from which the United Nations Organisation was to grow. However, it was still imbued with Roosevelt's characteristic caution. Moreover, joint British and American military and political action could not be effectively harnessed until the United States was at war with

Germany. In taking "all steps short of war", Roosevelt had been edging America closer to entering the conflict since March 1941 when Axis ships in US ports were seized. May had seen the transfer of oil tankers to the British. At the end of the month, following the torpedoing by a U-boat of the American freighter SS *Robin Moor*, Roosevelt had declared a state of unlimited national emergency. Axis credit in the United States was frozen and Axis consulates closed in June. In July, US Marines replaced British troops in Iceland, which the British had occupied after the fall of Denmark in 1940. In the Atlantic the US Navy was already engaged in a war of sorts, extending American protection of Britain-bound convoys in the Atlantic. At first, Roosevelt defined a neutrality zone which denied U-boats access to American waters, and from April 1941 he extended the zone to the mid-ocean boundary and allowed US warships to act as convoy escorts.

On 31 October 1941 a U-boat sank the old four-stack destroyer *Reuben James*, killing 115 American sailors. Within two weeks Congress had moved to arm merchantmen and permitted them to sail directly into war zones. But Roosevelt still did not act. A bigger shock was required to bring the United Sates into the war. Hitler seemed unlikely to oblige. His attention was now fixed on the Eastern Front as his armies drove ever deeper into the Soviet Union. Roosevelt was waiting to be pushed. When the shove came it was from a different direction, the Far East.

In the late 1930s the United States had stood aside from the expanding Japanese conquest and expansion into China. But in September 1940 it was extended to French Indochina, where Vichy France granted Japan military bases from which it could threaten Malaya, the East Indies and the US protectorate of the Philippines. Roosevelt chose an economic weapon to halt the Japanese advance, imposing an embargo on rubber, which was followed in July 1941 by the freezing in the United States of all Japanese assets and the announcement in the following August of an oil embargo against all aggressors, including Japan. At a stroke the Japanese were deprived of 90 per cent of their oil supplies and 75 per cent of their foreign trade. They were faced with a choice – diplomatic retreat from their Chinese conquest or war. They decided to play for time while planning for a surprise attack on the US Navy.

When it came on 7 December, at Pearl Harbor on the Hawaiian island of Oahu, it pitched the United States into Second World War. The immediate reactions of Churchill and Roosevelt to this momentous development are revealing. Churchill was at Chequers, dining with the Americans Winant and Averill Harriman, negotiating Lend-Lease, as part of his continuing Anglo-American charm offensive, when the news of the attack on Pearl Harbor started to come in. His fellow-diners were immediately obliged to restrain the Prime Minister from telephoning the Foreign Office and telling them to declare war on Japan. When Roosevelt heard the news on 7 December, he was lunching with Harry Hopkins, who noted his reactions: "The President discussed at some length his efforts to keep the country out of the war and his earnest desire to complete his administration without war, but if this action of Japan's were true it would take the matter entirely out of his hands, because the Japanese had made the decision for him." The situation was made infinitely more straightforward for Churchill and Roosevelt when four days later Adolf Hitler declared war on the United States.

Churchill realised this was a game changer. The British were now the allies of potentially, if not already, the most powerful nation in the world. A few days later he silenced a querulous colleague by observing, with something like a smirk on his face, that the fervent wooing of the United States was at an end. "Now that she is in the harem we talk to her quite differently." And talks were in prospect, as the Prime Minister was planning to visit Roosevelt in Washington within days. Churchill's moment of clarity shone like a searchlight slicing through clouds of strategic gloom. The Japanese were poised to cut a swathe through the Pacific, seizing colonies and protectorates controlled by the British, Americans and Dutch. In six months they carved out a vast Pacific perimeter stretching south to the Solomon Islands. To the north, they threatened the Aleutian chain and the approaches to Alaska. The British naval base at Singapore had been seized, Burma had fallen, opening the way to India, the jewel in the

British Imperial crown. The bad news was not confined to the Pacific. In Eastern Europe, only a week before Pearl Harbor, advanced German forces had fought their way to within 30 miles of Moscow. They could see the sun glinting on the towers of the Kremlin and the onion domes of St Basil's Cathedral. This was the high-water mark of the Axis' territorial expansion, although this was not known at the time. On 10 December, the diary of General Alan Brooke, now Chief of the Imperial General Staff, records:

Arrived at the War Office to be informed that both the Prince of Wales and [the battleship] Repulse had been sunk by the Japs! This on top of the tragedy of Honolulu puts us in very serious position in the prosecution of the war. It means that for Africa eastwards to America through the Indian Ocean and the Pacific, we have lost command of the sea. This affects reinforcements to Middle East, India, Burma, Far East, Australia and New Zealand!

Churchill set off for the United States on 12 December aboard the battleship *Duke of York*. He had much to ponder as the warship ploughed through heavy seas. Two possibilities, both of them alarming, presented themselves. First, that the flow of Lend-Lease materiel might be interrupted by America's entry into the war. Second that the "Germany First" agreement reached at Placentia Bay might be overridden by the demands of an oceanic war in the Far East and Pacific. On both counts Churchill's fears proved groundless. Pearl Harbor produced a surge in American war production that had a profound effect on the prosecution of the war. In 1939, the United States manufactured only a small amount of military equipment for its own needs. By 1944 it was producing 40 per cent of the world's armaments. In 1940, 346 tanks had been built in America; in 1944 the annual figure had risen to 17,500, most of them M4 Shermans, the tank which also became the mainstay of Britain's armoured divisions. In addition, the American High Command retained its position on "Germany

First". General Marshall and Admiral Ernest J. King, Commander-in-Chief of the US Fleet, took the position that "notwithstanding the entry of Japan into the war, our view remains that Germany is still the prime enemy and her defeat is the key to victory. Once Germany is defeated the collapse of Italy and the defeat of Japan must follow."[26]

Churchill disembarked from *Duke of York* at Hampton Roads and flew on to Washington, where in a singular honour he had been invited to stay in the White House. Roosevelt was determined to be the ideal host, even though throughout the visit he plied the Prime Minister with atrociously mixed dry martini cocktails, which the champagne and whisky-drinking Prime Minister, equally anxious to be the perfect guest, nevertheless downed with apparent gusto. The food and wine at the White House, usually supervised by the austerity-conscious Eleanor Roosevelt, was on this occasion of high quality. Harry Hopkins, who was a constant presence at Churchill's meetings with Roosevelt, noted that the wine always flowed more freely at the White House when Churchill was there.

Washington was the setting for the *Arcadia* Conference, as it was code-named. On the British side the business at hand was carried out in a blur of hustle and bustle, as if Churchill's team were intuiting their imminently diminishing role in the determination of global policy. The Americans, apparently infinitely more relaxed in spite of the onrush of disasters in the Pacific, were bemused by their British guests. The two leaders were also object lessons in differing styles of leadership. Churchill revelled in the whole business of war-making, spending his days and nights in constant contact with his military commanders. When he stayed in the White House in the winter of 1941-42, he immediately set up his own travelling map room displaying all the fronts in which the British armies and fleets were engaged. From the beginning of 1942, the potentially dangerous effects of the Prime Minister's

---

26. In spite of Churchill's initial misgivings, the United States' "Germany First" policy was retained until the fall of Berlin.

tendency to meddle in military matters big and small were happily mitigated by General Sir Alan Brooke, the Chief of the Imperial General Staff. In contrast Roosevelt, an invalid, remained aloof from the business of running the war. After Pearl Harbor he hardly altered the patterns of his life. Work in the White House seldom began before 10am, and he took few telephone calls at night. According to his biographer James MacGregor Burns:

He saw the Congressional Big Four – the Vice-President, the Speaker of the House of Representatives and the majority leader of each chamber – on Monday or Tuesday; met with the press on Tuesday afternoons and Friday mornings, and presided over a Cabinet meeting on Friday afternoons. There seemed to be no pattern at all in the way Roosevelt did his work. Sometimes he hurried through his appointments on crucial matters and dawdled through lesser ones. He ignored most letters altogether... He took many phone calls, refused others, saw inconsequential and dull people, and ignored others of apparently greater political and intellectual weight – all according to some mystifying structure of priorities known to no one, perhaps not even himself.

Apart from travelling to Allied conferences, Roosevelt's was a peacetime routine leading a nation that, Pearl Harbor apart, was physically if not psychologically untouched by the war but was also growing immeasurably rich through waging it.

As he celebrated Christmas in the White House, Churchill knew that he was in pole position at the heart of the command post of the free world. Addressing a large crowd from the White House balcony, the Prime Minister declared:

I spend this anniversary and festival far from my country, far from my family, yet I cannot truthfully say that I feel far from home. Whether it be the ties of blood on my mother's side, or the friendships I have developed here over many years of active life, or the commanding sentiment of comradeship in the common cause of great peoples who speak the same language, who kneel at the same altars and, to a very large extent, pursue the same ideals, I cannot feel myself a stranger here at the centre and summit of the United States. I feel a sense of unity and fraternal association which, added to the kindliness of your welcome, convinces me that I have the right to sit at your fireside and share your Christmas joys.

On Boxing Day, 26 December, Churchill spoke at a joint session of Congress, the first time he had addressed a foreign legislature. He got a thunderous response when, referring to the attack on Pearl Harbor, he asked his audience, "Who do they think we are?" Back at the White House, Roosevelt dryly opined that Churchill had done quite well. That night, while stretching to open a window, Churchill suffered a mild heart attack. For the first time his entourage included a physician, Sir Charles Wilson (later Lord Moran). The Prime Minister sought reassurance from Wilson that there was nothing about which to be alarmed, while at the same time insisting on his pulse being taken and then displaying considerable unease when he was presented with the result. Wilson concluded that a normal patient would be confined to bed for six weeks after such an incident, but Churchill was far from a normal patient. Within 36 hours he was due to meet the Canadian Prime Minister William Mackenzie King before addressing the Canadian Parliament.

Churchill caught the night train to Canada and on the 30th addressed the Canadian Parliament. The speech he gave was one of his most memorable. Referring to the catastrophe in France in 1940, he castigated the French High Command for misleading the French people: "When I warned them that Britain would fight on alone whatever they did, their generals told their Prime Minister and his Cabinet, 'In three weeks England will have her neck wrung like a chicken.' Some chicken! some neck!"

Fine words laced with robust humour could not disguise the gloomy prospects for 1942. Nevertheless, they failed to dampen the Prime Minister's spirits. Returning by train from Canada to

Washington, Churchill wished the attending Press Corps a glorious New Year: "Here's to 1942. Here's to a year of toil – a year of struggle and peril, and a long step forward towards victory. May we all come through safe and with honour!" Before he left Canada, Churchill fitted in a photocall with the portraitist Yousuf Karsh, who captured him at his bulldog best scowling defiantly at the camera.

On his return to the White House, and while still in his morning bath, Churchill was presented by his wheelchair-bound host with a draft document establishing the United Nations, then a framework for Allied wartime co-operation rather than the organisation for post-war security set up in San Francisco three years later. It was originally entitled "Associate Powers" before Roosevelt suggested the more resonant alternative. Churchill recalled its purpose was to state "who we were and what we were fighting for". The question of precisely who the Associate Powers were had been initially the source of some disagreement. Churchill the Imperialist had been less than enthusiastic about the inclusion of India. Cordell Hull, the American Secretary of State and a member of the anti-Gaullist faction in the American administration, objected to the inclusion of the "so-called Free French", as he referred to them. The Americans fretted that the inclusion of the phrase "freedom of religion" in the document would meet strenuous opposition from Stalin, which in fact it did not. In the end diplomacy won the day and on New Year's Day, 1 January, Roosevelt, the Prime Minister, T. V. Soong, representing China, and Maxim Litvinov, the Soviet Ambassador to the United States, signed the final document in Roosevelt's study. This simple ceremony confirmed America's assumption of the role of leader of the Western Alliance against the Axis while Stalin remained, with the help of Lend-Lease, the absolute leader in the East.

Several matters of immediate military concern were also settled at *Arcadia*. The first was the appointment of General Sir Archibald Wavell, Commander-in-Chief India, to the concurrent role of Allied Supreme Commander American-British-Dutch-Australian Command (ABDA) in the south-west Pacific. Churchill, no admirer of Wavell, was less than enthusiastic about this appointment. It was an impossible mission to fulfil at this stage in the war and was doomed to failure. With limited resources at his disposal, Wavell was unable to stem the Japanese tide and resigned a few weeks later. More to Churchill's liking was initial American approval of the British proposal to mount, when the numbers made it possible, an Anglo-American invasion of north-west Africa, initially code-named *Gymnast* and later *Torch*.

For the moment at least, the British and Americans were meeting as equal partners. Their respective Chiefs of Staff established a Combined Chiefs of Staff (CCS) and jointly agreed on a memorandum setting out the principal aims of Allied strategy. They included the support of American war industries, and those of the United Kingdom and the Soviet Union, the latter by extending to the Soviets the terms of Lend-Lease; to build up strength in the Middle East and secure the entire coast of North Africa; to undermine German morale by air bombardment, blockade, propaganda and a campaign of subversion in Occupied Europe.[27] All this came with the proviso that an Allied return to Europe was unlikely in 1942.

Churchill was immensely buoyed by the agreements reached at *Arcadia*. The Americans harboured serious reservations. Their philosophy of war differed markedly from that of their ally. At this stage in their mobilisation their High Command was disorganised, even incoherent. Nevertheless, the unerring view of the US High Command was that the defeat of Germany could only be achieved by beating its armed forces in the field by large-scale land operations in the manner of Ulysses S. Grant in the American Civil War. On 22 January 1942, General Dwight D. Eisenhower,

---

27. The last was to be undertaken by the British Special Operations Executive (SOE) established in the early summer of 1941. Its mission statement, in Churchill's words, was "to set Europe ablaze", wildly optimistic at first but nearer the mark as the war progressed. The US equivalent, in Europe and the Far East, was the Office of Strategic Services (OSS).

then the Chief of the US Army Operations and Planning Staff, wrote: "We've got to go to Europe and fight – and we've got to quit wasting resources all over the world. If we're to keep Russia in, save the Middle East, India and Burma, we've got to begin slugging with air at West Europe; to be followed by a land attack as soon as possible."

Churchill left Washington for home on 14 January. He was in buoyant mood in spite of the growing trickle of bad news from the Far East and North Africa. Before he left, Roosevelt expressed anxiety about the Prime Minister's return voyage from Bermuda aboard *Duke of York*, which, after his hardly low-key visit, might be targeted by the U-boat "wolf packs" lurking in the North Atlantic. This prompted one of the Prime Minister's inspired improvisations. At Norfolk, Virginia, he had boarded a Boeing Clipper flying boat bound for Bermuda. During the three-hour flight, Churchill sat in the cockpit befriending the chief pilot, Captain Kelly Rogers, who allowed him to take the controls. Churchill was enormously taken with the vast Boeing and asked Rogers if he could fly from Bermuda to England. Rogers replied that, with a good weather forecast and following wind, he could do it in 20 hours. Churchill then consulted the two senior officers travelling with him, Pound and Portal, reassuring them that there would be room on the flying boat for both of them and that passage aboard the Boeing would ensure a speedy return to England. Agreement was reached and the flying boat, stripped of its baggage bar a few vital papers, took off from Bermuda the following afternoon, carrying Churchill, Pound, Portal, Beaverbrook, who had also visited Washington, General Wilson and Colonel Sir Leslie Hollis of the Defence Staff.

The flying boat, heavily laden with fuel, struggled to get into the air, but Churchill, in characteristic fashion, was soon relishing its luxuries: "I had a good broad bed in the bridal suite at the stern with large windows on either side. It was quite a long walk, thirty or forty feet, downhill through the various compartments to the saloon and dining room, where nothing was lacking in food or drink."

Churchill woke at dawn. He went straight to the control room to find the Boeing cruising through mist over unbroken banks of cloud. Anxiety mounted before Portal intervened decisively to order a turn northward. Soon, Plymouth was sighted through breaking cloud. Later Churchill was told that had the flight continued for another five or six minutes the Boeing would have encountered the German anti-aircraft batteries at Brest. As it was, Portal's intervention had not prevented the scrambling of six Hurricane fighters with orders to shoot down a hostile bomber. Fortunately, they failed in their mission.

Five and a half months later, at 11.30pm on 17 June, Churchill and his entourage, including Brooke, took off once more under a full moon for the United States in the bijou Boeing flying boat piloted by Kelly Rogers. Churchill sat for two hours in the co-pilot's seat mulling over the see-sawing campaign in North Africa, where the key port of Tobruk, which had been relieved by the British in November 1941 in Operation *Crusader*, was now threatened by General Erwin Rommel's Afrika Korps. Early the next morning Brooke found Churchill "in tremendous form, and enjoying himself like a schoolboy", singing the old trench ditty "We're 'ere, because we're 'ere, because we're 'ere." After a 26-hour flight, the flying boat landed near Washington on the River Potomac to be greeted by the British Ambassador Lord Halifax and General George Marshall, the US Army's Chief of Staff. Churchill slept in the British embassy before flying on to Roosevelt's family estate at Hyde Park, standing on the bluffs overlooking the Hudson. The Prime Minister was met at the airfield by the President, who then took his guest all over the estate in his specially converted limousine, which he drove with surprisingly strong arms, reminding Churchill of those of a prizefighter. Roosevelt's biceps proved to be more impressive than his driving, which on several occasions left the limousine parked perilously close to the vertiginous drops into the Hudson below. Churchill fervently hoped that the brakes were in full working order.

Before he got down to work with the President, Churchill ran through a list of priorities with Harry Hopkins, of which the *Tube Alloys* project was the most important. *Tube Alloys* was the code-name for the British project to develop an atom bomb. In

1934 the physicist Leo Szilard, a Hungarian-born Jewish refugee from Nazi Germany, discovered that the nuclei of certain atoms could be split by bombarding them with atomic particles known as neutrons. In turn this would release more neutrons, which would split more nuclei, and so on in a chain reaction releasing huge amounts of energy. Scientists realised that the energy could be used to create a bomb of enormous power. In Britain, two more refugees from Nazi Germany, Otto Frisch and Rudolf Peierls, found that a rare form of uranium, uranium 235, was required to produce an instantaneous explosive chain reaction of the type required for a bomb. Meanwhile, physicists working in France discovered that an artificial element, plutonium, could also be used to make an atom bomb. Atomic research was also well advanced in Germany. Many scientists were fearful of the consequences of an atomic weapon being in the hands of a man like Adolf Hitler. In 1939, in the United States, Albert Einstein, the leading physicist of the day and another refugee from Nazi Germany, warned President Roosevelt that Germany might be planning to develop an atomic weapon. Prompted by Szilard, Einstein proposed an American research project to develop an atomic bomb. He was also of the opinion that the bomb should never be used. Roosevelt responded by setting up a Uranium Committee, which reported in 1941 that it would be possible to design and build an atomic bomb, which in any future war would be "determining". At the same time the British were working on *Tube Alloys*. The pace quickened after Pearl Harbor, and the British joined forces with the Americans in the race against the Germans. With greater economic resources than the British and secure from enemy bombs and aerial reconnaissance, the atomic project was transferred to the United States under the code-name *Manhattan Project*. By the summer of 1942, the point was reached at which a decision had to be taken about the construction of large-scale plants to construct a usable bomb. It was during this second visit by Churchill to the United States that the Prime Minister and the President met to make the decision in a small office at Hyde Park, shaded from the sun and dominated by huge desk behind which Roosevelt sat.

Harry Hopkins was perched in a corner. Roosevelt had been fully briefed and it fell to the President to make the grave decision to throw the weight of American science and finance behind the completion of the *Manhattan Project*. By the time plutonium was ready for testing, the cost had run to over two billion dollars.

Churchill rode the train from Hyde Park to Washington late on the evening of the 20th. The next morning after breakfast he went to see Roosevelt, accompanied by Generals Ismay and Brooke, the former ever the tactful emissary between the Prime Minister and the Americans. Churchill's conversation with Roosevelt was interrupted when a telegram was handed to him wordlessly by the President, bearing the news that Tobruk had surrendered and 25,000 men had been taken prisoner. Churchill later confessed that this was one of the heaviest blows he had taken during the war. He did not attempt to hide the shock he felt at that moment from the President, who immediately asked what he could do to help. Marshall, also in the meeting, offered 300 M4 Shermans and 100 self-propelled guns. Welcome though this gesture was, the surrender of Tobruk inevitably weakened Churchill's position at the White House. Far from being able to lecture his Allies on the conduct of the war, he was utterly dependent on their help in a theatre in which the British gains made in the summer of 1940 had been rolled back by Erwin Rommel in 1941-42. Rommel was now only 50 miles from Cairo.

In addition to the sobering news about Tobruk, Churchill had to contend with headlines in the New York papers about his own position at home, where a censure debate in Parliament awaited him on his return. The Prime Minister did not allow these developments to interfere with his planned trip to Camp Jackson in South Carolina, which had been arranged by Marshall. From the baking hot reviewing field, which reminded Churchill of his days in India, the Prime Minister and his entourage watched a display by some 600 paratroops. Brooke later noted that there were "only three casualties, one leg broken, one sprain and one suspected skull fracture". Churchill was handed a "walkie talkie", a device with which he was unfamiliar, and then viewed a divisional live-firing display. When he asked General Ismay's opinion of the demonstration, the general observed that to pit these American troops against battle-hardened German soldiers would be little short of murder. Churchill begged to differ, but nonetheless reminded his American hosts that it took two years to train a soldier. In this, both men were right. The American baptism of fire at the hands of Erwin Rommel at Kasserine Pass, Tunisia, in February 1943, was the start of a long learning curve which took the US Army to the heart of the Third Reich.

On the return flight to Washington on the 24th, Churchill changed into his siren suit and donned a Panama hat with its brim turned up all the way round, making him look like a small boy in rompers going down to the beach to build a sandcastle. This unusual sartorial display met with the disapproval of the Prime Minister's butler, Frank Sawyers, who had taken a few drinks too many during the display at Camp Jackson. Sawyers blocked Churchill's progress down the aisle of the flying boat and refused to move. When Churchill protested, Sawyers replied in slurred tones, "The brim of your hat is turned up, does not look well, turn it down! turn it down!" Churchill, red in the face, adjusted his hat and was allowed by his valet to pass with the words, "That's much, much, much better."

On the evening of 25 June, after meeting representatives of the Dominions and India and attending a meeting of the Pacific War Council, Churchill boarded his flying boat in Baltimore. His departure was not without incident. The narrow, closed gangway leading to the flying boat was guarded by a police detail, one of whom, a plain-clothes detective, had been arrested after he had been overheard threatening to kill the Prime Minister. When he was informed of the incident, Churchill dismissed him as a "crackpate". Having survived an assassination bid in America, Churchill returned to survive a censure debate in the House of Commons sparked by the fall of Tobruk. Just over two weeks later, General Marshall arrived in London with the mounting of a Second Front at the top of his agenda. Churchill weathered these storms, and in August set off for Egypt and the Soviet Union.

8

MISSION TO MOSCOW

On Saturday 21 June 1941, Sir John "Jock" Colville, Churchill's Assistant Private Secretary, travelled to Chequers for dinner with the PM, Mr and Mrs Eden, Mr Winant the US Ambassador and his wife, and Sir Edward Bridges, Secretary to the Cabinet. During dinner Churchill observed that a German attack on the Soviet Union was certain and that Hitler had calculated that capitalist and conservative interests in Britain and the United States would prevent the two nations coming to the aid of the Soviet dictator Josef Stalin. Churchill added that the Führer had miscalculated and aid would be forthcoming from both nations, a sentiment readily endorsed by Winant. Later that evening while walking on the croquet lawn, Churchill returned to the theme, prompting Colville to ask Churchill how he could square his dinner-table sentiments with his devout anti-Communism. Churchill replied that he was not troubled in the slightest: "I have only one purpose, the destruction of Hitler, and my life is much simplified thereby. If Hitler invaded Hell I would make at least a favourable reference to the Devil in the House of Commons."

At 4am in the morning Colville was awoken by a telephone message from the Foreign Office that Germany had attacked Russia. Mindful of the fact that Churchill had insisted that he should only be woken up in the small hours if England was invaded, he postponed the breaking of the news to the

Prime Minister to 8am. Churchill's only comment was "Tell the BBC I will broadcast at nine tonight." Churchill began drafting the speech at 11am, breaking only for lunch with Sir Stafford Cripps, Minister for Aircraft Production, Viscount Cranborne, a notable anti-appeaser, and Beaverbrook. Churchill finished the speech with 20 minutes remaining. The Prime Minister concluded in the sternest terms: "The Russian danger is therefore our danger, and the danger of the United States, just as the cause of any Russian fighting for his hearth and home is the cause of free men and free peoples in every quarter of the globe. Let us learn the lessons already taught by such cruel experience. Let us redouble our exertions, and strike with united strength while life and power remain."

At 3.30am on Sunday, 22 June 1941, the day after the 129th anniversary of Napoleon's invasion of Russia in 1812, seven German infantry armies, their advance spearheaded by four panzer groups, invaded the Soviet Union. The code-name for the operation was *Barbarossa*. Three million soldiers, supported by 3,600 tanks, 7,200 guns and nearly 2,000 aircraft were on the move along a front of 2,000 miles. The Red Army, in the middle of a wholesale reorganisation, and deployed forward to cover every curve and crevice in Russia's frontiers, was caught in a series of encirclements. At Minsk and Smolensk in July, the Germans took 400,000 prisoners. In September, 600,000 went into the bag, trapped in a wide bend of the Dnieper. However, sweeping success was bought at a heavy price. Deaths, wounds and sickness struck half a million men from the German order of battle. On 11 July, the commander of the 18th Panzer Division expressed fears that that the loss of men and equipment would prove insupportable, "if we do not intend to win ourselves to death."

In the British and American military, the overriding opinion was that Soviet defeat was inevitable. On the 22nd, while Churchill was composing his speech, the CIGS, General Dill, soon to be replaced by General Brooke, arrived with the news that in the opening German blow a large part of the Red Air Force had been destroyed on the ground.

Josef Stalin, the Soviet Union's Supreme Commander, Commissar for Defence and Chairman of the Council of People's Commissars, was shaken to the core by the opening of *Barbarossa* and came close to a nervous breakdown. Both he and the Red Army rallied. When Stalin regained his poise, his characteristic reaction was to consolidate the control of the war in his own hands. To have done otherwise would have been to cut himself adrift from the state and military systems he had built up around himself in the 1930s. Early in October 1941, the German Army Group North laid siege to Leningrad. Now Russia's seemingly endless spaces, primitive roads and punitive climate started to take their toll on the German Army. Scorching summer heat gave way to seas of autumn mud, the Russian *rasputitsa*. In October the first snows of winter began to fall. Hitler was now torn between driving straight for Moscow or reinforcing his extended southern flank to seize the raw materials and agricultural riches of the Ukraine. Winter – for which the German high command had not equipped its troops – arrived while Hitler was still shuttling forces up and down his battlefront. The German advance slowed amid blizzards and temperatures so low that they welded artillery pieces into immovable blocks on the rock-hard earth. Some German patrols reached a tram terminus on the outskirts of Moscow. On 6 December the Red Army counter-attacked with fresh and well-equipped divisions rushed from Siberia. They drove the German Army Group Centre back 200 miles before the offensive slithered to a halt in the glutinous mud of the spring thaw. *Blitzkrieg* had met its match.

In July 1941 Churchill established the framework for an alliance between Britain and the Soviet Union. At its heart was an undertaking to provide each other with mutual assistance of all kinds in the prosecution of the war against Germany and a pledge that neither side would negotiate or conclude an armistice or peace treaty with the enemy except by mutual agreement. In the same month Churchill authorised the shipment of Tomahawk fighter aircraft, millions of pairs of ankle boots, and scarce supplies of rubber, around the North Cape to the ports of Murmansk and Archangel to make good the grievous Soviet losses in the first phase of *Barbarossa*. This marked the start of the Arctic convoy system. Welcome as this assistance was to Stalin, his principal demand, made in July at the beginning of his correspondence with Churchill, was the opening by the British, and after December 1941 the Americans, of a Second Front in Europe. This contentious issue was the hot potato that Churchill had to juggle with his allies for the next 18 months.

On 30 July 1942, Anthony Eden, now Foreign Secretary, passed a message to Churchill from the British Ambassador to the Soviet Union, Sir Archibald Clark Kerr: "Although Molotov [the Soviet Foreign Minister] professes to have passed on faithfully to the Soviet government all that was to be said to him in London[28] and given him in writing ... it now looks as if he had to some extent failed to interpret to Stalin the mind of the Prime Minister." Kerr concluded that it was of the utmost importance for Churchill to meet Stalin face to face. When Eden showed the message to the Prime Minister, Churchill eagerly agreed, suggesting Cairo or Astrakhan as a possible meeting place. Stalin accepted the invitation to meet but protested that the pressures of war made leaving Moscow impossible. The meeting, code-named *Bracelet*, would have to take place in the Soviet capital. Eden was concerned that the exertions of such a trip would undermine the health of the sexagenarian Churchill. The Prime Minister would have none of it. Nonetheless, along with Sir Alexander Cadogan, who was to be one of his travelling companions, he submitted himself to tests at Farnborough on 31 July for high-altitude flying at 15,000ft while wearing oxygen masks. Both men were duly deemed fit. Before he set off for Moscow, Churchill received a message from Roosevelt: "Stalin must be handled with great care. We have got always to bear in mind the personality of our ally and the very difficult and dangerous situation that confronts him. No-one can be expected to approach the war from a world point of view whose country has

---

28. Molotov had visited London and Washington in the summer of 1942.

been invaded. I think we should try to put ourselves in his place." Churchill was to succeed in this task, but only with the greatest difficulty.

The first leg of the journey took Churchill and his party to Cairo via Gibraltar. In Cairo, important decisions had to be made about the British High Command in the Middle East. They took off from RAF Lyneham shortly after midnight on 2 August, flying in a B-24 Liberator bomber code-named *Commando* and piloted by an American, William Vanderkloot, of RAF Ferry Command.

Vanderkloot had assured the Chief of Air Staff Sir Charles Portal that he could make the flight with one stop at Gibraltar. The route he proposed would take *Commando* well away from land-based enemy aircraft in North Africa. The next day Vanderkloot was taken to Downing Street, where he was greeted by Churchill, clad in dressing gown and slippers, and offered a drink. It was the start of a long relationship in which Vanderkloot flew the Prime Minister on sensitive missions across Europe, Russia, North Africa and the Middle East. Conditions in the Liberator were markedly less comfortable than in the flying boats to which Churchill had grown accustomed. *Commando* was unheated, and sharp draughts whistled down the fuselage. There were no beds, sleeping accommodation being provided by two shelves in the after-cabin for Churchill and Cadogan. Nevertheless, Churchill embraced the rigours of travel with his customary brio. Escorted by four Bristol Beaufighters, *Commando* flew from Gibraltar at 6pm on the 3rd, at first avoiding the Mediterranean by crossing Spanish and Vichy territory in North Africa. Before turning in, Churchill briefly pondered the complications which would accompany a forced landing in these unfriendly parts. At sun-up on 4 August he rose from his shelf to watch the unfolding scene from the co-pilot's seat: " ... there in the pale, glimmering dawn the endless winding silver ribbon of the Nile stretched joyously before us. Often had I seen the day break on the Nile. In war and peace I had traversed by land or water almost its whole length... Never had the glint of daylight on its waters been so welcome to me."

Top of Churchill's agenda in Cairo was the replacement of General Sir Claude Auchinleck, a great Indian Army officer and Commander-in-Chief Middle East. Auchinleck had assumed personal command of British Eighth Army on 24 June and had inflicted a crucial defeat on the Afrika Korps in the First Battle of El Alamein. However, Churchill had never forgiven "The Auk", as he was affectionately known by his troops, for the loss of the North African port of Tobruk on 21 June. Churchill found the decision to sack Auchinleck painful, likening it to shooting a noble stag. He spent his time in Cairo between 4 and 10 August conferring over the Auk's successor with General Jan Smuts, the South African premier, the recently arrived Field Marshal Sir Archibald Wavell, Commander-in-Chief India, General Alan Brooke, appointed CIGS in December 1941, and Auchhinleck himself. A purge followed. On 15 August he replaced Auchinleck with General Harold Alexander as Commander-in-Chief Middle East. General Sir Bernard Montgomery was appointed commander of Eighth Army, the original choice, General W.H.E. "Strafer" Gott, having been shot down and killed by enemy aircraft on 7 August while flying to Cairo.

On 4 August Churchill telegraphed Stalin, informing the Soviet leader of his plan to fly to Moscow via the Persian city of Teheran. The next day he asked President Roosevelt to allow the prominent American businessman Averell Harriman, then in London negotiating the terms of Lend-Lease, to accompany him on the trip, adding "I feel that things would be easier if we all seemed to be together." Roosevelt concurred and Harriman immediately travelled to North Africa to join the Prime Minister. Late on the night of 10 August, Churchill's party left for Moscow in three aircraft. The party included Brooke, Wavell, who spoke Russian, Air Chief Marshal Sir Arthur Tedder, Commander-in-Chief Mediterranean Air Command, and Cadogan. Churchill and Harriman travelled together. At dawn, as they approached the mountains of Kurdistan, Churchill asked Vanderkloot the height at which he intended to fly over them. Vanderkloot, who was in high spirits, replied that nine thousand feet would be adequate. Churchill, having examined a map which displayed the Elburz mountains rising to a maximum of 20,000 feet, reassured himself that Vanderkloot could thread his way through them relatively easily, provided that they did not run into cloud, and donned his oxygen mask. Just before they landed, another mild shock was in store. Churchill recalled: "I noticed that the altimeter registered four thousand five hundred feet, and ignorantly remarked, 'You had better get that adjusted before we take off again.' But Vanderkloot replied, 'The Teheran airfield is over four thousand feet above sea level'."

It was now too late to attempt to fly over the northern range of the Elburz Mountains before night fell, and Churchill was invited to lunch with the pro-Allied 23-year-old Shah of Persia, Mohammad Reza Pahlavi, whose impressive palace was set in a forest on the spur of a mountain. Later, in the garden of the British Legation, Churchill discussed the handing over to the Americans of the recently completed Trans-Persian railway, built through mountain gorges by British engineers. On 12 August, Churchill flew northwards towards the Caspian Sea, passing over another mountain range. *Commando* had taken on two new passengers, Red Army officers, and the responsibility for the Prime Minister's safe arrival now passed into the hands of the Soviets. Churchill noticed that *Commando* was now flying alone, and was told that the aircraft carrying the CIGS, Wavell and Cadogan had been forced by engine trouble to turn back. Flying over the Caspian, Churchill recalled that over twenty-five years before, while Secretary of State for War, he had inherited "a fleet upon it, which for nearly a year ruled its pale, placid waters". As *Commando* lost altitude, Churchill could see in the distance Baku and its cluster of oil fields, the capture of which was a crucial element of Hitler's War Directive No. 45. This envisaged a German breakthrough in the Caucasus and then into the Near East. Key to the plan was the destruction of Stalingrad, the industrial city to the north-west of the Caucasus. The German High Command reckoned that the Stalingrad operation, launched on 19 August would take just over a week. On such miscalculations are the fates of armies and nations decided.

Keeping well away from the gathering storm at Stalingrad, *Commando* flew on to the Volga delta. Churchill's view from the aircraft was one of barely relieved monotony: "As far as the eye could reach spread vast expanses of Russia, brown and flat and with hardly a sign of human habitation. Here and there sharp rectilineal patches of ploughed land revealed an occasional state farm. For a long way the mighty Volga gleamed in curves and stretches as it flowed between its wide, dark margins of marsh. Sometimes a road, as straight as a ruler, ran from one wide horizon to the other. After an hour or so of this I clambered back along the bomb bay to the cabin and slept."

Churchill had much on his mind. He was about to visit a Bolshevik state which he had done his best to strangle at birth. What was he to say to its leaders now? Churchill was well aware that merely repeating "No Second Front in 1942", which from his point of view was a non-negotiable proposition, was rather like taking a block of ice to the North Pole. Until June 1941 he had been implacably hostile to the Soviet Union, just as Stalin had viewed with utter indifference the plight of the British in the summer of 1940. Churchill, the man of Empire, conjectured that Nazi victory in that year would have been followed by the rapid division of the spoils in the Far East between the erstwhile Non-Aggression allies of 1939. Now that the flail of *Blitzkrieg* had, albeit temporarily, brought Germany to the gates of Moscow, how was he to reach an active accommodation with Josef Stalin?

While the Prime Minister pondered these sobering obstacles to mutual understanding, the spires and domes of the Soviet capital came into view. *Commando* and its passengers were met by Vyacheslav Molotov at the head of a regiment of Russian generals, the bulk of the Soviet diplomatic corps and a swarm of photographers. Churchill and Harriman inspected a guard of honour and strode past a band playing the Soviet, British and American national anthems before they both delivered short speeches. Harriman then proceeded to the American Embassy. Accompanied by Molotov, Churchill was driven in a stuffy limousine through the deserted streets of Moscow to "State

Villa No. 7". Opening his window to get some air, he was surprised to find that the glass was over two inches think. He was told by the Russian interpreter, M. Pavlov, that Molotov considered this degree of protection "more prudent". In less than 40 minutes the limousine covered the eight miles to State Villa No. 7.

The preparations which Stalin had made for Churchill were impeccable and lavish. He was cordially greeted by a huge officer, apparently from an aristocratic pre-Revolutionary family, and several servants in crisp white coats who presided over a large table in the dining room laden with every conceivable Russian delicacy. The Prime Minister was then guided through a spacious reception room into a brilliantly lit bedroom and bathroom. The latter Churchill found particularly impressive after his gruelling flight: "The hot and cold water gushed. I longed for a hot bath after the length and heat of the journey. All were instantly prepared. In France I noticed that they were not fed by separate hot and cold water taps and that they had no plugs. Hot and cold turned on at once through a single spout, mingled to exactly the temperature one desired. Moreover, one did not wash one's hands in the basins but under the flowing currents of the taps. In a modest way I have adopted the system at home. If there is no scarcity of water it is far the best."

After bathing and eating and drinking his fill, Churchill was ready for a meeting with Stalin at 7pm on the 12th. As the second aircraft carrying the rest of Churchill's party had not yet arrived, those present at this initial meeting were Churchill, Stalin, Molotov, Marshal Klimenti Voroshilov, a member of the Bolshevik old guard and a Civil War comrade of Stalin, Harriman, the British Ambassador, Sir Archibald Clark Kerr, and the interpreters. The two leaders were an intriguing sight. Both men were about five and a half feet tall. Churchill was rubicund and bald, like a big baby, Stalin dark-haired and swarthy, with a pockmarked face and withered left arm (the result of a childhood accident), his immobile left hand rammed into the pocket of his tunic. They were both accustomed to dominating any room they entered.

Churchill began by stating that the opening of a Second Front in France could not happen until the arrival of a million US troops in Britain in 1943 at the earliest. By then the Americans would have at their disposal 27 divisions and the British 21, roughly half of them armoured. At present there were only two and a half American divisions in England. Furthermore, there were insufficient landing craft in Britain to mount a cross-Channel invasion of north-west Europe, and there was always the possibility that by 1943 the German Army in the West might be stronger. This statement failed to convince a morose Stalin, who asked if it was impossible to attack any part of the French coast. Churchill produced a map showing the extreme difficulty of providing air cover for the invasion force over the Channel and the French coast. Stalin considered this and then observed that there was not a single German division in France of any value. Churchill begged to differ, emphasising that he had brought Wavell and Brooke with him for the precise purpose of analysing these operational problems with the Soviet High Command (*Stavka*).

Churchill reminded Stalin of the folly of initiating premature action, which at this stage in the war would help no one. An increasingly restless Stalin responded by asking Churchill why he and his generals were apparently afraid of the Germans. In the Soviet leader's cruel universe, the only way of discovering the value of your troops was to commit them to battle. The Prime Minister then posed a question. Why was it that in the summer of 1940 Adolf Hitler, then at the height of his power, did not invade the south of Britain when all that stood in his way were 20,000 trained men, 200 guns and 50 tanks? Churchill then provided the answer. Crossing the English Channel was an operation fraught with danger. Stalin was unimpressed. A German landing in England would have been opposed by the British people. An Allied landing in France would have the support of the French people. The exchanges went back and forth. Churchill pointed out that a premature and unsuccessful landing would expose the French people to a terrible revenge exacted by Hitler. Silence fell. Then Stalin said he accepted Churchill's refusal to make a landing in

During Churchill's final illness, early photographs of his life were published including: four year old Churchill, full-length, standing, held by his mother, Lady Randolph Churchill (left) three-quarter-length, standing, and twelve year old Churchill, full-length, standing, attending Harrow School in England (right). (Library of Congress)

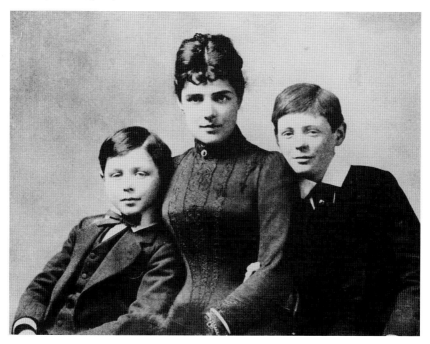

Jennie Churchill with her sons.

Left: Churchill on the campaign trail, 1899.

Below: Churchill at Blomfontein during the Second Boer War. (Library of Congress)

Churchill with Kaiser Wilhelm II during a military manoeuvre in 1906. (Library of Congress)

Churchill in the early 1900s.
(Library of Congress)

Churchill's wife, Clementine
Hozier, in 1915. (Library of
Congress)

Above: Winston Churchill, T. E. Lawrence and Emir Abdullah walking in the gardens of the Government House, Jerusalem, during a secret conference in 1921. (Library of Congress)

Right: Sir Herbert Samuel and Winston Churchill at tree-planting ceremony in 1921 on the site of Hebrew University, Mount Scopus, at the American Colony in Jerusalem. (Library of Congress)

Churchill calling on President Herbert Hoover at the White House in 1929.
(Library of Congress)

American and British military leaders at the Casablanca conference, 1943. Includes Winston Churchill (seated third from left), Franklin D. Roosevelt (fourth from left), and General Sir Alan Brooke (fifth from left). (Library of Congress)

On behalf of George VI, Churchill presents the Sword of Stalingrad to Stalin, for the citizens of Stalingrad, in the board room of the Russian Embasy at Teheran in December 1943. (Library of Congress)

Mary Churchill, Winston's youngest daughter, says goodbye to Harry Truman on the steps of the 'Little White House', Truman's residence during the Potsdam Conference of July 1945. Partially visible behind are Admiral William Leahy, General Dwight D. Eisenhower and General Harry Vaughan. (National Archives and Records Administration)

France in 1942 but remained unconvinced by the Prime Minister's arguments.

Churchill now attempted to draw Stalin's attention southward and away from the Channel, suggesting that a landing on a fortified coast in north-east France was not the only option open to the Western Allies. Might they oblige Hitler to defend the Pas de Calais in strength while mounting an operation in south-west France in the Loire or the Gironde, or the Scheldt estuary in Holland? Stalin remained sceptical but thawed when Churchill moved on to the strategic bombing campaign against Germany. At the end of May, Bomber Command had mounted the first "1,000 Bomber Raid" against the German city of Cologne and two follow-up raids on Essen, on 1 June and Bremen, on 25 June. All three raids were code-named *Millennium* and were a considerable propaganda coup. Stalin was impressed, pointing out the importance of striking at the heart of German civilian morale. The tension around the table was lifted and Churchill took advantage of this to introduce the subject of *Torch*, the Allied invasion of French North Africa, which he had agreed with Roosevelt to disclose secretly to Stalin. As Churchill went through the details of *Torch*, Stalin became animated, asking how the operation, when it went ahead, in October 1942, would be received in Spain and Vichy France. The Soviet leader considered the plan could be justified on military grounds but was concerned about its effects on metropolitan France.

Churchill went on to outline the strategic advantages which would flow from the freeing up of the Mediterranean and the opening up of another Allied front to attack the vulnerable belly of Nazi Europe. He chose to illustrate this point by drawing a sketch of a crocodile, whose "soft underbelly" he likened to the defensive Axis perimeter in the South of France, Italy and the Balkans. He may have been right about the first assertion but not the second and third. Progress up the Italian peninsula, from 1943 to 1945, was to prove slow and hard. Nevertheless, in the summer heat of Moscow in August 1942, Stalin warmed to the idea and observed, "May God prosper this undertaking."

This marked a turning point in the conversation, although Stalin continued to fire questions at Churchill. He was still concerned that an Anglo-American intervention in North Africa might be misunderstood in metropolitan France. He raised the question of de Gaulle, his relations with Churchill and his rivalry with General Henri Giraud (see p. 178). Churchill explained that the British did not favour de Gaulle's involvement in *Torch*, as the Vichy French troops in North Africa were likely to fire on him but not on the Americans. In this he was strongly supported by Harriman. Stalin then demonstrated his strategic grasp of the advantages of *Torch* with a quickfire summary. It would threaten Rommel from his rear; it would send a clear message to the Spanish; it would produce fighting between Germans and Frenchmen in France; and it would expose Italy to the full force of the war. Churchill later recalled: "Very few people alive could have comprehended in so few minutes the reasons which we had all so long been wrestling with for months. He saw it all in a flash."

In a scene reminiscent of Charlie Chaplin's capering in the movie *The Great Dictator*, Churchill, Stalin and their confederates gathered round a globe while Churchill, pressing home his advantage, continued to extol the advantages of clearing the Axis from the Mediterranean. He had seemingly weathered the storm of Stalin's displeasure about postponing the Allied return to north-west Europe, and the meeting, which had lasted four hours, broke up in an atmosphere of goodwill. Churchill returned to State Villa No. 7, dictated telegrams to his War Cabinet and Roosevelt and slept deeply and long.

On Thursday the 13th, Blenheim Day as Churchill fondly recalled, the Prime Minister met Molotov at noon to run over in detail the discussions of the night before, in particular the disagreement over the opening of a Second Front. Molotov listened cordially but offered no opinions beyond agreeing to a second meeting with Stalin at 11pm, which would also be attended by Harriman, Cadogan, Brooke, Tedder and Wavell, who had now arrived in Moscow in a Russian aircraft. Before leaving, the Prime Minister warned Molotov that Stalin would be making a major mistake if he treated the Anglo-American delegation roughly, as they had travelled so far. Molotov replied, "Stalin is a very wise man. You may be sure that, however he argues, he understands all. I will tell him what you say."

Churchill then seized the opportunity to take a walk in the summer sunshine around State Villa No.7's extensive grounds, which were heavily guarded by troops and police. He strolled through a fir wood and lay on the grass and piles of pine needles, walked past spouting fountains and a huge glass tank filled with goldfish, which he fed from his hand. About a hundred yards from the State Villa was an air raid shelter, where he was given a conducted tour. A lift took the Prime Minister some 90 feet underground where he inspected 10 large rooms inside a brilliantly lit, massively reinforced concrete box. Churchill reflected that on the whole, he preferred the goldfish.

At 11pm Churchill and his companions were back at the Kremlin, where they found Stalin in anything but a conciliatory mood. In a two-hour tirade, much of it aimed personally at Churchill, Stalin returned to the theme of the Western Allies' reluctance to open a Second Front, adding for good measure the poor quality of the weaponry they had sent the Soviets, the ineffectiveness, bordering on cowardice, of the Royal Navy, and the Allies' failure to appreciate the sacrifices made by the Red Army. It was, as Churchill recalled, "a most unpleasant discussion". Stalin's outburst was partly a negotiating tactic aimed at unsettling Churchill and his delegation, but it also reflected his genuine anger. The Soviet translator that day was Valentin Berezhkov, a shrewd judge of Stalin's modus operandi:

All those people that came to [Stalin] they immediately believed him, everything that he said. He could be severe, very severe, very unpleasant. And the next day he could be very cordial, very nice. This happened with Churchill, for example, when he came in '42 and I translated. Stalin was angry and he offended Churchill, saying that the British were afraid of the Germans, that they would never win this war.

Churchill also became angry and it was very unpleasant, both trying to offend each other. Then the next day Stalin [acted] like nothing had happened, he was so cordial. Churchill said he couldn't believe that this was the same Stalin that he'd seen the previous day. I think Stalin was a great actor.

Brooke was impressed by Stalin, but feared that Churchill would struggle to strike up the friendship which now existed between the Prime Minister and Roosevelt: "The two leaders ... are poles apart as human beings ... Stalin is a realist if ever there was one, facts only count with him, plans, hypotheses, future possibilities mean little to him, but he is ready to face facts even when unpleasant. Winston, on the other hand, never seems anxious to face an unpleasantness until forced to do so. He appealed to sentiments in Stalin which I do not think exist there."

Another factor governing Stalin's performance in Moscow was that the State Villa was almost certainly bugged, as was Churchill's accommodation in Yalta in 1945. Between his first and second meetings with Stalin, Churchill had told Tedder that Stalin was "just a peasant" and that he knew perfectly well how to handle him. This lofty attitude from Churchill must have been music to Stalin's ears, encouraging him to further needle his ally. Moreover, Churchill felt Stalin's barbs keenly, at one point threatening to boycott the official dinner on the 14th. He was eventually persuaded to turn up, inappropriately dressed in his siren suit. The official dinners on these occasions were always lengthy affairs, interrupted by endless toasts followed by short speeches. In his memoirs of the wartime years Churchill pointed out, not wholly convincingly, that there was no truth in the stories that they descended into prolonged drinking bouts: "The Marshal [Stalin] and his colleagues invariably drank their toasts from tiny glasses, taking only a sip on each occasion." Brooke's memory of the event differed from that of the Prime Minister:

From the beginning vodka flowed freely and one's glass kept being filled up. The table groaned under every description of hors d'oeuvres, fish etc. Stalin sat at the centre of the table with the Prime Minister on his right and Harriman on his left, then came an interpreter, then myself and Voroshilov on my left with a Foreign Office official. Molotov was opposite Stalin, and started proposing toasts within five minutes of our having sat down. These toasts went on continuously. My turn came about third or fourth and I replied proposing the health of the Red Army, after which I was left in peace... By the end of dinner Stalin was quite lively, walking round the table to click glasses with various people he was proposing the health of. He is an outstanding man ... but not an attractive one. He has got an unpleasantly cold, crafty dead face, and whenever I look at him I can imagine him sending people off to their doom without even turning a hair.

Given Churchill's fondness for whisky and champagne, and much evidence of this, particularly from the Yalta Conference, it is clear that drinking was the device that he habitually used to keep at bay the "Black Dog" depression from which he suffered throughout his life. In Moscow his mood had yawed between the melancholy and the manic. At one point he told the doctor who accompanied him, Sir Charles Wilson (later Lord Moran), "I ought not to have come... I am going to leave this man [Stalin] to fight his own battles." After his final hour-long meeting with Stalin on the evening of the 15th, he accepted the Soviet leader's invitation to accompany him to his private quarters for some drinks. The two men walked through a silent, deserted Kremlin to Stalin's surprisingly modest apartment where they were greeted by his red-headed daughter Svetlana, who kissed her father dutifully, prompting him to turn to the Prime Minister with a look that said, "You see, even we Bolsheviks have a family life." The dutiful Molotov was then summoned by Stalin, who explained that he was concerned about tidying up the post-summit communiqué, adding "There is one thing about Molotov – he can drink." As an aged housekeeper laid the table, it dawned on Churchill that a dinner was imminent, in addition to the drinks. It lasted from 8.30 to 2.30am the following morning.

The conversation quickly turned to the Arctic convoys, prompting Stalin to make a dismissive remark about the destruction of the PQ17 Arctic convoy by the Luftwaffe and U-boats in early July 1942. Fearing attack by the German battleship *Tirpitz*, the Royal Navy escort had been withdrawn and the ships were ordered to go on alone. Only nine ships out of thirty-four reached Soviet ports. Stalin was once again needling the Prime Minister, asking via the understandably hesitant Russian translator, "Has the British Navy no sense of glory?" Churchill shot back, "You must take it from me what was done was right. I really do know a lot about the Navy and sea-war." To which Stalin replied, "Meaning I know nothing." Churchill parried this thrust, observing that Russia is a "land animal" while the British are "sea animals". After a short silence, Churchill asked Stalin if was aware that Molotov, while recently in Washington, remarked that he was determined to make an unaccompanied visit to New York and that the delay in his return was not caused by a technical fault in his aircraft but rather because he was intending to set off on a jaunt of his own. Molotov glumly greeted this sally, before Stalin, recovering his sinister good humour, joked, "He did not go to New York. He went to Chicago, where the other gangsters live."

Equilibrium having been restored, talk ranged from the capture of the North Cape in northern Norway to ease the pressure on the Arctic convoys, one of Churchill's impractical hobbyhorses, Stalin's forcible establishment of collective farms and, according to Stalin, the all-round improvement in the Soviet food supply. Churchill thought about the suffering involved but decided not to repeat Burke's dictum, "If I cannot have reform without injustice, I will not have reform," as in the midst of a world war it seemed "vain to moralise aloud". At 1am Cadogan arrived with the draft communiqué, closely followed by a suckling pig. Up to this point Stalin had only toyed with the succession of dishes which had arrived at the table. As it was now his customary dinner hour, he fell upon the pig single-handed. Cadogan had happened on a scene of inebriated good fellowship "as merry as a marriage bell". He diplomatically declined Stalin's invitation to stay for the pig. From 2am Stalin attended to reports from every sector on the 2,000-mile front. At 2.30, with the communiqué agreed, Churchill took his leave. He had a splitting headache and begged the clearly exhausted Molotov not to see him off at the airport. Molotov gave him a reproachful look.

The communiqué stated:

> A number of decisions were reached covering the field of the war against Hitlerite Germany and her associates in Europe. This just war of liberation both Governments are determined to carry on with all their power and energy until the complete destruction of Hitlerism and any similar tyranny has been achieved. The discussions, which were carried on in an atmosphere of cordiality and complete sincerity, provided an opportunity of reaffirming the existence of the close friendship and understanding between the Soviet Union, Great Britain and the United Sates of America, in entire accordance with the Allied relationship existing between them.

Clark Kerr was at the State Villa to greet an exultant Churchill: "The P.M. began to chuckle and to kick a pair of gay legs in the air. I can't remember the words he used but it had all been grand. He had cemented a friendship with Stalin. My God! He was glad he had come. Stalin had been splendid. What a pleasure it was to work with that 'great man'… He was like that dog with two cocks." It remained to be seen how long this remarkable friendship would last. Churchill returned to Cairo, where he received congratulations from the King: "I am delighted that your talks with Stalin ended on such a friendly note. As a bearer of unwelcome news your task was a very disagreeable one, but I congratulate you heartily on the skill with which you accomplished it. The personal relationship which you have established with Stalin should be valuable in the days to come; and your long journey has, I am sure, been well worth while." On the following day Churchill replied that he was in the best of health and not at all tired, adding that he now had to deal with a number of important and urgent problems.

Top of the list was the pressure on the Mediterranean island of Malta, which in August 1942 had been awarded the George Cross in recognition of the civilian population's heroism under constant Axis air attack. The situation in Malta was now considered so critical that the decision was taken to run a convoy of 14 fast merchantmen to the island. The code-name for the operation was *Pedestal*, and the convoy was escorted by the battleships *Nelson* and *Rodney*, the carriers *Victorious*, *Indomitable* and *Eagle*, three cruisers, four anti-aircraft cruisers and 24 destroyers under the overall command of Vice-Admiral E.N. Syfret. The heavy ships were under orders to turn back when the convoy reached the Sicilian Narrows and thereafter it would have the protection of three cruisers, one anti-aircraft cruiser and 12 destroyers. Recognising its importance, Axis sea- and airborne forces strove to destroy the convoy in a running battle from 10 to 13 August. In spite of the heavy merchant marine and Royal Navy losses incurred in the operation, *Pedestal* restored Malta's ability to resist, reviving both its defensive and offensive capability.

Shortly afterwards, Churchill received news of the Dieppe raid of 19 August, Operation *Jubilee*, a "reconnaissance in force" which had been mounted in large part to soothe Soviet complaints about the lack of a Second Front and also to provide battle experience for the Commandos and the 2nd Canadian Division. *Jubilee* was little short of a disaster which suffered heavy losses and was a salutary warning about the dangers of a premature invasion of north-west Europe. Nevertheless, it taught the Allies many vital lessons in organisation and tactics. On the day of the Dieppe raid, Churchill had driven out past the Pyramids with Alexander and Brooke to the headquarters of Eighth Army at Burg-el-Arab, where they all swam in the sea with Montgomery. Churchill noticed that the troops swimming from the beach all wore white bathing drawers, which prompted him to question the unnecessary expense of providing them with swimwear. He recalled that when he marched to Omdurman it was unquestioningly accepted that at all costs the skin had to be shielded from the African sun. Special spine pads, pith helmets and thick underclothing were the order of the day. Forty-four years later the majority of the men went about their duties hatless and semi-naked. Most without harm.

Later, in his map wagon, Montgomery took Churchill and his companions on a masterly tour d'horizon, accurately predicting the axis of Rommel's next attack and the plans he had drawn up to meet and defeat it, after which he intended to go onto the offensive. He needed six weeks to complete his reorganisation of Eighth Army and break in the 250 American Sherman tanks which had been delivered. The next day Churchill was taken on a tour of what was to become the battlefield of El Alamein. At the Ruweisat Ridge, soon to become a key point in the battle, he surveyed

... the mass of our armour, camouflaged, concealed and dispersed, yet tactically concentrated, Here I met the young Brigadier Roberts, who at that time commanded the whole of our armoured force in this vital position... Although of course no gatherings of troops could be allowed under the enemy's continuous air reconnaissance, I saw a great many soldiers that day, who greeted me with grins and cheers. I inspected my own regiment, the Fourth Hussars, or as many of them as they dared to bring together – perhaps fifty or sixty – near the field cemetery, in which a number of their comrades had been newly buried. All this was moving, but with it all there grew a sense of the reviving ardour of the Army. Everybody said what a change there was since Montgomery had taken command. I could feel the truth of this with joy and comfort.

Lunch followed with the New Zealander General Sir Bernard Freyberg, a much-decorated veteran of the First World War, whom Churchill had encountered during that conflict. In the General's sweltering mess tent, "We had an enjoyable lunch, the centrepiece of which was a scalding broth of tinned New Zealand oysters." During the meal Montgomery arrived and was invited by Freyberg to join them. However, Montgomery, having made it a rule never to accept hospitality from subordinates, chose to sit outside the tent in his car eating a sandwich and drinking lemonade. The convivial Churchill pondered this self-imposed austerity: "Napoleon might also have stood aloof in the interests of discipline ... but he would certainly have had an excellent roast chicken, served him from his own fourgon [wagon]. Marlborough would have entered and quaffed the good wine with his officers – Cromwell, I think, too."

Churchill flew back to Britain on the night of 23 August. The enterprising Vanderkloot had one more surprise in store for him. After a long sleep, the Prime Minister clambered into the cockpit as *Commando* was nearing Gibraltar flying thirty feet above the sea through a thick early morning mist. Churchill was struck with a sudden fear that the American pilot would slam straight into a formidable obstacle, the Rock of Gibraltar. He asked Vanderkloot if he could climb *Commando* above the murk. Vanderkloot demurred and five minutes later *Commando* burst through the mist to present Churchill with a spectacular early morning view of the Rock. After some three hours flying in very poor visibility, Vanderkloot had been right on the button. *Commando* sped past the Rock, now only a few hundred yards away and made a perfect landing. As he later admitted, it was a fine performance.

9

CASABLANCA

On the Eastern Front, German Sixth Army had opened its assault on Stalingrad on 19 August 1942. Three months later it was still locked in a ferocious street-by-street battle with the defenders of the city, disrupting Hitler's plans for a drive into the Caucasus. The reduction of Stalingrad began to obsess Hitler, as it did Stalin. Not only was it the largest of the Soviet Union's cities to bear his name. It was also the place where in 1918 the "southern clique" – Stalin and Marshals Voroshilov, Budenny and Timoshenko – had defied Trotsky over the conduct of the war against the White Russians, the critical episode which marked his rise to power in the Communist Party.

Stalingrad became a tomb for Sixth Army. On 31 January 1943, its commander, Field Marshal Friedrich von Paulus, and 100,000 men went into captivity. The same month a massive Red Army counterblow, plans for which Stalin outlined to Churchill in Moscow the previous August, was launched between Orel and Rostock, threatening Kharkov and the German forces withdrawing from the Caucasus. The Soviet offensive was then halted in its tracks in February-March 1943 by a perfectly weighted riposte delivered by Field Marshal Erich von Manstein. When the fighting died down in the mud of the spring thaw, it left a huge fist-shaped salient, at whose centre lay the city of Kursk, in the heartland of the Ukraine, jutting westward into the German line.

The tide was also turning against the Third Reich in the Battle of the Atlantic after a period of sustained German success. In March 1943 the struggle for the sea lanes has reached crisis point for the Western Allies as Grand Admiral Dönitz's U-boat wolf packs savaged two Allied convoys. That month the number of ships accounted for by the U-boats in the North Atlantic was 108, a total that threatened the lifeline strung between Britain and the United States. The moment passed. The mid-Atlantic "air gap" – the stretch of water in which the U-boats had operated free of interference from Allied long-range patrol aircraft – was closed and a host of technical developments was introduced, ranging from centimetric radar to the breaking at Bletchley Park of the U-boats' *Shark* code. The wolf packs would soon be withdrawn from the North Atlantic to go in search of less dangerous hunting grounds.

By the spring of 1943 the tide was also turning in North Africa. The German high point in this theatre had been reached in August 1942 before Montgomery checked Rommel's Afrika Korps at Alam Halfa. Defeat followed at El Alamein in October-November, and on 8 November an Anglo-American army made a number of landings in French North Africa in Operation *Torch*. The response of the Axis was to send reinforcements from Germany. They joined hands with Rommel's retreating army and fierce fighting followed in the mountains of Tunisia. By March 1943 the Axis supply situation in Tunisia had become critical. Rommel was brought back to Germany to be decorated by Hitler and did not return to North Africa. German Army Group Africa was not so fortunate. By 12 May 1943, Axis resistance in North Africa was at an end and, with the fall of Tunis, some 240,000 Axis prisoners, nearly half of them German, passed into Allied captivity. Hitler had foreseen this reverse but, in a now regularly recurring pattern, found himself unable to liquidate a front. He had presided over another catastrophe.

Allied success made it all the more important to agree on a common strategy. On 12 January 1943 Churchill flew to Casablanca on the Atlantic coast of Morocco for an Allied conference code-named *Symbol*. Once again travelling in *Commando* provided its share of anxious moments. A petrol engine which had been installed in the aircraft to provide heating malfunctioned. Churchill woke up at 2am on the 13th with a burning sensation in his toes while *Commando* was flying at 8,000 feet over the Atlantic, 500 miles from anywhere. It looked as if his blankets might catch fire. Churchill struggled out of his bunk to alert Air Chief Marshal Charles Portal, Chief of Air Staff, who was sound asleep in a chair below the Prime Minister's berth. Both men set off on a search of the cabin for more hot points, of which they found two, before alerting the two men in charge of the heater. Their diligence prevented a mid-air conflagration had the petrol ignited. Churchill decided that he was happier to freeze rather than go up in flames and ordered the heating to be turned off. He returned to his bunk shivering with cold as icy drafts lashed *Commando*'s fuselage.

It was warmer when *Commando* touched down in Casablanca. The conference was to be held in a large hotel in the suburb of Anfa. Ringing the hotel were comfortable villas which were reserved for Churchill, Roosevelt, General Henri Giraud and, if he decided to come to Casablanca, General de Gaulle. While waiting for Roosevelt to arrive on the 14th, Churchill walked on the beach with Admiral of the Fleet Sir Dudley Pound and his Chiefs of Staff while 15-foot waves crashed in from the Atlantic Ocean. Their promenade was the preliminary to an 11-day conference, at which the decisions they made were underlaid by a number of clashing concerns about the conduct of the European and Pacific wars over the coming months. The bare bones of the agreement reached at the conference were as follows: the invasion of Sicily in the Mediterranean; the prosecution of a joint strategic bombing offensive against Germany; the acceleration of the build-up of US troops in Britain for an invasion of north-west Europe; and the demand, at the insistence of Roosevelt, of an unconditional surrender by Germany and Japan. These determinations were not reached without considerable misgivings shared by the two Allies, particularly by the British.

On 18 January Churchill despatched a report to Deputy Prime Minister Attlee and the War Cabinet. In it he outlined the Allied global strategy being decided in Casablanca theatre by theatre by the Anglo-American Combined Chiefs of Staff (CCS). Their meetings were not attended by the Prime Minister or the President, who were nonetheless kept in constant touch with the evolving picture. This process enabled Churchill and Roosevelt to address the most pressing problems facing the Allies at the start of the year. The first concerned the opening of a Second Front. In January 1943, with the Battle of Stalingrad still raging, Stalin needed urgent help from his Western Allies. The Soviet Union was still the only Allied power fighting the *Wehrmacht* in Europe. Operation *Torch*, the invasion of North Africa in November 1942, had not significantly slowed the transfer of fresh German divisions to the Eastern Front. Stalin continued to urge action from the British and Americans to establish a Second Front in Europe, which would force Hitler to withdraw significant forces from the war in the East.

The Americans had from the autumn of 1942 advocated an Allied return to Western Europe, the so-called *Sledgehammer* plan of which Churchill was extremely wary. In the spring of 1942, General George Catlett Marshall, Chairman of the US Joint Chiefs of Staff, had arrived in London to discuss the American military build-up in Britain, code-named Operation *Bolero*, and to hammer out with the British a timetable for the opening of the Second Front. Marshall, who believed that the Second Front should be mounted on the shortest route into Germany at the earliest possible date, was a formidable figure who deliberately and successfully unsettled his commander-in-chief, Roosevelt, by declining to laugh at any of the President's jokes, and not allowing the President to address him by his first name. He was equally stern with Churchill, remaining resolutely unenthusiastic about the Prime Minister's determined advocacy of an invasion of French North Africa, an operation which eventually saw the light of day as *Torch*. The dogged Marshall eventually obtained a grudging British commitment to a Second Front in 1943. Nevertheless, General Brooke in his diary noted that while the British Chiefs of

Staff retained their reservations about *Sledgehammer*, it remained a remote possibility, even in 1942, contingent on the unlikely event of a sudden German collapse.

The balance of this strategic tug-of-war had nonetheless shifted in the summer of 1942 with the arrival in Britain of General Dwight D. Eisenhower as Commanding General European Theatre of Operations (ETO). Eisenhower quickly grasped that the time was not ripe for *Sledgehammer*. Sensing the reluctance of Churchill and the British High Command, still haunted by memories of the Western Front in the First World War, to embrace *Sledgehammer*, and the enormous logistical problems the Allies faced in mounting such an operation, he estimated that a cross-Channel operation which could offer the best chance of achieving success could not be launched until the summer of 1944. At Casablanca, these considerations weighed heavily on Churchill, now fast becoming the junior partner in the Western Alliance. The Prime Minister was the determined advocate of an indirect, essentially peripheralist strategy which the British had perforce adopted after the summer of 1940. This aimed at nibbling away at the foundations of Hitler's fortress empire in the Mediterranean until a weakening in the edifice opened an indirect route, via the Italian peninsula and then the Balkans, to the greater prize of the Third Reich itself.

The Americans were now operating on a vastly wider scale than the British, and this meant that the demands in the Pacific theatre also had a bearing on the deliberations at Casablanca. When Marshall came to Britain in July 1942, he was accompanied by Admiral Ernest J. King, the US Navy's Chief of Operations, an Anglophobe and a single-minded supporter of the primacy of the Pacific theatre. Their visit sparked a heated strategic debate in which the Americans renewed their demands for the opening of a Second Front that year while the British Chiefs of Staff and War Cabinet understandably dug in their heels. At this point Roosevelt came to Churchill's aid, having been convinced by the Prime Minister's forcefully delivered arguments during his visit to Washington in June 1942.

Nevertheless, the protracted disagreements among the Americans between the Germany First and Pacific factions had not been fully resolved when the Allies met at Casablanca. To clinch the argument with Marshall, Churchill knew that a follow-up operation to *Torch*, preferably the invasion of Sicily as a preliminary to a landing on the Italian peninsula, could not be allowed to disrupt the schedule agreed in the summer of 1942 for the Second Front. For his part, Marshall believed that American incursions into the Mediterranean, essentially a secondary theatre draining Allied resources like a vacuum pump, had been justified by the clearing of French North Africa, completed in May 1943, and the securing of the Suez Canal, Britain's imperial artery at the eastern end of the Mediterranean. However, Churchill retained grave misgivings about the risks attached to the opening of a Second Front, were it to be launched later in 1943. In this he was correct. A continental incursion in 1943 would have faced much stronger opposition, on the land and in the air, than it did in June 1944 when the German Army and Luftwaffe had been fatally weakened by the attrition of the Eastern Front.

The most significant result flowing from *Symbol*, whether the Americans liked it or not, was that the Mediterranean strategy had secured a foothold in Allied strategic planning. The successful conclusion of *Torch*, the clearing of the North African coast, was to be followed by the invasion of Sicily (Operation *Husky*), another peripheral move but vital for Churchill, as its implementation would rule out the opening of the Second Front in north-west Europe until 1944. For the Americans, *Husky* was only one of a number of available options. Moreover, at this stage they did not commit themselves beyond Sicily to the invasion of peninsular Italy. However, in this particular game of military diplomacy they had been outmanoeuvred by the British, who were playing a longer game, although not one which ultimately would be to their military advantage.

By the end of *Symbol*, the British had secured, barring a German collapse, the postponement of the invasion of north-west Europe until 1944. Nevertheless, there was still an urgent need to demonstrate Allied willingness to take the pressure off Stalin. The answer at hand was the Anglo-American combined strategic bombing offensive, the principal aims of which were the dislocation of German war industry and preparing the way for an invasion of north-west Europe. At the heart of the offensive was "round the clock" bombing of Germany, the Americans by day and the British by night. By January 1943, RAF Bomber Command was on the point of receiving the radio navigation aids, notably H2S,[29] which were to reinvigorate its campaign against Germany, although bitter experience in 1941-1942 had obliged its leadership to adopt the policy of area bombing of German cities rather than the pinpoint bombardment of German war industry. The destruction of the morale of the civilians who worked in the war plants was deemed as important as the levelling of the factories themselves. By the beginning of 1943 this had not been achieved.

The United States Army Air Force (USAAF), which had arrived in England in July 1942 in the form of Eighth Air Force, had administered only a few pinpricks on Occupied Europe and none on Germany itself. It had spent the rest of 1942 in training, deployment and limited operations against targets in Holland, Belgium and northern France. On 17 August 1942 Brigadier-General Ira Eaker, the commander of Eighth Air Force Bomber Command, had flown in its first operation, a raid on the marshalling yards at Rouen. At Casablanca, Churchill spent some time with Eaker, now in overall command of Eighth Air Force, discussing the American strategy of the daylight precision bombing of German war industry. It was the firm conviction of Eaker and his subordinates that in the absence of long-range escort fighters their heavily armed B-17 Flying Fortresses, flying in formation, could fight their way to and from their targets without sustaining unacceptable losses. Churchill was sceptical about the Americans' confidence and suggested that

---

29. H2S was a downward-looking radar sending signals from the aircraft which were reflected back in progressively greater amounts by water, countryside and cities. This enabled the aircraft's navigator to build up a picture of the ground below.

their B-17 Flying Fortresses might be more usefully employed in night operations. Ignoring the colossal logistical effort the USAAF had necessarily made in establishing itself in England, Churchill reminded Eaker that his command had not dropped a single bomb on Germany. Eaker's measured and skilful response convinced Churchill to withdraw his criticism on the spot, although he later reflected that Eighth Air Force should have launched its campaign earlier with night operations. As the B-17 was a dedicated day bomber, wholly unsuited to nocturnal missions, this would have condemned the Allied strategic bombing offensive to failure at the outset.

Another delicate issue confronting the Allies at Casablanca was the hope of reconciling two French generals, Henri Giraud and Charles de Gaulle, to ease the passage of the Allies into North Africa. Giraud had been captured by the Germans in May 1940 and imprisoned in Königstein Castle, from which he had made a daring escape in 1942. He later became de Gaulle's rival for the leadership of the Free French. De Gaulle had been invited by Roosevelt to come to Casablanca but had repeatedly expressed his unwillingness to attend. Churchill urged Eden to pressurise de Gaulle, suggesting that if the General remained obdurate he could be replaced by someone from the French Liberation Committee in London. Churchill's instructions to Eden concluded: "Here I have been all these days fighting de Gaulle's battle and making every arrangement for a good reconciliation between the different sections of Frenchmen. If he rejects the chance now offered I shall feel that his removal from the headship of the Free French Movement is essential to the further support of the Movement by His Majesty's Government. I hope you will put as much of this as you think fit for him. For his own sake, you must knock him about pretty hard."

On 22 January de Gaulle arrived in Casablanca and was lodged in the villa next to Giraud's. At first the two men refused to speak to each other. De Gaulle, as ever, was haughty and imperious, Giraud politically inept and disdainful of his rival. Churchill despaired of de Gaulle. He knew that there was no love lost between the

General and the English, but he recognised in de Gaulle a kindred spirit: "The Germans had conquered his country. He had no real foothold anywhere. Never mind; he defied all. Always, even when he was behaving worst, he seemed to express the personality of a great nation, with all its pride and authority, and ambition."

Brooke immediately spotted the difference between the two men. He wrote of Giraud: "Poor Giraud! He was an attractive personality with great charm but with the very wildest ideas of what was possible, militarily. Politically he was no match for de Gaulle, whom I think he inwardly despised. He was one of those queer personalities that fortune occasionally throws forward into positions of responsibility they are totally unsuited for." Giraud spent his brief five minutes of fame in Casablanca before being shunted into the shadows by the Americans, his original backers, when they discovered that he was even more difficult to deal with than de Gaulle. As Roy Jenkins observed in his biography of Churchill, the photograph of the two men sitting uneasily with Churchill and the President at the end of the Conference casts them as two "determined duennas, a contest in which there could only be one winner, de Gaulle", for all his faults a great man.

The final outcome of the Conference, contained in paragraph 6 of Churchill's report to the War Cabinet on 20 January, was the declaration of the "firm intention of the United Sates and the British Empire to continue the war relentlessly until we have brought about the 'unconditional surrender' of Germany Italy and Japan." Four days later, on 24 January, Roosevelt announced at a press conference that unconditional surrender would be enforced on all the Alliance's enemies. Roosevelt suggested to his aide Harry Hopkins that the trouble he and Churchill had in getting de Gaulle and Giraud to talk to each other had put him in mind of the difficulty of arranging a meeting of Ulysses S. Grant and Robert E. Lee at the end of the American Civil War. Confronted with a press conference for which he and Churchill had no time to prepare, "… the thought popped into my mind that they had called Grant 'Old Unconditional Surrender', and the next thing I knew, I had said it."

This unguarded admission took Churchill by surprise, and in his history of the Second World War he devoted several pages to explaining it. The Prime Minister and the President both wanted to avoid the ambiguity which hung over the Allied victory in 1918 and the feeling amongst many Germans, prevalent at the post-war conference at Versailles in January 1919, that they had been "stabbed in the back" by their own political leaders. The apprehension that Germany could rise again to pose a new threat after defeat in a second global conflict loomed large in their minds. Many post-war critics of the expression "unconditional surrender" suggested that the proposition prolonged the war and made recovery after it more difficult.

In a Guildhall speech delivered on 30 June 1943, Churchill declared: "We, the United Nations, demand from the Nazi, Fascist and Japanese tyrannies unconditional surrender. By this we mean that their will-power to resist must be completely broken, and that they must be completely broken, and that they must yield themselves absolutely to our justice and mercy. It also means that we must take all those far-sighted measures which are necessary to prevent the world from being convulsed, wrecked, and blackened by their calculated plots and ferocious aggressions." Five months later, Roosevelt spoke out in less stentorian tones: "The United Nations have no intention to enslave the German people. We wish them to have a normal chance to develop in peace, as useful and respectable members of the European family."

Before the conference broke up, Churchill invited Roosevelt to spend two days with him in Marrakech, which he had visited in the late 1930s and where they could "see the sunset on the snows of the Atlas Mountains". A comfortable villa rented by the American Vice-Consul in Marrakech, Kenneth Pendar, accommodated the Prime Minister and the President who drove together to the "Paris of the Sahara", for centuries the magnet of caravans from central Africa and, as Churchill noted, the home of the most elaborately organised brothels on the continent. The five-hour journey took the two men along a road lined with American troops while fighter aircraft circled overhead. On arrival at the villa, Churchill took the President, carried in a chair, up a tower from which they enjoyed the sunset. The villa and its grounds were described in an evocative passage from another visitor, Alan Brooke: "Built in complete Moroccan architecture in the middle of what used to be an olive plantation. Very ornate and Moroccan with a wonderful garden around it. After lunch we climbed up into the tower to see the view. An astonishing mixture with palm trees and Arab Moroccan town in the foreground and lovely snow-covered peaks in the background!" It was during this brief interlude in Marrakech that Churchill painted his only picture of the wartime years.

On the morning of 25 January, Brooke was summoned by Churchill who announced that he wished to return to Cairo that evening. Even by his customary sybaritic standards, the Prime Minister presented an extraordinary sight tucked up in what Brooke assumed was the bedroom of the villa's American owner, a Mrs Taylor. The bed was covered with light blue silk fringed with lace, and Churchill greeted his CIGS wearing a green, red and gold dressing gown, his hair, or rather what was left of it, standing on end, and a large cigar clamped in his mouth. Brooke regretted that he did not have a camera to record the scene. When Brooke enquired where they might be going, Churchill replied, "I have not decided yet. I am either going to answer questions in the Commons tomorrow, or I am going to Cairo."

At 6.30pm two Liberators took off from the Marrakech aerodrome and headed over the peaks of the Atlas Mountains. At nearly 15,000ft the setting sun threw a pink glow over the mountain peaks. After a dinner of hard-boiled eggs and sandwiches, Churchill and his party buried themselves under piles of blankets to ward off the intense cold. Eleven hours later, at about 7.30am, they landed in Cairo. At the British Embassy, Churchill demanded breakfast. In the dining room the Ambassador's wife, Jacqueline Lampson, offered the Prime Minister a cup of tea. Churchill declined the offer and ordered a glass of white wine, which he drained before telling Jacqueline Lampson, "Ah, that is good, but you know I have already had two whiskies and soda and two cigars this morning."

While enjoying the hospitality of the Marrakech villa, Churchill had turned his attention to travelling to Turkey in an attempt to persuade its President, Ismet Inonu, to join the Alliance against Hitler. The Prime Minister had a particular obsession with Turkey, possibly the legacy of his intimate involvement in the Gallipoli campaign. However, it was not a topic that found favour with his Cabinet, who were eager for Churchill to return to London to give an account of the Casablanca Conference. Their protestations, conveyed by Anthony Eden, cut little ice with Churchill who "got quite upset by the obstruction of the Cabinet as I lay in my luxurious bed in the Villa Taylor, looking at the Atlas Mountains, over which I longed to leap in the 'Commando' aeroplane which awaited me so patient and contented on the airfield."

Churchill could not be gainsaid. At the suggestion of President Inonu, a secret meeting was arranged on Turkish territory, at Adana near the Turkish-Syrian frontier, aboard the Turkish President's special train. On 30 January two Liberators made the four-hour flight across the Mediterranean carrying Churchill and his party, including Cadogan and Generals Brooke, Alexander and Wilson.[30] After a bumpy trip they were greeted by the Turkish Prime Minister, Sukru Saracoglu and the Foreign Minister, Numan Menemencoglu and taken by train some 20 miles west to meet the President in his train. The two rickety trains were drawn up tail to tail in the middle of a rain-drenched open plain, guarded, the Turks assured their visitors, by a screen of sentries. Brooke, by no means confident of his hosts' security measures, took a stroll outside. There he discovered two soldiers squatting in the rain on their haunches under their blankets. He found Churchill's personal detective, Walter H. Thompson, eating his head off in the dining car, and told him that the security arrangements were abysmal and that he and his assistant should mount regular night-time patrols

---

30. Sir Henry Maitland Wilson, who in 1943 succeeded Alexander as Commander-in-Chief Middle East. In January 1944 he was appointed Supreme Allied Commander Mediterranean Theatre.

outside Churchill's sleeping car. Thompson bristled at having to work a night shift, to which Brook replied that he had travelled in the same comfort as the rest of the party and should now do the job for which he was paid. Perhaps the Cabinet's reservations about the Prime Minister's trip to Turkey were not without foundation.

Nevertheless, the dinner party that evening was a resounding success. Churchill was at his most ebullient, addressing the assembled company in a combination of flowery French and English words delivered in a French accent. He was so pleased with himself that he proposed to stay another day and had to be dissuaded from this by Brooke, who was still rattled by the Turks' shambolic security measures. Churchill delighted in the mild anarchy of revising long-laid plans, but the exasperated CIGS pointedly reminded the Prime Minister that, as things stood, it would be a simple matter to blow him up in his sleeping car bed. Churchill gave his berth a quizzical look and remarked, "Oh, do you think so?" Brooke added that he had instructed the Prime Minister's detectives to take every precaution against such a contingency and bade him goodnight. Later he reflected fondly on the Prime Minister's addiction to changing travel plans on a whim but less fondly on his predilection for meddling in grand strategy in similarly Quixotic fashion.

From the outset of the talks Churchill offered the Turks a wealth of modern weaponry to modernise their army. Top of the list was 25 RAF fighter squadrons plus engineers to overhaul their crumbling aviation infrastructure. Next came two armoured divisions, and instructors to train the Turks in their employment. In return the Prime Minister requested access to Turkish airfields from which raids could be mounted on the Romanian oilfields at Ploesti, a vital source of oil for the German armed forces. As far as security allowed, he informed the Turks of the conclusions reached at Casablanca, all of which enjoyed the full support of Stalin who, he claimed, was most eager to see Turkey well-armed and ready to repel any foreign aggression. At the end of the war Turkey would be guaranteed a place at the Peace Conference. Churchill brought his address to an end by referring to the long history of friendly relations between Britain and Turkey while also regretting that in the First World War the two nations were "brave and honourable opponents". The delivery of Allied weaponry never materialised. The Turks, fearful of the formidable German military presence in neighbouring Bulgaria, ensured that the British military delegation, headed by General Sir Henry Maitland Wilson, was swaddled in red tape. The training of Turkish tank crews had to start with basic information about the workings of the internal combustion engine. The upgrading of airfields proceeded at a snail's pace. Inonu, a foxy-faced and wily operator, ensured that Turkey retained its neutrality.

The discussions which immediately followed Churchill's arrival in Turkey also focused on arrangements for the post-war world, particularly relations with the Soviet Union. President Inonu observed that Churchill's remarks indicated he was concerned that a post-war Soviet Union might harbour imperialistic ambitions. The Prime Minister assured him that a new international organisation to secure peace and security, the fruit of the Atlantic Charter, would prove stronger than the League of Nations in defending democracy.[31] He added that his record proved that he was no friend of Communism. This did not go down well with Mr Saracoglu, who observed that Europe was awash with Slavs and Communists, a combination guaranteed to alarm the Turks, sitting on the southernmost border of the Soviet Union. If all the European countries subjugated by Hitler regained their freedom, they would all become Bolshevik or Slav, the two seemingly being interchangeable in Saracoglu's eyes. Churchill told Saracoglu to be more optimistic and reminded him that in the United Kingdom and the United States the Turks enjoyed true friends.

Early the next morning Churchill lay awake in his sleeping car bed mulling over the exchange of opinions with the Turks on

---

31. In 1944, at Quebec, Churchill and Roosevelt agreed to start work on the creation of a permanent United Nations Organisation, successor to the ill-fated League of Nations.

post-war security. He gathered together his reflections in a paper, "Morning Thoughts", which contained the following words: "It is the intention of the Chiefs of the United Nations to create a world organisation for the preservation of peace, based on the conceptions of freedom and justice and the revival of prosperity." He had failed to draw Turkey into the war against the Axis but in characteristic fashion managed to convince himself that he might still have managed to do so before the end of 1943 without inflicting any damage to the Allied cause, and with all kinds of advantages to the Allies and Turks alike. Brooke was doubtful of this. His assessment of the Turkish Army's C-in-C, Field Marshal Fevzi Cakmak - "he had no conception of the administrative aspect of handling armies" - betrays his misgivings. The CIGS concluded that the Turks had "a long way to go before they can be considered as [a] real efficient force, and how we are to provide them with the necessary equipment in spite of their poor communications is a mystery!" This lofty assessment of Turkish capabilities, as opposed to British effectiveness, was rudely undermined in the autumn of 1943 by the German continued possession of the Dodecanese Islands, 12 miles off the Turkish coast, after attempted British landings. The embarrassing fiasco convinced the Turks that they had been correct in retaining their neutrality.

10

TRIDENT AND EUREKA

The *Trident* conference, in Washington in May 1943, was held in the aftermath of General Alexander's defeat of the Axis forces in Tunisia. To all intents and purposes, the Mediterranean was now open and Italy was teetering on the edge of collapse. The British urged that, following a successful invasion of Sicily, Allied landings should follow in Calabria, in the toe of southern Italy, with a view to expanding eastwards into the southern Balkans. In the event of a sudden Italian capitulation, the Italian peninsula should be occupied as far north as Rome; a bridgehead established on the coast of Yugoslavia; and the Dodecanese Islands, lying off the south-west coast of Turkey, should be seized and pressure exerted on the Turks to enter the war on the Allied side. The British anticipated that this would force the Germans to dispatch more troops either to the Balkans or to Italy, in all likelihood the former, abandoning Italy to the Allies, who could use its airfields to raid central and south-eastern Europe, particularly the Axis' Romanian oil fields at Ploesti.

Trident also saw the first formal discussions between the British and American staffs about the invasion of southern France. However, the principal item on the agenda was the operation which was to become *Overlord*, the cross-Channel invasion of north-west France, which had drifted in the Allied timetable into the late spring of 1944. This presented the Allies with a problem. The proposed date for the execution of *Overlord* left the Americans with little or no opportunity to lock horns with the Germans on land for approximately nine months. The Joint Chiefs of Staff therefore cast around for other potential targets in the Mediterranean theatre which would divert German attention from northern France without impeding the Allied build-up.

In Algiers on his return from *Trident*, Churchill joined the continuing Allied debate about the strategic options open to the Allies in the Mediterranean. At the end of May a series of meetings were held in the villa occupied by General Eisenhower, now commander of US troops in Europe, and were attended by, among others, the Prime Minister, Generals Brooke, Alexander and Ismay, Admiral Sir Andrew Cunningham, Air Chief Marshal Sir Arthur Tedder, General Marshall, and General Bedell-Smith, Eisenhower's Chief of Staff. Churchill, ever the opportunist, argued for an attack on mainland Italy after the conclusion of the campaign in Sicily. Marshall responded guardedly, observing that the Allies should carefully consider their next move.

When it came, the next major strategic move of the war was made not in the Mediterranean but thousands of miles away, at Kursk, in the Ukraine, where on 5 July Hitler launched an operation, code-named *Zitadelle*, *Citadel*, to pinch out the huge fist-shaped salient driven into the German line in the spring of 1943. The build-up for *Citadel*, aimed at clawing back the initiative after the surrender of the German Sixth Army at Stalingrad, had taken three months. The Red Army, reorganised and re-equipped after the disasters of 1941-42, was well-informed of German intentions and, under the direction of Marshal Georgy Zhukov, Stalin's Deputy Commissar for Defence, had prepared to defend the salient's shoulders in massive strength and depth. A week after the German offensive had opened, on 12 July, the Red Army launched a series of co-ordinated counter-offensives which drove the Germans back 150 miles on a front of 650 miles.

Sicily was retaken by the Allies by 17 August and on 3 September the British Eighth Army landed in Calabria on the Italian mainland. A week later, German forces, catching the Allies napping, occupied

Rome. On the Eastern Front, Smolensk, keystone of the German defences in Russia, fell to the Red Army at the end of September. It was against this strategic background that preparations were underway for the first Allied conference attended by the Allied triumvirate of Churchill, Roosevelt and Stalin.

The proposed meeting place was the Persian capital, Teheran. However, getting the "Big Three", as they were dubbed in the press, together at the same place and at the same time proved difficult. There were two barriers to Roosevelt's attendance: his physical infirmity; and the demands placed on him by the American constitution, which called for action on legislation, by written approval, within ten days of its passage through Congress. Roosevelt suggested Basra as an alternative venue. Stalin, notoriously reluctant to stray far from home, insisted on Teheran. On 11 November, Churchill wrote to Stalin, pointing out that "It is very difficult to settle things by triangular correspondence, especially when people are moving by sea and air." The next day Roosevelt informed the Prime Minister that all was set fair for the Teheran meeting as the constitutional problems had been overcome. Prime Minister and President would meet in Cairo before the Allied conference in Teheran code-named *Eureka*.

On 12 November the Prime Minister set sail from England aboard the battlecruiser *Renown*. He was far from well, nursing a heavy cold and an adverse reaction to the inoculations administered before his departure. He arrived in Alexandria nine days later, flying on to Cairo where he met General Chiang Kai-Shek, the leader of Nationalist China and his wife. Churchill was unimpressed by the champion of the "New Asia" but found his wife "remarkable and charming".

Not so charming for Churchill were the growing cracks in the Anglo-American alliance, particularly in Italy, where progress towards Rome was agonisingly slow. Another potential point of discord lay in the yet-to-be-decided command of *Overlord*. The British had envisaged a combined command, but Roosevelt and the American Chiefs of Staff made it clear that they favoured the appointment of a Supreme Commander, working under the

Combined Chiefs of Staff, who would co-ordinate operations in both north-west Europe and the Mediterranean. Churchill and the British Chiefs of Staff, who assumed that this role would fall to General Marshall, considered the proposal a certain recipe for muddle and delay. The decision was taken to defer the decision to the heads of government meeting at Teheran.

On 25 November, Thanksgiving Day, Churchill and his daughter Sarah were treated to a display of American abundance at Roosevelt's villa. Two colossal turkeys were carved with panache by the President, prompting Churchill to wonder if there might be anything left for Roosevelt when the two carcasses were borne away. Harry Hopkins, noting his anxiety, leant over and informed the Prime Minister that "we have ample reserves." After the meal the company listened to dance music played on a gramophone. Sarah, the only woman present, had her work cut out and the Prime Minister shook a leg with "Pa" Watson, an old crony of the President, to the great amusement of his boss, watching from a sofa. At the crack of dawn on 27 November, Churchill and his entourage took off for Teheran.

At Teheran, Churchill was dismayed at the security arrangements, or rather lack of them, which greeted him on his arrival. He was driven for three miles from the airport by the head of the British Legation past Iranian cavalrymen posted every 50 yards, a blatant advertisement of the Prime Minister's arrival but providing little or no protection against a potential assassin. A police car driving 100 yards ahead gave ample warning of Churchill's approach, which proceeded at a snail's pace. Presently, large crowds, unsupervised by police, gathered on either side of the road, pressing to within a few feet of the Prime Minister's limousine. Approaching the Legation, the car was brought to a halt by the curious crowd. Churchill grinned at them and they grinned back. Finally, he gained the safety of the Legation, which was ringed by Anglo-Indian troops. The Legation was almost adjacent to the even more heavily guarded Soviet Embassy. However, the American Legation was more than a mile away, which would have obliged the three Teheran principals to make dangerous trips through narrow, crowded streets during the course of the Conference. Moreover, Molotov, the Soviet Foreign Minister, was hinting darkly of a plot uncovered by Soviet intelligence to assassinate the "Big Three". Molotov and Churchill persuaded Roosevelt to move into the greater safety of the Soviet Embassy, although this would inevitably have exposed him to Soviet listening devices, the lesser of two evils.

The Teheran Conference was dominated by Stalin. He was still basking in the Red Army's victory at Kursk, which had tripped off a series of massive convulsions on the Eastern Front. After five months of concerted fighting, almost two-thirds of the territory once occupied by Axis forces had been cleared, enabling Stalin to contemplate the future after the defeat of Nazi Germany. On his journey to Teheran he had passed through the oil city of Baku where two aircraft awaited to fly him on to the Conference, one piloted by a general, the other by a colonel The cautious Stalin opted for the latter on the sound basis that generals do not fly that much. He took off with an escort of 27 fighter aircraft. At the first plenary meeting of the Conference, he appeared in the uniform of a Field Marshal.

Churchill, coughing, spluttering and peevish, initially presented a distracted figure. Stalin and Roosevelt had a preliminary meeting without him, which left the Prime Minister childishly anxious that they were "ganging up" on him. The interpreter at the meeting recalled that the two leaders enjoyed an easy rapport. After the opening pleasantries, Roosevelt made it clear that it was the aim of the United States to establish a front in north-west Europe which would divert up to 40 German divisions away from the Eastern Front. Stalin responded by observing, with some understatement, that "It would be very good if that were done."

At the first plenary meeting, on the afternoon of 28 November, Stalin urged the launching of a cross-Channel invasion. Brooke, who attended the meeting, was struck by the incisiveness of the Soviet leader: "During this meeting and all the subsequent ones we had with Stalin, I rapidly grew to appreciate the fact that he has a military brain of the very highest calibre. Never once in any of his statements did he make any strategic error, nor did he ever fail to appreciate all the implications of a situation with a quick and unerring eye." Stalin confirmed this insight, suggesting that *Overlord* was an operation of such seriousness that it should be preceded by an invasion of the South of France. He pointed out that the experience gained in two years of fighting on the Eastern Front demonstrated that a major offensive, if undertaken on only one axis, rarely achieved positive results. If launched from a number of directions simultaneously, it would oblige the enemy to disperse his forces while simultaneously prove a force multiplier for the attacker if the thrusts were not too far dispersed.

In Brooke's estimation, neither Churchill nor Roosevelt matched this perceptiveness. Roosevelt never pretended to fully grasp the finer points of waging war, relying on men like Marshall to advise him. Churchill was more difficult to handle, brilliant at times but impulsive and liable to favour unsuitable military plans without thinking them through. Brooke was also sceptical of Churchill's obsession with the Eastern Mediterranean, his persistent attempts to coax Turkey into the war, and his oft-repeated preoccupation with thrusting into the Third Reich by way of the Balkans. Brooke's scepticism about the Balkans was shared by the Americans. They regarded the region much as medieval cartographers saw the terra incognita beyond the boundaries of the known world - "Here Be Dragons". The US Army Planning Staff harboured a deep dread of the region, associating it with the lingering Imperialism with which Churchill's approach to grand strategy was fatally infected. Little good could come from venturing into this minefield.

Churchill was, perhaps, understandably irked by the Americans' lack of interest in the Eastern Mediterranean. The Prime Minister's extensive and highly romantic knowledge of British history was informed by many past events in this theatre, from Admiral Horatio Nelson's victory in the Battle of the Nile to the deaths of the poets Byron at Missolonghi and Rupert Brooke in a hospital ship off Skyros. On a more immediate contemporary note, the ancient city of Alexandria was the base of the British Mediterranean Fleet and departure point for the westbound Malta relief convoys.

Crucially, in Churchill's mind, the Suez Canal was Britain's Imperial lifeline, briefly threatened by Rommel in 1942. Brooke's calm interventions nevertheless did much to restrain the Prime Minister's freewheeling strategic forays. In part these were prompted by Churchill's growing awareness of the retreat of British power and influence. Churchill was, in Brooke's words, "inclined at times to put up strategic proposals which, in his heart, he knew were unsound, purely to spite the Americans... It was usually fairly easy to swing him back on the right line. There lay, however, in the back of his mind, the desire to form a purely British theatre where the laurels would be all ours." Brooke was not alone in his criticism of the Prime Minister. Both the Foreign Office and Churchill in his more reflective moments realised the inexorable tide of war in the form of the Red Army would place the Balkans squarely in the Soviet sphere of influence at the end of the conflict. In October 1943, when peace feelers were extended to the Western Allies by King Michael of Romania, Foreign Secretary Anthony Eden and the US Secretary of State Cordell Hull agreed that, "The Soviet Union was entitled to decide any such questions concerning Romania and Hungary, and Finland as well, since only its forces were engaged in active warfare against these countries."

The formal meetings at Teheran were punctuated by informal exchanges between the principals at luncheons and dinners. On the evening of 28 November, Churchill drew Stalin aside to review with the Soviet leader a range of post-war political perspectives. Stalin ventured a worst-case scenario in which he predicted that Germany would recover from defeat within 15 to 20 years. In that context he proposed that the Allies would have to impose severe manufacturing constraints across the board on their defeated enemy. Churchill's response was that the duty of the Allies was to make the world safe for at least 50 years by means of German disarmament, strict supervision of her industry, the forbidding of aviation and the close monitoring of territorial changes. Stalin observed that there had been control after the First World War under the terms of the Versailles Treaty, to which the Soviet Union was not a party, but it had failed. Churchill insisted that this would not happen again. Prussia must be isolated from the less toxic German elements of the Third Reich to prevent a recrudescence of militarism. Stalin averred this was all very well but quite insufficient. Churchill reminded Stalin that the Allies were the trustees for the peace of the world. Failure would precipitate a century of chaos.

During this informal meeting, Churchill and Stalin mapped out in rough and ready fashion the post-war frontiers of Poland, the nation for which Britain had declared war in 1939. Stalin secured a western frontier with Poland which ran along the so-called "Curzon Line", the border he had negotiated with the German Foreign Minister Joachim von Ribbentrop in 1939. Poland was to be compensated for this loss of territory by receiving 44,000 square miles of eastern Germany to the east of the Oder and Neisse Rivers. In the process several million Poles and Germans would have to migrate westwards, a consequence about which the Poles were not consulted. To Churchill and Stalin, poring over a map of Eastern Europe, this merely seemed a minor detail in a much bigger picture. On 30 March 1939, Neville Chamberlain had written out, in his own hand, a guarantee against aggression toward Poland which Colonel Joseph Beck, the Polish Foreign Minister, had accepted "between two flicks of the ash off his cigarette". Now, in equally casual fashion, Poland's post-war future was settled. This agreement was formally acknowledged after a meeting at the Soviet Embassy on 1 December of Churchill, Roosevelt, Stalin, Molotov and Eden. A Foreign Office minute recorded:

At this point Mr Molotov produced the Russian version of the Curzon Line and a text of a wireless telegram from Lord Curzon giving all the place names. The Prime Minister asked whether Mr Molotov would object to the Poles getting the Oppeln district. Mr Molotov replied that he did not foresee any objection. The Prime Minister said that the Poles would be wise to take our advice. They were getting a country 300 miles square and that he was not prepared to make a great squawk about Lvov, and (turning to Marshal Stalin) he added that he did not think we were very far off in principle. President Roosevelt asked Marshal Stalin whether he thought a transfer of the population on a voluntary basis would be possible. Marshal Stalin said that it probably would be. Here the discussion about Poland came to an end.

On the morning of the 29th the British, American and Soviet military chiefs met to discuss strategy. Churchill seized the opportunity to suggest a private lunchtime meeting with Roosevelt in the Soviet Embassy before the second plenary meeting in the afternoon. Roosevelt declined and despatched Harriman to explain that he did not want Stalin to think that he and Churchill were plotting behind the Soviet leader's back. This unsettled the Prime Minister, who noted that after the lunch the President attended a further session with Stalin, who was accompanied by Molotov, at which he outlined his plans for the post-war world. Roosevelt proposed that there should be "Four Policemen", the Soviet Union, the United States, Britain and China. Stalin's immediate, and wholly correct, reaction was that the inclusion of China in this arrangement would be unwelcome to the small nations of Europe, whose feelings for the Chinese and Chiang Kai-shek were far from friendly.

Before the start of the second plenary session at 4pm, a ceremony was held in which Churchill presented Stalin with the Sword of Stalingrad, a longsword made of Sheffield steel with a jewel-encrusted hilt, which had been commissioned by King George VI to honour the heroic Soviet defence of that city. The delegations assembled in the Embassy's conference room while British and Soviet honour guards lined the walls and a Soviet military band played "God Save the King."

Churchill, wearing the uniform of an air commodore, unsheathed the sword and then handed it to Roosevelt, who held it aloft, affirming "Truly, they had hearts of steel,"[32] before handing it to Stalin who replaced the sword in its scabbard and passed it on to Marshal Voroshilov who, taken by surprise, promptly dropped it. Sword and scabbard were then removed with great solemnity.

Thereafter the conference was resumed. Brooke summarised the available options in the Mediterranean theatre, concluding with the proposed landings in northern and southern France, respectively *Overlord* and *Anvil* (later *Dragoon*) He was followed by Marshall who emphasised that the principal problem facing the Western Allies when it came to launching *Overlord* was not one of men or material but rather the lack of landing craft, particularly tank-landing ships (LSTs). At this point Stalin abruptly lobbed a large rock into the calm pool of Allied consensus by asking who was to command Operation *Overlord*. Roosevelt replied that the decision had not yet been taken. Stalin shot back with the observation that *Overlord* would remain no more than hot air if a single man was not placed in charge of it. Roosevelt attempted to temporise by explaining that a British officer, General Sir Frederick Morgan, had been charged in January 1943 with producing plans for the invasion of Europe. This did not satisfy Stalin, who pointed out that planning was one thing, execution quite another. The Supreme Commander, when he was appointed, might disagree with Morgan's carefully laid plans. Churchill then pitched in, explaining that in the Mediterranean, where the British deployed the preponderance of military assets, the overall command of operations devolved on a senior British officer. The opposite was the case with *Overlord*. Stalin replied that the Soviet Union had no interest in the appointment of a Supreme Commander beyond knowing who exactly it was to be. The Prime Minister, rattled by Stalin's intervention, concluded by assuring him that a decision would be reached within 14 days at the very latest.

---

32. Stalin means "Man of Steel".

Marshall, the original favourite for the job, was retained in Washington, where his presence was deemed indispensable, and the post of Supreme Commander of the Allied forces for *Overlord* was filled by his protégé, General Eisenhower, not a fighting soldier but a man whose soldierly skills were diplomatic, oiled by an ability to weld a co-ordinated team from a collection of powerful individuals with conflicting views and personalities. Before the meeting broke up, Stalin fixed Churchill with a steady stare across the table and posed a final, searching question. Did Churchill and the British Chiefs of Staff actually believe in *Overlord*? Churchill, placed firmly on the spot, improvised a high-flown answer: "Provided the conditions previously stated for *Overlord* are established when the time comes, it will be our stern duty to hurl across the Channel against the Germans every sinew of our strength." With that, the meeting broke up.

At dinner that night, Stalin had more surprises in store. Toast succeeded toast, in the Russian manner, while the Soviet leader indulged in some teasing of the Prime Minister in suitably sinister tones before embarking on a description of what awaited the German nation after its defeat at the hands of the Allies. The German General Staff would have to be liquidated and 50,000 officers rounded up and shot. Taken aback, Churchill observed that the Stalin must understand that the British public would never tolerate mass executions. He would rather be shot in his own garden than besmirch his honour, and that of his country, with such infamy. Roosevelt, in a misjudged attempt at humour, then proposed a compromise death list of 49,000. Eden attempted, using sign language, to suggest that Stalin was merely joking. However, an awkward situation was then made worse by Roosevelt's tactless son Elliott, a recent arrival, who had joined the table and rose to support Stalin, assuring the company that the US Army would be right behind the Soviet leader on this issue. Churchill stalked into the semi-darkness of an adjoining room. Shortly afterwards he felt a hand on his shoulder and turned to find Stalin and Molotov, wreathed in smiles and confessing that they were only joking. Churchill was not remotely fooled but consented to rejoin the company.

For two reasons, the next day, 30 November, was of particular significance to the Prime Minister. First it was his 69th birthday – and he spent it dealing with some of the most important decisions in his life. He believed that Stalin had convinced himself that he and the British High Command were bent on invading the Balkans, which the Soviet leader rightly regarded as within his sphere of influence, rather than committing wholeheartedly to *Overlord*. Moreover, the quibbling about landing craft was merely a smoke screen to camouflage an Allied plan, previously unmentioned at Teheran but favoured by Roosevelt, for a projected major landing in the Bay of Bengal, Operation *Buccaneer*,[33] in March 1944 to aid Chiang Kai-shek. Churchill discussed all these issues with Stalin at a private meeting before the third plenary session began at 4pm in the afternoon.

Roosevelt now pre-empted the debate about *Overlord* by baldly stating at the beginning of the session that it would be launched by the Western Allies in May 1944, together with an operation in the South of France. Stalin remained impassive but remarked in the softest of tones, "I am satisfied with this decision." He then committed the Red Army to a simultaneous offensive on the Eastern Front. At Churchill's suggestion a communiqué was drafted and agreed upon by all present: "Our Military Staffs have joined in our round table discussion, and we have concerted our plans for the destruction of the German forces. We have reached complete agreement as to the scope and timing of the operations which will be undertaken from the east west and south."

That night the third dinner was held in the British Legation. It was preceded by a rigorous security search by the NKVD (The People's Commissariat for Domestic Affairs) whose men left no stone unturned in the Legation before Stalin arrived, accompanied by 50 armed Soviet policemen who posted themselves by every door and window. American security was also much in evidence. The dinner was of great significance to Churchill. On his right was

---

33. *Buccaneer* was never launched.

the President, on his left Stalin: "Together we controlled a large preponderance of the naval and three-quarters of all the air forces in the world, and could direct armies of nearly twenty millions of men, engaged in the most terrible of wars that had yet occurred in human history."

Stalin, however, persisted with questions about the command of *Overlord* and, referring to Brooke, observed that he seemed to dislike Russians, recalling his seemingly hostile manner at the Moscow meeting in 1942. Churchill replied that military men often appeared abrupt and somewhat blunt when dealing with professional problems. Stalin agreed with this sentiment while staring pointedly at Brooke. The dinner proceeded in the Russian fashion, with endless toasts. At one point Roosevelt proposed Brooke's health, referring to the time when Brooke's father had visited his father at Hyde Park. The compliment was interrupted by Stalin, who then repeated his earlier accusation that the General had displayed no warmth towards the Red Army. When it was Brooke's turn to propose a toast, he thanked Roosevelt for his kind words before turning to Stalin and reminded him of Churchill's observation earlier in the day, when referring to Allied deception measures: "In war the truth must be accompanied by an escort of lies to ensure its security." Brooke told the Soviet leader that the Red Army was no stranger to these tactics – the Russian word for them is *maskirovka* – the massing of dummy tanks and aircraft on a front that is not going to be activated or the stealthy movement of troops under the cover of darkness. By the same token, he added, sometimes one's outward appearance could deceive even close friends. Might the Marshal have fallen into the same trap and failed to grasp Brooke's deep regard for the sterling qualities of the Red Army? After the dinner, Churchill glimpsed Brooke and Stalin standing face to face in a small circle of guests. Brooke later confirmed that he had raised the matter again, knowing full well that backing down would only confirm Stalin's low estimation of him. The Marshal's reply came via the Soviet translator Pavlov: "The best friendships are those founded on misunderstandings."

Significantly, at the end of the dinner Stalin had toasted the Western Allies referring to "My fighting friend, Roosevelt" and "My fighting friend, Churchill". Churchill was more circumspect in his toasts: "Roosevelt, the President, my friend" and "Stalin, the Mighty", the different emphases obvious to even the most tin-eared members of the audience. In truth, Teheran's apparent success, concluding on Churchill's birthday, masked a shifting in the underpinning of the Anglo-American alliance. For the first twelve months after they joined the war the Americans had, as a rule, deferred to their British allies, relied on their strategic and tactical advice, and raised no major objections to Churchill's peripheralist strategy. By 1943, they commanded the largest war economy and the military make-up of the Allied forces was becoming more decidedly American. By the spring of 1944 there were nearly six million Americans under arms, more than double the numbers deployed by the British. British strength was in decline as its industrial and manpower resources became ever more stretched. British ammunition production had been falling since late 1942. Production of vehicles had started to dip in mid-1943 and by the end of the year the same was true of artillery and small arms. In 1940 Britain was producing just over 90 per cent of the Commonwealth's munitions while purchasing 5.6 per cent from America. By the beginning of 1944 the British share of production had fallen by 30 per cent, the slack largely taken up by Lend-Lease material from America.

The inevitable tensions that arose between the two Western Allies were to complicate their return to the European mainland. Stalin saw this as clearly as he saw that the Americans had naively imagined that the British would go for the Balkan option at Teheran, in concert with the Soviets, rather than *Overlord* and *Anvil*. He was determined to keep the British away from Eastern Europe and this he achieved by his solid support for the operations in France, pushing Churchill and Brooke into the awkward position of making a commitment about which they continued to harbour deep anxiety. Brooke wrote in his diary that he was "torn to shreds with doubts and misgivings ... the cross-Channel operation is just eating into my heart," and feared that its failure could prove "the most ghastly disaster of the war".

In spite of Brooke's misgivings about *Overlord*, the landings in Normandy began on 6 June 1944. After a month-long air offensive and an Allied deception plan which convinced Hitler that the main attack would come in the Pas de Calais, where he held back a powerful armoured reserve, the largest amphibious operation in history got underway. In the small hours of that Tuesday, Allied airborne troops landed to seize bridges and coastal batteries on the flanks of the invasion zone. The first Allied troops came ashore at 6.30am. On only one of the five invasion beaches did the Germans mount fierce resistance. On Omaha Beach the US Fifth Corps took heavy casualties from experienced and well-dug-in infantry. When they broke out of their beachhead on "Bloody Omaha", Fifth Corps left 2,400 dead behind them. By midnight 57,500 US and 75,000 British and Canadian troops had gone ashore.

In the long build-up to *Overlord*, Churchill had taken a keen, almost boyish interest in the many ingenious engineering innovations underpinning the operation: among them Mulberry Harbours, swimming and flail tanks, and the submarine Pluto pipeline providing fuel for the invasion forces. The Prime Minister's enthusiasm for these devices, both large and small, prompted some ideas of his own, the great majority of which were, to say the least, wildly impractical. Typical was a suggestion to stage "some form of reverse Dunkirk", in which the initial assault landings would be followed by the arrival of small civilian boats bearing symbolic loads of troops. Predictably, Churchill also wanted to observe the bombardment of the Normandy coast on 6 June from the bridge of the heavy cruiser *Belfast*. He bypassed Brooke, knowing that the CIGS would overrule this foray, but justified it on the grounds that he was the Minister of Defence. Four days before D-Day, King George VI stepped in with a deftly worded letter: "My Dear Winston, I want to make one more appeal to you not to go to sea on D-Day. Please consider my own position. I am a younger man than you, I am a sailor,[34] and as King I am the head of all the services. There is nothing I would like better than to go to sea but I have agreed to stay at home; is it fair that you should then do exactly what I should have liked to do myself?"

Churchill had to wait until D+6, 12 June, before he could set foot in France. Accompanied by Field Marshal Jan Smuts,[35] General Marshall and Brooke, he boarded the destroyer *Kelvin* at 8am. The Prime Minister was in high spirits, having received encouraging news from Stalin about the imminent Red Army offensive, *Bagration*, which was to be launched on 22 June. *Kelvin* ploughed across the Channel past scenes of intense activity, convoys of landing craft, mine-sweepers busily at work, component parts of Phoenix floating breakwaters being towed towards the French coast. As they neared the shore, past rows of anchored LSTs *Kelvin* nosed into a "Gooseberry" Harbour, a crescent of sunken ships. They were met by the barge of Admiral Sir Philip Vian, Naval Commander of the Eastern Task Force. They transferred from the barge to a DUKW amphibious cargo carrier which ran Churchill and his companions up to the beach, where they were met by General Montgomery, commander of the Allied ground forces in Normandy.

Jeeps then drove Churchill and his companions to Montgomery's headquarters at Bayeux, where they were given a crisp summary of Allied dispositions and plans from Monty at his most schoolmasterly. Over lunch, Brooke's thoughts ran back to the dark days of May 1940 when both he and Montgomery, and their

---

34. As Duke of York the King served on HMS *Collingwood* in the Battle of Jutland and was mentioned in despatches.

35. An opponent in the Boer War, Smuts had long been a favourite of Churchill and attended the Paris Peace Conference in 1919. In 1939 he was elected Prime Minister of South Africa. In 1945 he attended the San Francisco Conference at which the UN Charter was formulated.

commands, were "kicked out" of France: "… if anyone had told me that in four years time I should return with Winston and Smuts to lunch with Monty commanding a new invasion force I should have found it hard to believe it." After lunch, the party drove to the headquarters of Lieutenant-General Sir Miles Dempsey, commander of British Second Army. The landscape, verdant and seemingly unscathed by war, prompted Churchill to observe: "We are surrounded by fat cattle lying in luscious pastures with their paws crossed!" It was also clear to these visitors that the French peasants labouring impassively in the fields did not seem overjoyed at their liberation.[36] The Allies had brought war and desolation to disrupt their rural calm.

After a further inspection of Allied activity from Admiral Vian's barge, Churchill spotted an Allied gunship with a 14in gun peppering targets inland. The Prime Minister insisted on climbing aboard to fire the gun himself but the ascent from the barge was judged too hazardous. Undeterred, Churchill tried again, also unsuccessfully, when back aboard *Kelvin*, which was bombarding the Norman countryside without drawing any enemy fire. Nevertheless, he was able to brag to Roosevelt that "We went and had a plug at the Hun from our destroyer." By 9.15pm Churchill was back in England and boarding a train in Portsmouth. He dined on the train with Brooke, Marshall and Admiral King and was in Downing Street shortly after midnight. It had been a day of some significance. The Allied bridgehead in Normandy had become continuous when US 101st Airborne Division captured Carentan, which commands the estuary of the River Vire. This closed the last gap in the Allied front between Omaha and Utah beaches, linking their land forces together in a beachhead 42 miles wide. That night the first of Hitler's "revenge weapons", the V-1 flying bombs, crossed the Channel, landing in London and the Home Counties.

---

36. Some 30,000 French civilians were killed by Allied bombing in the build-up to and aftermath of D-Day.

By mid-July, the V-1s were arriving in greater numbers, by which time the British public had been informed of the existence of this new weapon, a forerunner of the modern cruise missile, by the Home Secretary Herbert Morrison. In the small hours of the 19th a flying bomb had landed near Brooke's flat in central London, blowing out the window frames in the sitting room while the CIGS, who had been woken by its spluttering approach, took cover behind his bed to avoid flying glass. Later that day Brooke was on the receiving end of a comparably explosive outburst from the Prime Minister. The CIGS had planned to fly to Normandy to see Montgomery, but heavy fog had grounded his aircraft. At 9.30am he was summoned by Churchill, whom he found in bed in a towering rage and a fetching blue and gold dressing gown. The Prime Minister had also been planning to go to France but had been told by Eisenhower that Montgomery did not want to have any visitors during the next few days. Churchill protested vehemently that as Defence Minister he had the right to visit France whenever he liked. In the last war, when he was Minister of Munitions, Haig had never stood in his way and always placed a chateau at his disposal. Why was Montgomery picking on him? Reeling from this verbal onslaught, with the Prime Minister frothing at the mouth, Brooke could only think that Churchill had become completely unbalanced.

Later that day, after a meeting of the Chiefs of Staff, the fog had lifted and Brooke flew from Northolt to Normandy in an aircraft loaned to him by Air Chief Marshal Sir Arthur Tedder, Deputy Supreme Commander of the Allied Expeditionary Force. In Normandy, Brooke asked Montgomery to write a note to the Prime Minister, explaining that he did not know of Churchill's desire to visit and inviting him to come to France. Then he went further, warning Monty that the Prime Minister considered his conduct of the fighting in Normandy was over-cautious and risk averse, adding that Churchill had a vindictive side to his nature and was considering transferring the Guards Tank Brigade from Normandy to Alexander's front in Italy. Montgomery took all this in and informed Brooke that he was making excellent progress east of Caen.[37] He also supplied Brooke with the missing piece of the jigsaw that had occasioned Churchill's outburst. It was a visit by the US Secretary for War Henry Stimson to the headquarters of General Omar Bradley, commander of US First Army, which went on so long that Bradley had to postpone for 24 hours an important attack scheduled for that day. After this, Montgomery had asked Eisenhower to halt visitors for the present. Eisenhower had passed the request on to Churchill, who immediately assumed that this proscription was aimed only at him. The emollient note to the Prime Minister written by Montgomery, but effectively dictated by Brooke, did the trick. Brooke returned to London to find Churchill, who had been fuming all day, now all smiles having received the message from Monty. Peace and goodwill had been restored but, given the combustible chemistry generated by Churchill's finest fighting general, the relief was only temporary.

On 22 July Churchill arrived on the Normandy bridgehead. He visited the Americans at Cherbourg and Utah Beach and then went to the principal British landing area, Gold Beach at Arromanches, where he inspected the two artificial Mulberry Harbours. These comprised off-shore and flanking breakwaters consisting of huge ferro-concrete caissons towed by tugs across the Channel. Sadly, heavy storms over the previous four days had badly damaged the Mulberry at Saint Laurent, effectively putting it out of action. That night Churchill slept aboard the cruiser *Enterprise*. During his two days in Normandy, Churchill spent time at Montgomery's headquarters and visited Caen where two holding operations in June and July, *Epsom* and *Goodwood*, had enabled the Americans to launch their successful break-out, Operation *Cobra*. He also met the four British corps commanders and General Omar Bradley, mastermind of the rapid American

---

37. After fierce fighting, Caen was not taken by Montgomery until 20 July.

build-up in Normandy and shortly to become commander of the US Twelfth Army Group.

Churchill returned from Normandy to be faced with the problem of the V-1 flying bombs, or "doodlebugs" as they were now dubbed by the British public. As the V-1 offensive continued, Londoners cultivated a determinedly casual attitude to the new threat. One woman recalled, "having lunch one day in a small restaurant in Baker Street when the ominous sound of a doodlebug was heard and it got nearer and louder. Everyone in the restaurant gradually stopped talking and eating and froze, with knives and forks poised in mid-air until we all looked like statues. Then the usual bang was heard as a doodlebug landed somewhere nearby, and it was wonderful to see everyone carrying on eating and taking up their conversations without even referring to what had happened."

The V-1s frayed the nerves of war-weary civilians but they had no discernible effect on the progress of the war. Churchill, blessed with reserves of physical courage and excited rather than terrified by loud explosions, was unperturbed by Hitler's "revenge weapon", continuing with dictation even as doodlebugs signalled their approach. He told Stalin that the new weapon "had no appreciable effect upon the ... life of London ... the streets and parks remain full of people enjoying the sunshine when off work or duty." This was, perhaps, stretching a point as the summer of 1944 was, even by British weather standards, exceptionally dismal. Churchill resisted the temptation to accelerate the campaign in France to eliminate the V-1 launching sites, most of which were in the Pas de Calais. However, he did explore the possibility of retaliatory measures against the German civilian population, among them a resort to chemical warfare and the carpet-bombing of 100 medium-sized German towns one after the other, but he was persuaded by RAF Bomber Command to stay his hand.

By the beginning of September 1944, the worst of the V-1 offensive was over. The launching sites in northern France had been captured by the Allies, forcing the Germans to fire the V-1s at longer ranges from Holland or air-launch them from converted bombers. Success came at a price. It has been estimated that for every pound that the Germans spent on the V-1 programme, the British spent five in combating it – the combined cost in civilian casualties, air defence and damage repair. However, there was no relief for Londoners. On 8 September the first V-2[38] rocket, fired only minutes before from a site in Holland, fell on the London suburb of Chiswick with a shattering roar that could be heard all over the city.

---

38. Unlike the V-1, the V-2 gave no warning of its approach. Just over 1,000 V-2s fell on England, the last of them on 27 March 1945. They killed nearly 9,000 people and seriously injured another 25,000.

II

THE BATTERED BULLDOG

In June 1944 Germany was facing defeat on two fronts. In the East, German Army Group Centre still held the "Vitebsk Gate", the gap between the headwaters of the Dvina and Dnieper Rivers. From Vitebsk to Berlin was a distance of 750 miles, only 100 miles further than the distance from Normandy's Cotentin peninsula to the capital of the Third Reich. In Normandy the Allied lodgement had become continuous on 12 June along a front of 42 miles. Once the Allies had established their bridgehead in Normandy, the inevitable outcome was hastened by Hitler's refusal to listen to the advice of his High Command or to release divisions of German Fifteenth Army, stationed north of the Seine, because of his lingering belief that the Allies would make a second landing in the Pas de Calais. Hitler's absolute determination to deny the Allies access to the open country beyond the Normandy bridgehead, wearing them down by a process of attrition, only ensured the piecemeal destruction of his best armoured forces at the forward point of contact with the enemy. In the slugging match which developed around Caen, it was not the British who were annihilated, as the Führer had promised, but the massive concentration of SS armour at Cheux, 12 miles west of Caen, which on 29 June was savagely mauled by an intense air and artillery bombardment as it launched a counter-attack on the right flank of British Eighth Corps.

By the end of June, Cherbourg had been secured and the Allies prepared to swing eastward against a German left flank weakened by the concentration of seven of its ten panzer divisions in the fighting at Caen. During the night of 7 July, 467 Lancasters of RAF Bomber Command dropped approximately 2,600 tons of bombs on the city, reducing much of it to rubble and inflicting heavy civilian casualties. By 20 July the Germans had been cleared out of Caen. On 31 July, Avranches, at the base of the Cotentin peninsula, fell to the US Eighth Corps. The recently appointed Commander-in-Chief West, Field Marshal Gunther von Kluge, informed Hitler, "Whether the enemy can still be stopped at this point is questionable. The enemy air superiority is terrific and smothers almost all our movements." In the next two weeks the American break-out surged ahead as US Third Army, commanded by the hard-fighting General George S. Patton, fanned out almost unopposed, along the roads from Avranches, driving west to Brest, south to Nantes and east to Le Mans and beyond. An attempt by German armour to cut the American lines of communications at Avranches failed after fierce fighting, leaving 100,000 men of Fifth Panzer Army, Seventh Army and Panzer Group Eberbach trapped in a salient between Falaise and Argentan, which was being sealed off in the north by Canadian First Army and in the south by Patton's Third Army. By the evening of 17 August, the jaws of the Allied pincer were only six miles apart. Three days later they snapped shut on 50,000 troops, thousands of trucks and over 5,000 armoured vehicles.

These Allied successes were a vindication of the arguments made by Marshall and Roosevelt since 1943 for the establishment of a full-blooded Second Front in France as opposed to the more cautious peripheralist approach adopted by Churchill and Brooke. *Anvil*, over which the British and Americans had blown hot and cold at differing times, remained a point of contention. Churchill, eyeing the Italian peninsula and the Balkans, had always opposed *Anvil*, but the invasion of Southern France (now code-named *Dragoon*) had survived with American support, albeit postponed to mid-August. The Americans had convinced themselves that they had been hoodwinked into the Italian campaign, a secondary theatre, by the British who were now junior partners in the Western Alliance. In June and July, the disagreements simmered on at Chiefs of Staff and Prime Minister-President levels. The latter prompted a number of frosty exchanges, which concluded with a solemn protest by Churchill against a decision which left his hopes for the Italian campaign "dashed to the ground".

It was a bitter pill for the British to swallow, made even more unpalatable when a decrypt on 17 June at Bletchley Park[39] suggested that Hitler intended to prevent the Allies from breaking into the Po plain by moving formations away from the front in northern France rather than those on the French Riviera. When this was put to Marshall, he replied that while such decrypts were immensely valuable, if absolute value was to be attributed to them at all times Operation *Overlord* might never have been launched. Churchill's irritation with his Allies was exacerbated by his conviction that, at the end of June, Roosevelt had suggested Stalin as an arbitrator on the growing British and American divergences over strategy, particularly with relation to *Anvil/Dragoon*. It is clear from Roosevelt's message that he had suggested no such thing, but Churchill, nursing his cherished Balkan dream, saw the invasion of the South of France, requiring the transfer of troops from Italy to the Western Mediterranean, as a threat to the "back door" strategy which, it was hoped, would take the Allies all the way to Vienna, a route which recalls his thinking in the Gallipoli campaign.

The row over *Anvil* almost brought Churchill to the point of resignation. His state of mind was captured in Brooke's diary entry of 30 June:

---

39. Bletchley Park, a country house in Buckinghamshire and pre-war home of the British government's Codes and Cypher School. In the Second World War it housed the Ultra interception and decoding service vital to Allied victory and in Churchill's words "the goose which laid the golden eggs".

Just back from a meeting with Winston. I thought at first we might have trouble with him, he looked like he wanted to fight the President. However in the end we got him to agree to our outlook which is: 'All right, if you insist on being damned fools, sooner than falling out with you, which would be fatal, we shall be damned fools with you, and we shall see that we perform the role of damned fools damned well!'

Churchill's opposition to *Anvil/Dragoon*, and his enthusiasm for his Balkan adventure, was in large part fuelled by his growing concern over the Red Army's penetration into Eastern Europe, a development about which he had been previously relatively insouciant. His doctor, Lord Moran, noted that in the early summer of 1944, "Winston never talks about Hitler these days; he is always harping on the dangers of Communism. He dreams of the Red Army spreading like a cancer from one country to another. It has become an obsession and he thinks of little else." The Americans were less than impressed with Churchill's counter-arguments over *Anvil*, and their views were hardened by the fierce Channel storms at the end of June, which wrecked one of the Mulberries. This made Eisenhower even more determined to secure the ports of Southern France to ensure that the Allied build-up in Normandy was not overtaken by a German counterblow similar to the one which bottled up the Allied bridgehead at Anzio. The Vienna option was out of the question. Equally whimsical alternatives suggested by Churchill, such as a landing near Bordeaux, on France's Atlantic coast, were given short shrift.

The disagreements over *Anvil/Dragoon* consolidated a new phase in Anglo-American relations. When dealing with Roosevelt, Churchill was now very much the supplicant. At the height of the quarrel he wrote to the President plaintively, "I am sure that if we could have met, as I so frequently proposed, we should have reached a happy agreement." The happy agreement Churchill sought with the President, and also in a different fashion with Stalin, lay behind his obsessive need to find solutions by way of face-to-face encounters, which in turn was driven by his unashamed addiction to travel. The excitements and anxieties of arrival and departure were the moving parts of his mental make-up. An inter-Allied summit was his sovereign remedy for any difficulties confronting the tripartite alliance. Significantly, however, Churchill was almost always the visitor in these encounters.

The drawback of this ceaseless domestic and international schedule was the strain it imposed on the Prime Minister's fragile health. This produced a recurrent testiness in Cabinet, which Brooke found increasingly taxing. On 6 July, he endured a meeting which began at 10pm and lasted until 2am. Churchill was exhausted by a speech in the House of Commons dealing with the doodlebugs, after which he had resorted to drink to keep himself going. This only made the Prime Minister alternately irritable and maudlin, taking offence at all-comers, particularly the Americans and Montgomery. The normally emollient Brooke flared up, demanding that Churchill trusted his generals for more than five minutes rather than continually ranting against them, a charge Churchill vehemently denied. The Prime Minister ploughed on, ignoring the scheduled agenda, a discussion of the war in the Far East, and opened a debate about the raising of a force in the Middle East akin to the Home Guard. When Brooke's colleagues, Eden and Attlee, attempted to steer Churchill back on course, they only succeeded in provoking another outburst, which culminated in a row with Attlee about the future of India. Brooke ruefully observed that Churchill's bruised colleagues left under the cover of a smokescreen, having achieved precisely nothing in four hours of bickering. He later recalled the "ghastly evening as if it were yesterday".

There is little doubt that the continual strain of wartime leadership, coupled with physical exhaustion, exacerbated in Churchill what would now be called a bipolar condition. Churchill was well aware of this frailty, telling Moran: "I don't like standing near the edge of a platform when an express train is passing though. I like to stand back and, if possible, get a pillar between me and the train. I don't like to stand by the side of a ship and look down into the water. A second's action would end everything. A few drops of desperation." Debilitating despair, which from time to time confined Churchill to bed, was often followed by periods when he would be charged with fits of manic energy, dictating into the small hours to weary secretaries the books on which his reputation as a writer rested. Self-medication through alcohol only worsened this condition, which in the wartime years Moran attempted to ameliorate with amphetamines during the day and barbiturates at night. Moran's biographer, Professor Richard Lovell, identified the drugs administered at night as quinalbarbitone tablets, which the Prime Minister dubbed "reds". The daytime drugs were d-amphetamine sulphate, which Churchill nicknamed "Morans". Brendan Bracken told Moran that Churchill "has always been a 'despairer'". Sir William Orpen, who painted him after the Dardanelles disaster, used to speak at the time of the misery in Churchill's face. He called him the man of misery:

Winston was so sure then that he would take no further part in public life. There seemed to be nothing left to live for. It made him very sad. Then, in his years in the wilderness, before the Second War, he kept saying: 'I am finished.' He said that about twice a day. He was quite certain that he would never get back to office, for everyone seemed to regard him as a wild man. And he missed the red boxes awfully. Winston has always been wretched unless he was occupied.

The summer of 1944 provided Churchill with an abundance of opportunities to remain occupied. Having failed to lure Roosevelt to visit him in Britain, with or without Stalin, he nevertheless secured an agreement to a bilateral meeting (code-named *Octagon*) with the President in Quebec. This enabled him to take a three-week August jaunt to Italy. On 12 August, he arrived in Naples in his Avro York aircraft *Ascalon*, fuming over the extended Anglo-American debate over the invasion of Southern France and with eyes still firmly fixed on the Balkans. The trip mixed pleasure – swimming in the Bay of Naples – with business – two meetings with the

Marshal Tito,[40] the leader of the Yugoslav Communist partisans. The Communist partisans in Yugoslavian were uniquely reluctant to submit themselves to domination by Stalin and had succeeded in driving out the Germans single-handed without any help from the Red Army. Throughout the war, Stalin had supported Tito's rival, the royalist guerrilla leader General Draga Mihailovich. After some dithering, the British had put their weight behind Tito, who was fighting the Germans while Mihailovic was not. When Fitzroy Maclean, the British representative with Tito, warned Churchill that he was a Communist, the Prime Minister replied, "Are you going to live in Yugoslavia after the war? No, neither am I." Communist or not, the Yugoslavs saw no reason to exchange German occupation for Russian domination. This independence was eventually to lead to Yugoslavia's expulsion from the Cominform, the successor organisation to the Comintern, which Stalin had disbanded in 1943 as a gesture to his Western Allies.

Pierson Dixon, the Foreign Office official who accompanied Churchill on his meetings with Tito, noted in his diary:

> Tito was cautious, nervous and sweating a good deal in his absurd Marshal's uniform of thick cloth and gold lace. The PM pitched into Tito a good deal towards the end, and told him that we would not tolerate being used against rival Yugoslavs. But Tito must have known there was no real threat against him, since we have consistently done nothing but court him... We went straight from the conference room into a lunch in Tito's honour... The PM, looking pasty and ill, lurched to his feet and made a highly laudatory speech about Tito's exploits, welcoming him as an ally.

Churchill also undertook a number of expeditions during his trip, including one to the outskirts of Florence, still held by the

---

40. Tito was the nom de guerre adopted by the Yugoslav Communist leader Josip Broz who became post-war President of his country.

Germans, several nights in the British Embassy in Rome and an audience with Pope Pius XII, at which the Pontiff and the Prime Minister both heartily agreed on their anti- Communism. He also visited the British front line at Ancona and on 15 August sailed on a Royal Navy cruiser to within a few miles of the *Dragoon* landings that he had so bitterly opposed. He was back in London for a week before departing for Quebec on the liner *Queen Mary*, suffering from a patch on his lung and the after-effects of anti-malarial drugs administered following his trip to Italy. The Prime Minister's recurring bouts of ill health would make the voyage to Quebec a miserable one, which began on 5 September, three days before the first German V-2 rocket fell on London.

Throughout the voyage the principal victim of Churchill's mood swings was Brooke, who wrote in his diary of the difficulties of dealing with the Prime Minister at his most volatile. On 7 September, Brooke noted that at lunch Churchill looked listless and unwell, attributing this to the drugs he had been taking. At a meeting the next day Churchill appeared haggard, unable to concentrate and frequently held his head in his hands. He accused the Chiefs of Staff of misleading him about the transfer of troops from the European to the Far Eastern theatre by insisting that the redeployment was dependent on the defeat of Hitler. Brooke, reining in his temper, began to feel sorry for the Prime Minister: "He gave me the feeling of a man who is finished, can no longer keep a grip on things, and is beginning to realise it. We made no progress and decided to go on tomorrow. He finished up by saying: 'Here we are within 72 hours of meeting the Americans and there is not a single point that we are in agreement over!'"

The frustrations of those working under Churchill were customarily offset by the affections of men like Brooke who were often prepared to forgive the Prime Minister much that in any other man would have been considered intolerable. George Mallaby, the Under-Secretary to the Cabinet Office, recalled:

Anybody who served anywhere near him was devoted to him. It is hard to say why. He was not kind or considerate.

He bothered nothing about us. He knew the names of only those very close to him and would hardly let anyone else come into his presence. He was free with abuse and complaint. He was exacting beyond reason and ruthlessly critical. He continuously exhibited all the characteristics which one usually deplores and abominates in the boss. Not only did he get away with it but nobody really wanted him otherwise. He was unusual, unpredictable, exciting, original, stimulating, provocative, outrageous, uniquely experienced, abundantly talented, humorous, entertaining – almost everything a man could be, a great man.

Neither the sticky heat of steaming through the Gulf Stream nor the alienating effects of his medication dimmed Churchill's prodigious appetite. On his third night at sea his dinner comprised oysters, consommé, turbot, roast turkey, canteloupe melon on ice, Stilton cheese, fruits and petits fours lubricated by 1929 Mumm champagne, Liebfraumilch and 1870 brandy. On 10 September, he resumed the running argument with Brooke, demanding the acceleration of operations in Europe to enable transfers to the Far East. Brooke, tested to the limit of his patience, found it hard to remain civil. He reflected that while Churchill was seen by the greater part of the public as a master of strategy, much like his great ancestor John Churchill, Duke of Marlborough, it was fortunate that very few of them knew that their idol had feet of clay. Without Churchill, Britain would almost certainly have lost the war, yet with him the nation had courted disaster on numerous occasions. Brooke concluded, "Never have I admired and despised a man simultaneously to the same extent. Never have such opposite extremes been combined in the same human being."

Churchill's spirits, hitherto lethargic, improved immeasurably on arrival in Quebec. Once more he found himself warmed by the blaze of Allied friendship. The principal item on the Quebec agenda addressed the need to ensure that Germany did not produce a Fourth Reich and precipitate a new world war. The French and the Soviets, having been invaded by Germany twice in the previous 50 years, were determined that this should never happen again. Several different schemes had been hatched to prevent a resurgence of German territorial ambition. General de Gaulle, now the head of the French provisional government, had proposed that Germany be split into a large number of small independent states. This resembled an American plan, devised by Henry Morgenthau, the US Treasury Secretary, under which post-war Germany would be stripped of its industry and converted to an entirely agricultural economy. When the Germans got wind of the plan, Josef Goebbels, Hitler's Minister of Propaganda, had made much of the fact that Morgenthau was a Jew and his plan provided ample warning of the fate which awaited Germany if it lost the war. On 15 September, the plan was formally endorsed by Roosevelt and Churchill, but was swiftly killed by the opposition of Eden and Hull. The Americans, for their part, were happy to assure Churchill at Quebec that there would be no immediate calls made on the Allied armies in Italy. Their principal aim was the destruction of the German army on the central front in Western Europe while the British preoccupation was increasingly the Soviet penetration of Eastern Europe. The British objective was the securing of Trieste, at the head of the Adriatic, and Vienna, while the Americans did the same in Prague, the Czechoslovak capital. The devout British wish, not to be realised, was to see themselves joining hands with the Americans in Berlin before the arrival of the Red Army.

Octagon also revealed the gulf between the Americans and the British over the war in the Far East and Pacific. The British were reluctant to be relegated to the jungles of Burma and were keen, once Germany had been defeated, to commit the Royal Navy to the final assault on the Japanese home islands. The Americans, ever suspicious of lingering British Imperial ambitions and the recovery of territories lost to the Japanese in 1941-42, were notably reluctant to shore up the British Empire. This was a view shared by the President, who nevertheless spent two amicable days with Churchill at Hyde Park after the conclusion of *Octagon*. With the exception of a brief encounter in Malta on the way to the Yalta Conference, this was the last time the Prime Minister had the President all to himself. Churchill returned home at the end of September in notably high spirits. The news in London was less than triumphant. Operation *Market Garden*, the Allied attempt to secure a crossing of the Rhine in the immediate aftermath of the German collapse in Normandy, had ended in failure and the virtual annihilation of the British First Airborne Division.

Within two weeks the Prime Minister set off for a meeting with Stalin in Moscow. His stated reason for the trip was a desire, after *Octagon*, not to leave Stalin out in the cold, although it seems more likely that the Prime Minister's growing addiction to summitry had gained the upper hand. He flew to the Soviet Union via Naples and Cairo, arriving on the morning of 9 October. Eden and Brooke made the same journey but in a different aircraft. In Moscow the Russians had provided the Prime Minister with a town house and a country house, but from the night of 11 October, with one day's exception, he preferred the former. Churchill embarked on his Moscow venture intending to cement a relationship with Stalin which would reflect their status and experience as world statesmen and would permit a sly degree of "ganging up" on Roosevelt. On 13 October he wrote to Clementine, "The affairs go well... I have had very nice talks with the old bear. I like him the more I see him." He added a caveat, "I have to keep the President in constant touch and this is the delicate side." He also wrote to the King, referring to himself in the third person: "The Prime Minister attended a special performance of the ballet, which is very fine, and received a prolonged ovation from an enormous audience... At or after the very lengthy feasts, and very numerous cordial toasts, it has been possible to touch on many grave matters in an easy fashion. The nights are very late, lasting till three or even four o' clock, but the Prime Minister also keeps late hours, and much work is done from about noon onwards."

The most important meeting with Stalin was the first, beginning at 10pm on 9 October, the day of Churchill's arrival, when he was tired after many hours of flying. The Prime Minister and Stalin were not alone. There were two interpreters present plus Eden,

Molotov, and Sir Archibald Clark Kerr, the British Ambassador in Moscow. The principal issues were intended to be the settlement of the Polish question and the respective post-war "spheres of influence" in Eastern Europe and the Balkans to be exercised by Britain and the Soviet Union. On a piece of paper Churchill had scrawled the suggestion that the Russians should have 90 per cent influence in Romania – for a trade-off of 10 per cent influence in Greece – 75 per cent in Bulgaria and 50 per cent in Yugoslavia and Hungary, the remaining percentages to be controlled by Britain. Churchill recalled, "I pushed this across to Stalin... Then he took his blue pencil and made a large tick upon it and passed it back to us... At length I said: 'Might it not be thought rather cynical if it seemed we had disposed of these issues ... in such an offhand manner? Let us burn this paper.' 'No, you keep it,' said Stalin."

At no point had Poland appeared on Churchill's note or been mentioned in the exchange between the two leaders. Churchill had envisaged a post-war democratic future for the Poles and had admired the bravery displayed by Polish fighter pilots in the Battle of Britain and Polish infantry in the Italian campaign. However, he had also accepted without question Stalin's cynical explanation of his failure to come to the aid of the Polish Home Army in the Warsaw uprising of the previous August.[41] The Prime Minister's sentimental attachment to Poles fighting for the Allies did not extend to the Polish politicians in exile in London, three of whom had come to Moscow at his request. Five days later he gave them a harsh lesson in realpolitik at the British Embassy. The Polish record states that he told them:

You are no Government if you are incapable of taking any decisions. You are callous people who want to wreck Europe. I shall leave you to your own troubles. You have no sense of

---

41. The Warsaw uprising began in August 1944 and was suppressed by the Germans by the following October. Stalin chose not to intervene but let the *Wehrmacht* do its work for him before liberating the shattered city on 17 January 1945.

responsibility when you want to abandon your own people at home, to whose sufferings you are indifferent. You do not care about the future of Europe, you only have your own miserable interests in mind. I will have to call on the other Poles and this Lublin government [the Soviet-backed Poles in Moscow] may function very well. It will be the Government. It is a criminal attempt to wreck, by your ... veto, agreement between the Allies. It is cowardice on your part.

In fact, Churchill had nothing but contempt for the Lublin government, calling them "the greatest villains imaginable". In Moscow, however, he seemed overawed by Stalin, who had no illusions about the post-war future of Poland, the age-old invasion route into Russia. It would remain under Soviet control. Beyond the boundaries of an enlarged Soviet Union would stretch a protective buffer of satellite Eastern European states which the Red Army had either liberated (Poland and Czechoslovakia) or invaded (Hungary, Romania, Bulgaria).

Churchill left Moscow on the morning of 19 October, flying back to London via the Crimea (where he was treated to a sumptuous dinner), Cairo and Naples. On 10 November he flew to Paris for the first time since May 1940. There he was to meet General de Gaulle, a man with whom he had shared a tempestuous relationship since the fall of France but was now a European figure possibly second only in stature to himself. During the darkest days of the war Churchill had promised de Gaulle that they would walk down the Champs-Élysées together. Now that promise was kept on the 11th, the anniversary of the 1918 Armistice. The Prime Minister was given a hero's welcome by the people of Paris and installed in a superb apartment, complete with gilded bath, in the Quai d'Orsay. His splendid quarters prompted the Prime Minister to remark to Brooke that the last time he was there a small army of decrepit civil servants were burning stacks of files in the courtyard. On the day of the parade Churchill was studiedly cheerful while de Gaulle was stiffer and haughtier than ever. The General disliked sharing occasions, particularly with a portly man dressed in the unbecoming uniform of an air commodore. Brooke later recalled a conversation he had the next day with senior officers who had fought in the Resistance. These men were less than impressed with de Gaulle. One of them told Brooke, "De Gaulle! What did he do? Evacuated his family to London from the start, where he followed them. There he lived comfortably throughout the war whilst we were risking our lives daily in contact with the Germans, living in cellars with them overhead and expecting daily to be apprehended by the Gestapo. Meanwhile in his safe position he had the impertinence to say 'Je suis la France'. They were very bitter and had little use for him."

The trip to France showed Churchill at his worst and his best. On 13 November he flew at his valet Sawyers, reprimanding him in the foulest language for forgetting to remove the belt from his air commodore's tunic before a public appearance. Mary Churchill, who witnessed the incident, sauntered away with a smile on her face. On the same day, having travelled in frigid winter weather to inspect the front held by First French Army, Churchill arrived at lunch frozen to the marrow and rolled up in a greatcoat like a hedgehog. He proceeded to sit down on a chair with a hot-water bottle at his feet and another wedged behind him. After a reviving brandy thawed him out somewhat, he made a speech in his idiosyncratic French, which disarmed his audience.

The agreement he had reached with Stalin in Moscow enabled the Prime Minister, on his return from France, to turn his attention to Greece, which had suffered cruelly from famine and German occupation. Now it was ravaged by what amounted to a civil war between supporters of the Greek monarchy, represented by King George II in London, and the Communist-controlled political Resistance force EAM and its military wing ELAS. On the evening of 4/5 December, Churchill instructed the commander of the 5,000 British troops in Athens, General Scobie, to crush EAM-ELAS, which controlled a large part of the country. His telegram to the General contained the telling phrase: "Do not however hesitate to act as if you were in a conquered city where a local rebellion is in progress."

Unfortunately, the telegram was also despatched to the Italian headquarters of the British C-in-C Mediterranean, General Wilson, without the code "Guard", which signified that it should not be shown to the Americans. The US Ambassador in Rome forwarded the telegram to the US State Department, which in turn leaked it to the *Washington Post* columnist Drew Pearson. A first-class row ensued in which Admiral King, the US Chief of Naval Staff, threatened to withdraw the American landing craft which the British were using for transport to and from Greece. Roosevelt was notably reluctant to defend Churchill, sending a distinctly unhelpful message on 13 December: "No one will understand better than yourself that I, both personally and as Head of State, am necessarily responsive to the state of public feeling. It is for these reasons that it has not been possible for this Government to take a stand along with you in the present course of events in Greece."

Eden and the majority of the War Cabinet urged that a regency be established under Archbishop Damaskinos, the Greek Orthodox Metropolitan. Churchill, assessing the heavily bearded prelate as a likely Leftist troublemaker, would have none of it. Coupled with the German offensive in the Ardennes, launched on 16 December, the Greek crisis cast a pall over the coming Christmas season, which Churchill had planned to spend with his family at Chequers. However, driven by the desire to be at the centre of events, the Prime Minister tore up his plans and spent Christmas Day en route to Athens in a Douglas C-54 Skymaster. In Churchill's scheme of things boredom always took second place to danger and he was sure that the force of his personality would prevail on the spot. That evening a meeting with Damaskinos convinced the Prime Minister that this was not an Hellenic version of Charles de Gaulle but an emerging strongman, a magnificent figure, seven foot tall in his episcopal hat and a former champion wrestler.

Damaskinos agreed to chair a constitutional conference on 26 December attended by all the principal Greek political players. It was convened in the chilly, unheated Greek Foreign Ministry lit by flickering Hurricane lamps while intermittently advancing and receding gunfire rattled around outside. Churchill's opening address was well under way when three piratical figures, representatives of ELAS, appeared in the gloom. Churchill, who later chose later to describe them as wearing British battledress, decided not to shake their hands. Nevertheless, the ELAS men expressed satisfaction that the British Prime Minster had judged the situation in Greece worthy of his personal attention, although it did little to prevent the eruption of a full-blown civil war, which lasted until October 1949. It also showed Churchill as an extraordinary mixture of world statesman and Boy Scout adventurer. He was back in London on 29 December, reporting to the War Cabinet and then spending hours with Eden forcing the Greek King to accept the regency.

By the end of December, the Allies had recovered from the initial shock they had suffered two weeks earlier when Hitler had launched his final offensive in the West through the heavily forested and fogbound hills of the Ardennes and aimed at Antwerp, splitting the British and American fronts. After four days of confused fighting, the Americans, who had initially borne the brunt of the 44-division attack, pulled themselves together, squeezing the Germans into an extended salient the tip of which was halted just south-west of Dinant, the so-called Bulge, which subsequently gave to the battle its popular name. To the north of the salient, Eisenhower gave Montgomery temporary command of all Allied forces in the sector while Bradley commanded US VIII Corps in the south and Patton's Third Army drove north to slam into the Bulge's southern shoulder. The fog cleared, allowing Allied fighter-bombers to regain air supremacy. As early as 22 December, Rundstedt, mindful of the threat in the East and the acute fuel problems slowing the German offensive, begged Hitler to call off the operation. With his customary sublime lack of tact, Montgomery could not resist the opportunity, on the verge of victory, "to tweak our Yankee noses", as Bradley later put it. One of Monty's staff officers recalled that he had arrived at the headquarters of US First Army like "Christ come to cleanse the temple". After the battle Montgomery made things worse at a press conference by claiming the entire credit for the

Allied victory, which had been completed by the end of January. Churchill was obliged to mollify the outraged Americans with a generous speech in the House of Commons.

The Ardennes offensive delayed the Allied drive to the River Rhine by some six weeks. In April the Allies closed on the Rhine. Standing in the way was the West Wall (popularly known as the Siegfried Line) an uncompleted defensive feature, a German equivalent of the Maginot Line, running along the Dutch and French borders from near München Gladbach to the Swiss border near Freiburg. In Operation *Grenade*, launched at the end of April, Montgomery broke through the northern section of the West Wall, and on 2 March Churchill flew out to inspect his handiwork.

Accompanied by Brooke, Montgomery, General William Simpson, commander of US Ninth Army, and a convoy of pressmen, the Prime Minister motored in a Rolls-Royce to inspect the West Wall and its celebrated dragon's teeth defences. The journey was enlivened by a surreal episode in which the Prime Minister's limousine was halted to take delivery of his dentures, left behind and rushed up by a jeep. These he unconcernedly dropped into his mouth before waving the driver on. At the West Wall the Prime Minister was at his most theatrical. Clad in the uniform of the Fourth Hussars, his old regiment, he walked purposefully towards a row of dragon's teeth, opened his fly, and invited his distinguished companions "to urinate on the great West Wall of Germany". Turning to the press photographers aiming their cameras, while he aimed a jet of urine at the concrete below him, he shouted, "This is one operation connected with this great war which must not be reproduced graphically." Brooke recalled, "I shall never forget the childish grin of inner satisfaction that spread all over his face as he looked down at the critical moment."

On 23 March, Brooke joined the Prime Minister at Northolt to fly in a C-54 to Brussels before driving to Montgomery's headquarters near the aerodrome. That night the crossing of the Rhine, Operation *Plunder*, began on a two-army front, US Ninth Army on the right and British Second Army on the left. After dinner Montgomery went to bed, leaving Churchill and Brooke to take a moonlight stroll and to reminisce about their early struggles in the war and Brooke's appointment as CIGS. They then went back to the Prime Minister's caravan to examine his communications box. A telegram from Molotov about the secret talks which Karl Wolff, Himmler's former liaison officer at Hitler's headquarters and later Military Governor in North Italy, had opened with Allan Dulles, Roosevelt's envoy in Switzerland and an agent of OSS.[42] Churchill immediately suspected, wrongly as it turned out, that the Americans wanted to make a separate peace with Germany on the Western Front, cutting the Soviets out of the equation. Churchill decided to sleep on this news.

The next morning the Prime Minister and Brooke drove out to a viewing point near Xanten to survey the progress of *Plunder*. They took up position surrounded by artillery batteries pounding German anti-aircraft guns on the opposite bank before the arrival of Allied airborne formations, 22,000 men in 1,696 aircraft and 1,348 gliders, the largest single day's operation of its type in the war. Over the bridgehead an air umbrella was formed by 900 Allied fighter aircraft while deeper into Germany fighter formations swept the skies clear of the Luftwaffe. At 10am, in sunshine obscured by the great clouds of dust raised by another massive bombardment, the first airborne wave flew in. Churchill, watching on the western bank with Brooke and Eisenhower, turned to the Allied Supreme Commander and observed, "My dear General, the German is whipped. We've got him. He's all through."

---

42. OSS, the Office of Strategic Services, the US equivalent of the British SOE (Special Operations Executive) set up with Churchill's enthusiastic encouragement in the summer of 1940, was established in 1942 to gather intelligence and support Resistance movements.

12

THE RIVIERA OF HADES

Arrangements for the second wartime summit between the "Big Three" had been agreed by the Soviet and American leaders, principally to forestall any objections from the British Prime Minister. For his part, Stalin had insisted on Yalta, on the Black Sea coast of the Crimea, as the site of the summit, citing ill health and the pressure of military operations as reasons which would not permit him to leave the Soviet Union. The resort towns of the southern Black Sea littoral, dubbed the "Romanov route" as it was dotted with a string of Imperial palaces, would play host to the Allied leaders. It was only after Stalin had got his way that Churchill was invited to attend the conference, which was scheduled for the beginning of February.

In January 1945, the outlines of the post-war world were taking shape. The Americans and British had liberated large parts of western Europe, Italy and Greece, and had installed sympathetic regimes in countries formerly occupied by the Third Reich. In Eastern Europe the Red Army had liberated Romania, Bulgaria and Poland and, in similar albeit more ruthless fashion, installed regimes which remained under tight Russian control. Hungary looked likely to go the same way, but Yugoslavia, where Tito's partisans had liberated the country with little outside help, seemed set to retain a substantial measure of independence. Stalin had a pragmatic view of these developments, summed up in an observation delivered in July 1944: "Everyone imposes his own system as far as his army can reach. It cannot be otherwise."

Six months later, these words weighed heavily with Churchill as he prepared to leave for what was to be the last great Allied conference of the European war. What evidence could he offer the Russians of Western support for the massive offensives the Red Army was mounting in the East? Diplomatic imperatives combined with the dynamic of area bombing to revive the 1943 *Thunderclap* scheme to destroy German morale in a series of cataclysmic air raids. The target, on the night of 13/14 February 1945, in effect two days after the Yalta conference ended, was the ancient city of Dresden, which had survived the war virtually unscathed but was now deemed a significant transport and war industry hub. The resulting death toll, estimated at up to 130,000, still reverberates today. On 28 March 1945, in the bitter aftermath of the raid, Churchill wrote that if the bombing continued there was the possibility that "we shall come into control of an utterly ruined land."

Before their rendezvous with Stalin, Churchill, Roosevelt and the Combined Chiefs of Staff met in Malta, the British stronghold in the central Mediterranean, on the morning 1 February, to discuss military and political strategy before flying the 1,400 miles to the Crimea. Accompanied by his daughter Sarah Oliver,[43] an aerial reconnaissance intelligence analyst in the Women's Auxiliary Air Force, and wearing the uniform of the Royal Yacht Squadron, Churchill puffed a cigar awaiting Roosevelt as he paced the deck of the light cruiser HMS *Orion*, the warship which had fired the first shell during the D-Day landings. Roosevelt, who arrived in Valetta harbour a little later aboard the heavy cruiser *Quincy*, cut a contrasting figure, drawn but dignified, wearing a civilian suit

---

43. Churchill's daughter was estranged from but still married to the comedian Vic Oliver. Also present at Yalta and performing similar unofficial roles were the Russian-speaking Kathleen (Kathy) Harriman, daughter of Roosevelt's Ambassador in Moscow, and Anna Roosevelt Boettiger, FDR's eldest daughter.

and wheelchair-bound as he saluted his opposite number, who as a matter of courtesy had now dispensed with his cigar. The war had taken its toll on both men. Churchill's stamina and powers of concentration had been noticeably sapped, as was clear to his wartime deputy, the Labour Party leader Clement Attlee, who had taken the Prime Minister to task on 19 January 1945, writing to him that, "It is very exceptional for you to have read your papers. More and more often you have not even read the note prepared for your guidance. Often half an hour is wasted in explaining what could have been grasped in two minutes of reading the document. Not infrequently a phrase catches your eye which gives rise to a disquisition on an interesting point only slightly connected with the subject matter. The result is long delays and increasingly long Cabinets imposed on Ministers who had already done a hard day's work."

Roosevelt cut a haunting figure. His health had been in rapid decline since the beginning of 1944. A thorough medical examination at Bethseda Hospital in March 1944 confirmed that he was suffering from acute congestive heart failure, a diagnosis that was kept secret, even from the President himself, although he remained markedly incurious about his health. Howard Bruenn, the young cardiologist who had conducted the examination, took Roosevelt's daughter Anna into his confidence, stipulating that her father must work for only four hours a day. The President's wasted limbs and gaunt features now lent him an almost spectral appearance. In Malta he had been closely observed by Charles Wilson, now Lord Moran, Churchill's doctor and President of the Royal College of Physicians. Shortly before his departure for Malta, Moran had received a letter from his American counterpart, Dr Roger Lee, President of the American Medical Association, indicating that the President's heart condition was now advanced. Moran noted in his diary that Roosevelt was clearly "a very sick man... He has all the symptoms of hardening of the arteries of the brain [sic] in an advanced stage, so that I can only give him a few months to live," a conclusion which was not shared with the President's entourage. An exhausted

Churchill and a moribund Roosevelt rang alarm bells for the British Foreign Secretary Anthony Eden, who feared that the two Western leaders were ill-prepared for their approaching encounter with Stalin, "a bear who would certainly know his own mind." Churchill harboured his own misgivings about the imminent encounter, fretting – correctly as it happened – that the scheduled week of negotiations would be insufficient to deal with the host of geopolitical problems demanding attention as the war came to an end.

Shortly before midnight on Friday 2 February, the first aircraft in a long procession bearing 700 Allied officers and officials took off from Luqqa in Malta for Saki airfield in the Crimea, which the Americans had code-named *Albatross* because of its uncomfortably short runway. They were followed in the small hours by Churchill and Roosevelt, flying in separate Douglas C-54 Skymaster transports, blacked out and maintaining radio silence. The Skymasters and their Lockheed P-38 Lightning escorts touched down at Saki, situated in a featureless, frozen and foggy steppe, just after midnight on 3 February. They were greeted by a white-gloved guard of honour, a Red Army band, lines of Lend-Lease Packards, hearse-like Soviet limousines, and a tented compound boasting a lavish breakfast buffet complete with brimming tumblers of brandy, which the teetotal General George Marshall, Chairman of the US Joint Chiefs of Staff and an earlier arrival, had eschewed before pressing on to Yalta.

Churchill arrived at Saki wearing a military greatcoat and officer's cap. He was greeted by the Soviet Foreign Minister Vyacheslav Molotov, who was dressed from head to toe in black, and the two men stood together awaiting the arrival of Roosevelt's Skymaster, dubbed the "Sacred Cow". The President descended from the Skymaster on an elevator and was gently lifted into a jeep by his secret service officer Mike Reilly, his frailty underlined by his Brooks Brothers boat cloak which enveloped his shrunken physique. Roosevelt's evident fragility was noted by the Soviet doctors unobtrusively placed at Saki by Stalin to observe and report on the President's condition.

After the reception ceremonies, Churchill and Roosevelt were driven in their limousines the 70 miles to Yalta over bruising, bumpy roads and past the litter of wrecked weaponry left in the wake of the German retreat from the Crimea ten months earlier. The bleak landscape through which the convoy threaded its way reminded Moran of snow-covered moorland. After an hour of lurching over rutted roads past gloomy knots of Red Army troops, many of them women who had been withdrawn from the front line, Churchill turned to his daughter Sarah and said, "Christ, five more hours of this," before cheering himself by reciting from memory long passages from Byron's *Don Juan*.

After four more bladder-straining hours, the convoy drew up at a rest house, where the British and American visitors were confronted with tables groaning with vodka, wine, caviar and a host of other delicacies. Roosevelt, who had long been placed on a strict invalid's diet, was obliged to enlist the help of his daughter Anna and that of Vladimir Pavlov, the Russian interpreter, to decline the hospitality as graciously as possible and push on to Yalta. However, diplomacy demanded that Churchill and his daughter Sarah, who was acting as an unofficial aide de camp, were in no position to refuse the Soviet leader's prodigal generosity and by so doing insult the ingratiating Molotov. In spite of travel exhaustion and a hearty sandwich luncheon en route, they were obliged to sample a spread which put the rigours of ration-bound Britain to shame where wartime austerity and belt-tightening had taken a grim toll.

Churchill's mood had lightened somewhat by the time his party arrived in Yalta, with its backdrop of low mountains sloping down to the Black Sea through cypress and orange groves, vineyards, and tobacco plantations. The British delegation was housed in the Vorontzov Palace, a combination of Scottish baronial and Arabian Nights fantasy built in 1837. Its interior was largely intact and Churchill was delighted to discover in the dining room a portrait of Count Vorontzov's daughter with her

English husband, George Herbert, eleventh Earl of Pembroke. In spite of these reminders of home, an oppressive atmosphere clung to the Palace. In a letter to her mother, Sarah Oliver conceded that it commanded sweeping views of mountains and valleys, but she confessed that "... the whole landscape is rather like a woman who has all the attributes of beauty, yet no charm – no power to move on." Churchill's inner feelings at this stage in the war, when British status as a great power was inexorably slipping away, can be sensed in his gloomy observation to Sarah when gazing at the view from the Vorontzov: "Behold the Riviera of Hades."

Taking a sanguine view of Soviet sanitary habits, the British Military Mission in Moscow had advised the delegation to take "plenty of flea powder and toilet paper". Churchill, at least, was housed in some comfort, with sole access to the only bathroom in the Palace which had a flush toilet. Conditions were crowded for everyone else. The Chiefs of Staff in the Vorontzov had to queue for the other facilities, often standing in line to urinate in a bucket. The Chief of Air Staff, Sir Charles Portal, was seen jumping up and down in the corridor to get a glimpse through the transom above the door of exactly which one of his fellow military panjandrums was lingering too long in the bathtub.

Thousands of Russian workers and Axis prisoners of war had been hard at work in the Yalta palaces which were to house the delegations. The retreating Germans had plundered the conference palaces' interiors, and the Red Air Force had been obliged to fly in fresh furniture, carpets, curtains and even wallpaper. Cracking the whip was the pudgy, bespectacled, yellow-toothed Laventi Beria, chief of the NKVD, the Soviet Secret Service, and like Stalin a Georgian, the man responsible for the deportation of 200,000 Crimean Tatars suspected of wartime collaboration with the Nazis. Beria, a figure almost unknown in the West but universally feared in the Soviet Union, had also overseen the elaborate bugging of the British and American delegations, a task assigned to his son Sergo, an electronics student at a Leningrad military academy. From Roosevelt's arrival at Saki, Sergo had been listening to the President's conversations,[44] deploying powerful directional microphones. At Yalta, bugs in the gardens of the Livadia Palace occupied by the Americans provided Soviet intelligence with a steady stream of information. It was typical of Stalin that throughout the war he spent as much time spying on his Western allies as he did on his Axis enemies. He came to Yalta armed with detailed information on the British Foreign Office's strategy and the dealings and disagreements between Roosevelt and Churchill provided by the Cambridge spies Guy Burgess and Donald Maclean and the American State Department official Alger Hiss, who was also at Yalta. He was to deploy this wealth of inside information with great skill.

The Livadia Palace, built of white Crimean stone, had been the infrequently visited summer home of Tsar Nicholas II and his family. After the Bolshevik Revolution, it became a workers' sanatorium, from which all traces of the Romanovs had been removed. From 1942, it functioned as the *Wehrmacht*'s Crimean headquarters before being stripped bare in 1944 during the German withdrawal. The conference's plenary sessions were to be held in the Palace's white ballroom to the right of the spacious reception hall. To the left were Roosevelt's quarters in what had been a suite of the Tsar's private offices, more accessible by wheelchair than the upstairs imperial bedroom.[45] Elsewhere in the Palace the representatives of the American High Command were sleeping eight generals to a room. General Marshall and Admiral Ernest J. King, the US Navy's C-in-C and from 1942 Chief of Naval Operations, a unique double appointment, were sharing the Tsarina's suite, Marshall in her bedroom and King in her boudoir, which had a staircase reputedly used by Rasputin.

Stalin was quartered in the relatively modest Koreiz Villa, midway between the British to the south and the Americans to

---

44. Roosevelt's conversations contained many unflattering remarks about Churchill. Sergo Beria was fluent in English.
45. The Tsar, fearful of assassination, was in fact rumoured to sleep in a different bedroom every night.

the north. Under Beria's watchful eyes, a bomb shelter with a two-metre-thick concrete ceiling had been built in the basement. Stalin had arrived at Yalta before Churchill and Roosevelt, the better to amass intelligence before and during the Conference. However, on the first morning he turned up late, pointedly setting the tone and reminding his allies who was in charge. As Anthony Eden had observed, Stalin was better placed than his allies to command and control proceedings as they unfolded. The Prime Minister was exhausted, reluctant to read his briefings, and liable to embark on impromptu Imperialistic perorations which tried the patience of both Stalin and Roosevelt. The President was a dying man, slack-jawed, often silent and prone to random personal reminiscences which bore little or no relation to the matter immediately under discussion.[46] Moreover, he clung to the belief that he could personally "handle" Stalin and reserved most of his suspicions, as the conference progressed, for Churchill's crusty Imperialism. However, the President's attempts to strike up a personal rapport with the Soviet leader frequently misfired. At the tripartite dinner on 4 February, Roosevelt observed that in America Stalin was known as "Uncle Joe", a remark which nearly sent the Soviet leader stalking from the room in a rage, apparently stung by the vulgarity of the nickname. Churchill contrived to draw him back to the table with a toast.

Tired though he was, there is no doubt that the nightclub manager's hours imposed on the principal negotiators at Yalta suited Churchill far better than the ailing Roosevelt. According to Alexander Cadogan, Permanent Secretary at the Foreign Office, the Prime Minister was sustained throughout the conference by "buckets of Caucasian champagne which would undermine the health of any ordinary man." The plenary sessions at Yalta began

---

46. One of Roosevelt's odder digressions, delivered on the final evening of the Conference, was a series of observations, by no means critical, on the Ku Klux Klan.

in the late afternoon and lasted up to five hours with a short break during which Churchill fortified himself with whisky and soup. Dinner was at 9.30pm, three of them formal tripartite affairs punctuated by florid toasts larded with flowery compliments and mutual backslapping.[47] On the other evenings Churchill dined at the Vorontzov with his daughter Sarah, Anthony Eden and a shifting cast of generals, admirals and civil servants. At midnight the Prime Minister took delivery of the diplomatic pouch, scanned the morning newspapers it contained and worked on for several hours before retiring to bed. On waking, Churchill remained in bed until the early afternoon, brunching heartily at 11.30am. During the conference, the Prime Minister telegraphed his deputy Clement Attlee:

This place has turned out very well so far, in spite of our gloomy warnings and forebodings. It is a sheltered strip of austere Riviera with winding cornice roads, and the villas and palaces more or less undamaged of an extinct imperialism and nobility. In these we squat on furniture carried from Moscow and with plumbing and road-making done regardless of cost in a few days by our hosts, whose prodigality exceeds belief. All the chiefs of staff have taken a holiday to see the battlefield at Balaclava. We are not stressing this in our contacts with our friends.

---

47. At the Soviet tripartite dinner Churchill said of Stalin, "I walk through this world with greater courage and hope when I find myself in a relationship of friendship and intimacy with this great man, whose fame has gone out not only over all Russia but the world." Stalins's reply was a masterclass in insincerity: "I am talking as an old man; that is why I am talking so much. But I want to drink to our alliance, that it should not lose its intimacy, its character of free expression of views. In the history of diplomacy I know of no such close alliance of three Great Powers as this... I know that some circles will regard this remark as naïve."

The visit to Balaclava, made on 7 February, was not without its alarms. The Chief of the Imperial General Staff, Sir Alan Brooke, was studying a map of the battlefield when

> ... someone discovered a complete human skeleton within five yards of us, one of the victims of the last campaign [the retreat of the Wehrmacht]. We could see Balaclava port quite clearly and could imagine its working organisation as a base, the mud, the storms, the frightful difficulties, the awful sufferings, etc. And then on top of it all, as if this small corner of the world had not witnessed sufficient human suffering, there were ample signs of the vast recent conflicts to capture Sebastopol and then to free it! A grave beside a wrecked aeroplane here, a broken-down tank there, rows upon rows of shell and bomb craters ... tangled basket wire, odd graves, and the usual rubbish of a battlefield. It is very strange how history can repeat itself under a different guise.

Writing about the Yalta Conference years later, Churchill wistfully evoked a kindred sense of history now rapidly retreating beyond recall: "We had the world at our feet. Twenty-five million men were marching at our orders by land and sea. We seemed to be friends." Nevertheless, the major items on the agenda inevitably exacerbated the underlying tensions inherent in the Grand Alliance against the Axis: the future of Poland; the post-war dismemberment of Germany; the terms of the Soviet entry into the war against Japan; and the structure of the emerging United Nations Organisation, the one topic that animated the ailing Roosevelt the most.

Poland's post-war boundaries had been crudely mapped out at the Teheran Conference in November-December 1943. Stalin was to be ceded a slice of eastern Poland up to 185 miles wide, an area traditionally claimed by Russia. Poland was to be compensated with a tranche cut from Germany's eastern boundary extending to the Oder and Neisse Rivers. At Yalta the first argument was over the proposal for the German-Polish border. Had Poland been allotted territory up to the eastern branch of the Neisse – as

Churchill and Roosevelt believed – or to the western branch, sixty miles closer to Germany, which was Stalin's interpretation? A decision was put off until an eventual European peace conference, which never met.

There was little common ground between Stalin and the Western Allies over the political future of Poland. The Americans submitted a "Declaration on Liberated Europe", a well-meaning but woolly document, among the provisions of which were the right of all peoples to choose the form of government under which they wanted to live. Poland's prospects of democratic government had already been extinguished. Stalin was determined that in Poland, an age-old invasion route into Russia, any future government would be a "friend of the Soviet Union". In 1943 the Polish government-in-exile in London had demanded a Red Cross inquiry into the massacre of more than 10,000 Polish soldiers and civilians whose bodies had been uncovered by the Germans in the forest of Katyn, near Smolensk.[48] The Soviet Union had immediately broken off relations with the London Poles and had set up a puppet Polish government in Moscow, which moved to Lublin in 1944 and was subsequently installed in Warsaw.

At Yalta, the London Poles were abandoned by Churchill and Roosevelt. Stalin made one small concession, suggesting that the Lublin government be widened to include a few London Poles, but in all other respects he got his way. The promised "free elections" in Poland would be monitored by his own stooges, the Lublin Poles, with only minimal outside monitoring. At the plenary session on 8 February, Churchill had undermined all his and Roosevelt's arguments by suddenly declaring, "I do not care much about the Poles myself," a disarming display of frankness, perhaps, but an ill-advised negotiating stance. In truth, however, Churchill and Roosevelt had no hand to play over Poland and were obliged to recognise the Soviet Union's powers to determine matters there

---

48. It is now established beyond doubt that the Poles were killed by the Red Army during the Soviet occupation of eastern Poland, 1939-41.

on the ground. They came away clutching the face-saving formula of "free elections" but could have been under no illusions that such a concept was anything other than entirely alien to Stalin.

At Yalta the geopolitical grandstanding was accompanied by gourmandising on a colossal scale.[49] The Grand Banquet on the evening of the 8th was hosted by Stalin at the Koreiz Villa. Even by the standards of Yalta the menu was remarkable: red caviar, herring, dried and salted fish, cold pork, assorted cheeses, duck, salmon in champagne sauce, grey mullet, mackerel, lamb kebabs, fillets of veal, quail pilaf, grouse, Chicken Kiev, cauliflower in breadcrumbs, fruits, coffee and, in honour of Stalin, Georgian candied fruit. Because of the endless toasting most of the food arrived at the table stone cold. Stalin, nevertheless, remained in high good humour throughout. When Roosevelt's interpreter, Charles "Chip" Bohlen, emboldened by too much vodka, proposed a toast, "Interpreters of the world, unite, you have nothing to lose but your bosses," there was sudden, shocked silence, which was broken by Stalin's laughter as he strode around the table to salute the bold young American. The mood was further lightened by Churchill, who declared to the assembled company, "Interpreters of the world unite, you have nothing to lose but your audience!"

As well as settling boundaries – and recognizing realities – in Eastern Europe, the Allies had to decide what do with Germany itself. As early as 1943 the British had been working on a plan, code-named *Rankin C*, for a three-way post-war division of Germany and joint occupation of Berlin. Better a divided Germany than the prospect of an energetic nation of 80 million people at the heart of Europe rising again as a Fourth Reich. The British plan gave Stalin control of almost 40 per cent of Germany's post-war area, 36 per cent of its population and 33 per cent of its resources. Since *Rankin C* had been first mooted, however, another plan for

---

49. There were many demonstrations of Soviet prodigality. When Sarah Oliver hinted that a slice of lemon might accompany the lavish helpings of caviar provided by the Russians, a lemon tree appeared overnight.

post-war Germany had come and gone. As mentioned earlier, at the Quebec Conference in September 1944, Henry Morgenthau, Roosevelt's Secretary of the Treasury, presented a proposal under which Germany would have been stripped of her industrial assets and converted into an agricultural economy. This provided the Nazi propaganda chief Josef Goebbels with a handy weapon with which to rally his countrymen, not least because Morgenthau was Jewish. Although the plan had received initial support from Churchill, it was eventually shelved by Roosevelt.

At Yalta the Allies formally agreed to the zones outlined in *Rankin C*, with the addition of a small French zone in the Saarland, carved out of the British and American sectors. Churchill had argued that France should be restored as a counterweight to Germany, not least because an indefinite American presence on the continent of Europe could not be guaranteed. Berlin, deep in the Soviet zone, was to be divided into four sectors and was to house the Allied Control Council for supervising the occupying powers. Stalin gave informal guarantees of access by air, road, canal and rail through the Soviet zone to the sectors of Berlin occupied by the Western powers. Austria was to be divided in similar fashion, with Vienna providing the headquarters of a four-power commission.

Like Henry Morgenthau, Stalin had his own designs on German industry. On 5 February Ivan Maisky, formerly the Soviet Ambassador in London and now the Deputy Commissar for Foreign Affairs, presented a plan which proposed the reduction of German industry to one-fifth of its present size, with all arms factories and synthetic oil plants to be dismantled within two years. To this was added ten years of reparations payments, to be followed by the establishment of a tripartite international control commission which would take command of the entire German economy. Stalin also demanded additional monetary compensation of 10 billion dollars, a figure he had cooked up with Roosevelt. Churchill woke up at this point, recalling that the reparations imposed on Germany after the First World War had played no small part in hastening the Second, and suggesting that Germany would be hard pressed to meet just the Soviet demands. After much blustering, he agreed that the matter should be remitted to a reparations commission, to be established in Moscow.

One thorny problem which was not on the agenda of the plenary sessions, but which had been rumbling away since the summer of 1944, was the repatriation by the Soviets of hundreds of thousands of Russian prisoners of war who had either been impressed into the *Wehrmacht* or, like the Cossacks and other Soviet minorities, had volunteered to fight the Allies. There was no easy solution as this was linked to the return of some 60,000 British and American prisoners of war who had been liberated but were still held by the Red Army during its westward drive into Europe. The numbers of the former category had been swelled by many thousands of displaced persons steamrollered westward by the Red Army advance. Few of them wished to be thrown back into Stalin's less than welcoming embrace. These unfortunates became bargaining chips in a gigantic game of bluff in which Stalin prevailed. The matter was settled on the morning of 11 February when the British Foreign Secretary, Anthony Eden, John Russell Deane of the US Military Mission in Moscow and Lavrenti Beria signed a document agreeing to the handover.[50] Therein lay the difference between Stalin and the Western democracies.

Stalin emerged triumphant from the Yalta Conference. Where Churchill was long-winded and Roosevelt vague, Stalin remained incisive, playing a strong hand with masterly skill. As the delegates assembled for farewell photographs on the sunlit terrace of the Livadia Palace, the Soviet leader was in fine fettle, barking out the only four English phrases he knew: "So what!" "What the hell goes on around here?" "You said it!" and, perhaps with the Poles in mind, "The toilet is over here." In contrast, Churchill had subsided into the black mood in which had arrived in the Crimea, referring to the joint communiqué issued on the 11th as "this bloody thing" and adding, "Grand to be back to English fare after

---

50. The State Department declined to take part in this transaction.

the suckling pig and the cold fatty [Soviet] approach to all their meals."

Like a boarding school pupil at the end of term, Churchill's only thought was to get away from Yalta immediately, throwing all the carefully laid plans for the departure of the British delegation into chaos. Roosevelt, who had left the conference an hour before Churchill, departed in relatively good order. In the words of Sarah Oliver, Stalin, "like some genie, just disappeared". Churchill spent the next two days resting on the troopship *Franconia* and then flew to Athens and on to Alexandria, lunching with Roosevelt on the *Quincy*. They never saw each other again.

Yalta had succeeded in temporarily papering over the cracks in the wartime alliance between East and West. The British and American delegations chose to believe that they understood Stalin,[51] but they viewed the negotiations through flawed perspectives which were abruptly wrenched out of kilter on 13/14 February with the firebombing of Dresden by Bomber Command and US Eighth Air Force. The destruction of much of the city's war industry was seen by the Soviets as a violation of the undertakings given by the British and Americans on post-war reparations, an issue over which there had been substantial disagreement at Yalta. The Soviet diplomat Rostislav Sergeev concluded that, "... the Allies soon revealed their dissatisfaction with agreements they had signed and the true colours of their attitude towards the USSR ... they had wiped Dresden from the face of the earth - and with it vast quantities of the industry and material that the Yalta accords had just agreed would go to the Soviet Union."

---

51. Roosevelt's confidant, Harry Hopkins, the only man at Yalta who was in worse health than the President, hailed the conference as "the dawn of a new day" and a new era in which Americans could live peacefully with the Russians "as far into the future as any of us could imagine".

13

ENDGAME

Queasy misgivings about the obliteration of Dresden in February 1945 by RAF Bomber Command and the US Eighth Air Force went all the way to the top. Six weeks later, on 28 March, Churchill minuted the Chiefs of Staff: "It seems to me that the moment has come when the question of bombing German cities simply for the sake of increasing the terror, though under other pretexts, should be reviewed ... The destruction of Dresden remains a serious query against the conduct of Allied bombing."

The Prime Minister was concerned, rather late in the day, that the Allies, now on the brink of victory over Germany, would occupy a wasteland. The great European power of 1941, straddling an empire from Bordeaux to Belarus, had ceased to exist. Savage fighting had washed back and forth over its borders, bringing with it waves of countless refugees, at first fleeing east away from Anglo-American bombing and then cascading west away from the Red Army. Bombing had gouged the heart out of German cities and industries. For every ton of bombs dropped on Britain, 315 had fallen on the German heartland. The writer Mervyn Peake, despatched to Germany as a war artist, wrote home to his wife about the cities through which he had passed: "They are no more. They are relics. Terrible as the bombing of London was, it is absolutely nothing – nothing – compared with this unutterable destruction. Imagine Chelsea in fragments with not a single house with any more than a few weird-shaped walls where it once stood, and you will get an idea in miniature of what Mannheim or Wiesbaden are like – yet these are only two of the towns we have seen."

The end of the war in Europe was not long in coming. At about 3.20pm on the afternoon of 30 April, Hitler and Eva Braun, his mistress and bride of barely 48 hours, committed suicide in the Führer's last refuge, the Berlin bunker. Hitler's successor, Admiral Karl Dönitz, broadcast a stark message to the German people: "My first task is to save Germany from destruction by the advancing Bolshevik enemy. It is to serve this purpose that the struggle continues." Dönitz's vain hope was to surrender in the West while holding off the Red Army in the East. The Allies would have none of this. At 5pm on 4 May, Admiral Hans von Friedeburg and his delegation arrived at the headquarters of Field Marshal Sir Bernard Montgomery's 21st Army Group on Lüneberg Heath to surrender all German forces in Holland, north-west Germany and Denmark. Photographs of the event show grim-faced German officers looking faintly ludicrous as they creak their way across the windy heath, escorted by their British counterparts who look like bank managers in uniform. For the signing, Montgomery was at his most brisk. As he recalled, the business was conducted on "a trestle table covered with an army blanket, an inkpot, an ordinary army pen that you could buy in a shop for tuppence ... The Germans were clearly nervous and one of them took out a cigarette ... I looked at him and he put the cigarette away."

On 7 May General Jodl, Chief of Staff of the German armed forces with the exception of the Eastern Front, signed an instrument of unconditional surrender at Eisenhower's war room in Rheims, which was dominated by a giant thermometer mounted on a background of swastikas and bearing a running total of German prisoners in Allied hands. On the 8th, in Berlin, Field Marshal Wihelm Keitel, chief of the High Command of the German armed forces, signed an instrument of surrender at the headquarters of Marshal Georgy Zhukov, commander of the Red Army's First Belorussian Front These proceedings were confirmed at an inter-Allied meeting in Berlin on 10 May. The German capital lay in ruins. Taking the city, in an assault which lasted from 16 April to 2 May, had claimed the lives of some 305,000 Red Army soldiers, the heaviest loss sustained by the Soviets in any battle of the war.

Among the first British soldiers to enter Berlin after the German surrender was a Colonel Byford Jones, who had known the German capital before the war:

The Unter Den Linden, now embankments of burnt-out buildings that were once stately palaces, the pavements littered with wreckage. Between these embankments, where the proud Wehrmacht had marched, were hundreds of ex-Wehrmacht prisoners, unshaven ... filthy, tattered, empty food tins tied to the string that girt their waists, their eyes empty. Like an army of zombies, they moved silently, their feet bound in sacking, as if propelled by some external power... Rising in the heat of the day came a hideous smell of dampness, of charred remains, of thousands of putrefying bodies.

On 7 May, VE Day, Churchill made what was effectively his last wartime speech to the British people from the balcony of the Ministry of Health in Whitehall. He concluded on a rousing note: "When shall the reputation and faith of this generation fail? I say that in the long years to come not only the people of this island, but from all over the world, wherever the bird of freedom chirps in human hearts, they will look back to what we have done, and they will say 'Don't despair, don't yield to violence and tyranny. March straight forward, and die, if need be, unconquered.'" As the cheering died away, Churchill led the crowd in singing "Land of Hope and Glory".

By the end of the war in Europe, the political and social consciousness of the great majority of the British people was higher than at any time before or since. This mood provided the background to the election of July 1945. After discussions with Attlee, Churchill presented the wartime coalition with two choices. Either it should continue until the end of the war in the Pacific – a prospect which still seemed about 18 months away; or it should be disbanded immediately and an election held in July. To complicate matters, Churchill also suggested that a referendum on the matter should be held. The Labour and Liberal Party leaderships – both of which had failed fully to grasp the changing public mood – were extremely reluctant to agree on an immediate election, fearing a repeat of Lloyd George's "Khaki Election", which would return Churchill as Prime Minister with a handsome majority. Attlee and Ernest Bevin, both members of the wartime Coalition Cabinet, urged the Labour Party's National Executive Council (NEC) to accept Churchill's offer of a continued coalition, but they were voted down and the NEC's decision was endorsed in Blackpool by the Labour Party Conference. Also rejected was the idea of a referendum, and Attlee's reply to Churchill contained the astringent observation that a referendum had "only too often been the instrument of Nazidom and Fascism". It was the opening shot in what was to become an increasingly bitter campaign, which culminated in polling day on 5 July.

Churchill tendered his resignation to the King on 23 May, and a caretaker government, principally composed of Conservatives, replaced the Coalition. Parliament was dissolved on 15 June, by which time the campaigning was well under way. There was some confusion about compiling the new electoral register, which was compounded by wartime movements and evacuations and the creation of 25 new constituencies. Woodford was one of the new constituencies and its Conservative candidate, one Winston Churchill, found himself without a vote. He was not on the electoral roll for his home at Westerham, for Chequers or for Downing Street. Churchill had been out of the country in the summer of 1943 when the buff identity cards from which the register was compiled were exchanged for new ones. A new card had been issued for the Prime Minister but the old one had not been handed in and thus he was disenfranchised.

Churchill initially thought that the Conservatives would win the election by between 30 and 80 seats. He had misjudged the mood of the British people. Polling, then an infant discipline, began to detect a significant swing to Labour. Churchill might still have been respected as a great wartime leader, but there were reservations about his ability to win the peace. Most people were now preoccupied with housing, employment, social security, and the nationalisation of key sectors of industry, the "Giants of the Road to Recovery", issues which had been identified and advocated by the Beveridge Report in 1942. A majority of the electorate associated the Labour Party with these issues rather than the Conservatives, whose support for radical post-war domestic reform seemed, at best, half-hearted. Moreover, the Conservatives' campaign leaned too heavily on a Churchill cult of personality. Their most familiar poster in the election did not even bear the name of the Party but carried the legend, "Vote National – Help Him Finish the Job" under a pugnacious image of The Man with the Big Cigar. In the words of Angus Calder, "Like naked heathens, they proclaimed the unique virtues of their tribal idol, a man whom most of them had spurned and ignored in the 1930s. The irony was not missed." Churchill then compounded his Party's strategic misjudgement with a colossal campaigning gaffe, claiming that an incoming socialist government would inevitably employ "some form of Gestapo" to enforce its programme. Nobody could have been more unlike Heinrich Himmler than the mild-mannered Old Haileyburian Clement Attlee, who responded to the Prime Minister's assertion with the telling reproof that Churchill "feared lest those who had accepted his leadership in war might be tempted out of gratitude to follow him further. I thank him for disillusioning them so thoroughly."

The cautious Attlee had judged that Labour's chances of victory were "no more than fair". The result was to be declared on 26 July to allow for the counting of the votes of troops serving overseas. Churchill, confident of victory, flew from Hendaye, where he and Clementine had enjoyed a brief break, to Berlin on 15 July to attend the last great Allied conference of the war, appropriately code-named *Terminal*. It was held in Potsdam, a Berlin suburb sprinkled with palaces, parks and lakes, the historical stamping ground of Prussian royalty until the abdication of Kaiser Wilhelm II in November 1918. It was Churchill's hope that the conference would enable him to join the new American Preisdent Harry Truman (Roosevelt had died in April 1945) in a stand that would prevent the spread of Communism across Europe. However, before leaving for Potsdam, the Prime Minister was disturbed by a premonition that he might suffer a political demise as abrupt as that of Wilhelm II. He told Moran: "I dreamed that that life was over. I saw – it was very vivid – my dead body under a white sheet on a table in an empty room. I recognised my bare feet projecting under the sheet. It was very lifelike ... Perhaps this is the end."

Terminal was held in the Soviet zone of Berlin.[52] Potsdam was largely unscarred by RAF Bomber Command, the USAAF and the Red Army, and Churchill was housed in the handsome Villa Urbig, designed by Ludwig Mies van de Rohe and built during the First World War for the German banker Franz Urbig. Mindful of their experience at Yalta, the British brought a large amount of kitchen equipment, including cutlery, glasses, plates and dishes. On arrival, Churchill complained that his bed was broken, and repairs were hastily improvised. A plague of mosquitoes then descended on the villa and its grounds, requiring heavy spraying of the entire complex. In spite of all these efforts, an atmosphere of brooding menace hung over the villa and its grounds. Moran recalled: "The Prime Minister had called for a glass of whisky. Then we sat in silence for a long time looking at the lawn that sloped to a lake, into which, so it was said, the Russians had thrown some German soldiers who could not walk because of their wounds. Beyond the lake a field rose sharply to a wood. The only sign of life we could see was a Russian sentry who came out of the woods, looked round and disappeared into the trees. When the light had gone, a

---

52. The Allies had agreed at Yalta a plan for the post-war dismemberment of Germany. There were to be four sectors, American. British, French and Soviet. Berlin, in the middle of the Soviet sector, was divided into four zones and was to be the headquarters of the Allied Control Council. Austria was divided in similar fashion.

rifle shot, that seemed to come from the wood, broke the silence that had fallen over everything."

Eden, recovering from a duodenal ulcer which had kept him from electioneering, accompanied Churchill to Potsdam, where they met Harry Truman for the first time. The US President, lively and alert, was a welcome contrast to the moribund Roosevelt. Churchill noted that he used "many expressions at intervals in our discussion that I could not easily hear unmoved. I felt that here was a man of exceptional character and ability ... simple and direct methods of speech and a great deal of self-confidence and resolution."

Churchill and Truman made separate tours of Berlin before the opening of the conference, shepherded by Soviet minders through the ruins of the Reichstag and Hitler's bunker. The Prime Minister was unusually subdued during this macabre sight-seeing tour. In Hitler's bunker, he descended to the room occupied by Eva Braun, where a vase still contained the dried remains of a bunch of flowers placed there just before the end. Recovering his breath on a chair in the Chancellery garden, Churchill mopped his brow and observed that Hitler must have come up there to get some air and heard the Russian guns getting closer and closer. Moran attempted to raise Churchill's spirits by showing him a souvenir Iron Cross he had scooped from the floor of the Chancellery building. The Prime Minister's only response was "poor devils". Outside the Chancellery, Churchill had encountered some inquisitive Berliners: "In the square outside the Chancellery there was a considerable crowd. When I got out of the car and walked about among them, except for one old man who shook his head disapprovingly, they all began to cheer. My hate had died with their surrender, and I was much moved by these demonstrations."

Although Churchill could draw some satisfaction from this display, two topics, one domestic, the other with colossal international implications, were dominating his mind. Referring to the first, he told Moran: "I shall be glad when this election business is over. It hovers over me like a vulture of uncertainty in the sky." In addition, something far bigger filled his horizon.

Shortly afterwards, he further unburdened himself to Moran. On 23 July he informed him, in wildly unscientific terms, of the culmination of the Manhattan Project, the Anglo-American development of an atomic bomb: "I am going to tell you something that you must not tell any human being. We have split the atom. The report of the great experiment has just come in. A bomb was let off in some wild place in New Mexico. It was only a 13lb bomb but it made a crater half a mile across." Moran replied, "It is H. G. Wells stuff. It is the second coming." Churchill continued, "The secret has been wrested from nature... It gives the Americans the power to mould the world. If the Russians had got it, it would mean the end of civilisation. It is to be used on cities, not on armies."

On the same day, Churchill told Brooke in excited tones of the atomic breakthrough:

At 1.30pm we went round to lunch with the PM, just three chiefs of staff ... Ismay and Anthony Eden, who came in later. I was completely shattered by the PM's outlook! He had seen the reports of the American results of the new TA [Tube Alloys, the British code-name for the atomic bomb project] secret explosive experiments... He had absorbed all the minor American exaggerations, and as a result was completely carried away! It was no longer necessary for the Russians to come into the Japanese war, the new explosive alone was sufficient to settle the matter.[53] Furthermore we now had something in our hands which would redress the balance with the Russians. The secret of this explosive, and the power to use it, would completely alter the diplomatic equilibrium, which was adrift since the defeat of Germany! Now we had a new value which redressed our position (pushing his chin out and scowling) now we could say if you insist on doing this or

---

53. A reference to the testing of the first atom bomb device on 16 July, 1945 at Alamagordo in the New Mexico desert

that, well we can just blot out Moscow, then Stalingrad, then Kiev, the Kuibyshev, Kharkov, Sebastopol etc etc. And now where are the Russians!

The next day Truman casually mentioned to Stalin that "we had a new weapon of unusual destructive force. The Russian premier showed no special interest. All he said was that he was glad to hear it and hoped we would make good use of it against the Japanese." Stalin certainly was taken aback but his masterly ability to control and conceal his emotions came to his aid. Marshal Zhukov, who was present at Potsdam, later recalled the immediate aftermath of Truman's revelation in the Soviet camp: "Churchill and many Anglo-American authors subsequently assumed that Stalin had really failed to fathom the significance of what he had heard. In actual fact, on returning to his quarters after this meeting, Stalin, in my presence, told Molotov [the Soviet Foreign Minister] about his conversation with Truman. Molotov reacted almost immediately. 'Let them. We'll have to talk it over with Kurchatov [head of the Soviet atomic bomb programme] and get him to speed things up.'" Igor Kurchatov and his team had from 1942 been the beneficiaries of a stream of intelligence on the Manhattan Project delivered by Soviet spies. After the attacks on Hiroshima and Nagasaki in August 1945, Stalin urged Kurchatov to accelerate his programme: "Hiroshima has shaken the world. The balance has been broken. Build the Bomb – it will remove the danger from us." However, the Soviets would not be able to conduct the first test of their own bomb until August 1949, in part because the paranoid Stalin had convinced himself that the technical detail he had received from his espionage sources was riddled with Western disinformation.

Churchill had arrived in Potsdam in a curmudgeonly mood. Eden reflected on his performance in the opening exchanges: "W. was very bad. He had read no brief and was confused and woolly and verbose. We had an anti-Chinese tirade from him. Americans not a little exasperated … have never seen W. worse … he is again under Stalin's spell. He keeps repeating 'I like that man.'" It is doubtful if any of this mattered a great deal. Britain was an increasingly diminished nation, dilapidated by five years of war. Its status as a global power was now dwarfed by the economic might of the United States, massively stimulated by the war, and the seemingly infinite manpower reserves of the Soviet Union, which had taken the Red Army all the way to Berlin. Britain was no longer one of the "Big Three" but rather a junior partner in the radically transformed geopolitical landscape of 1945.

The conference at Potsdam conformed to a depressingly familiar pattern which had evolved from 1942. Churchill would try to organise a preliminary meeting with the Americans to thrash out a common position. The Americans would sidestep this move to avoid, as they saw it, "ganging up" on the Russians. In turn, this fuelled Churchill's irritation with the Russians and generated milder annoyance with the Americans. Nevertheless, having got off to a sticky start at Potsdam, Churchill hit his stride as the Allies sought to settle the outstanding issues stemming from the conflict, principally the best way to handle Germany in the post-war world.

Churchill's participation in the conference was interrupted by the announcement of the result of the British General Election. It is clear from the many agitated telephone requests for information he made from Potsdam that the Prime Minister was by no means wholly confident of a successful outcome. In contrast Moran was so sure that he and Churchill would return victorious that he left all his luggage in the Villa Urbig. In Downing Street, in the small hours of the 26th, Churchill woke just before dawn, "suddenly with a sharp stab of almost physical pain. A hitherto subconscious conviction that we were beaten broke forth and dominated my mind." He went back to sleep and woke at 9am just as the first ballot boxes were being opened.

Churchill stayed in his bed, then bathed, clambered into his siren suit and settled into a chair in the Map Room to contemplate the unfolding disaster engulfing the Conservatives. Labour had won a landslide victory with 393 seats against the 231 won by the Conservatives and their allies. The scale of Churchill's defeat astonished friends and enemies alike. Brooke confessed that "The thought that my days of work with Winston had come to an end was a shattering one. There had been very difficult times, and times when I felt I could not stand a single more day with him, but running through all our difficulties a bond of steel had been formed uniting us together." Churchill remained philosophical in defeat. Harold Nicolson wrote in his diary: "Winston was in magnificent form and took defeat with humour. He confessed that it was distressing after all these years to abandon the 'reins of power'. Someone said, 'But at least, Sir, while you held the reins you managed to win the race.' 'Yes,' said Winston, ' I won the race – and now they have warned me off the turf.'"

Attlee, who had accompanied Churchill to Potsdam on 15 July, concluded the talks, which effectively settled the future of European governments in the post-war world, a process initiated at Yalta. The anti-Communist "London Poles" were to play no part in the future of Poland, where occupation by the Red Army was ten-tenths of the law. In addition, by endorsing the westward resettlement of Eastern European Germans in Poland and Czechoslovakia and the scattered settlements of German commercial, agricultural and intellectual interest in the Slav and Baltic states, the ethnic frontiers in Europe became largely those that had prevailed at the time of Charlemagne in the ninth century. The creation of an "Iron Curtain" dividing non-Communist states to the west of the Elbe from Communist states to the east dominated by the Soviet Union, was the legacy of Potsdam vividly identified by Churchill in 1946, in his speech at Fulton, Missouri.

At the resignation audience in Buckingham Palace, King George VI, dismayed by the rejection of the Prime Minister, offered Churchill the Order of the Garter. Churchill declined, suggesting that the recipient should be Anthony Eden.[54] Later, a dignified farewell was broadcast on the nine o' clock news: "The decision of the British people has been recorded in the votes counted today ... Immense responsibilities at home and abroad fall upon the new

---

54. Eden also refused but both men were awarded the honour in the 1950s.

Government and we must all hope that they will be successful in bearing them. It only remains for me to express to the British people, for whom I have acted in these perilous years, my profound gratitude for the unflinching, unswerving support which they have given me during my task, and for the many expressions of kindness which they have shown towards their servant."

14

DYING FALL

After the 1945 election, on 26 July, Moran spoke out against the "ingratitude of the people". Churchill, sunk deep in gloom, roused himself to reply. "Oh, no, I wouldn't call it that. They have had a very hard time." Later that day he told Noel Coward that there was nothing so mortifying as to step forward as victor and drop through the stage trap-door. On the same day Brooke wrote in his diary: "It is probably all for the good of England in the long run, any government in power during the next year is not going to last long. But what a ghastly mistake to start elections at this period in the World's History! May God forgive England for it."

The arrival of a Labour government did not hasten the Bolshevik revolution dreaded by many diehard Tories. There was, however, a social revolution presided over by a Cabinet with an average age of well over 60. The new Prime Minister, Clement Attlee, had been Churchill's wartime deputy and was a pragmatist who once remarked of his Party's intelligentsia that they were people who could be relied on to take the wrong view on anything. A public school man given to long silences and cricketing metaphors, he was the embodiment of a long line of "safe" politicians, among them Stanley Baldwin and Harold Wilson, to whom the British people can become addicted over long periods. Churchill, for all his qualities, was never "safe".

Establishment figures like Brooke,[55] who were more at home with Churchill's gleefully theatrical style or Anthony Eden's fashion plate elegance, initially found it hard to come to terms with Attlee's unobtrusive presence on the world stage. At the Paris Peace Conference in 1946, the writer and politician Harold Nicolson was dismayed by the appearance of the new Prime Minister: "Molotov and Vyshinsky stride across the stage with all the consciousness of power ... and then trips in little Attlee, hesitates on finding himself on stage, tries to dart back through the door through which he has come, and is then rescued by an official who leads him across the stage with a hand on his elbow... How different from Lloyd George and Balfour – how terribly different from Winston."

The restrained public face which Churchill presented to the world belied the stressful effects that his loss of power had on himself and his family. At the end of August, Clementine wrote to her daughter Mary about the problems at Chartwell: "I cannot explain how it is but in our misery we seem, instead of clinging to each other to be always having scenes.... He is so unhappy and that makes him very difficult. He hates his food (hardly any meat)... I can't see any future. But Papa is going to Italy."

On 2 September 1945, accompanied by his daughter Sarah, a doctor, dictating secretary and valet, Churchill flew to Milan en route to a villa on Lake Como which Field Marshal Alexander[56] had placed at his disposal, a generous act which nonetheless might raise a few eyebrows today. Alexander also provided two aides de camp and 24 guards from the Fourth Hussars. Thereafter Churchill moved on to the South of France, taking the ADCs with him, staying in the Hôtel de Paris and finally in an Antibes villa provided by Eisenhower and all the while painting again. Churchill returned to England in the first week in October, having told Clementine: "I am much better in myself and am not worried about anything... This is the first time for very many years that

---

55. Brooke became Lord Alanbrooke in December 1945.
56. The patrician Alexander, created First Earl of Tunis after the war, was Churchill's favourite general but by no means the best.

I have been completely out of the world. The Japanese War being finished and complete peace and victory achieved, I feel a great sense of relief which grows steadily, others having to face the hideous problems of the aftermath."

Having tumbled down the trap door, Churchill was now brooding about the menace of Soviet expansion. The sole reason for the wartime alliance of Britain, the United States and the Soviet Union had been the defeat of Nazi Germany. Once the Germans had surrendered, that reason vanished. When the Big Three met for the last time in Potsdam, the cracks in the wartime alliance had become a yawning gulf. In Eastern Europe, Stalin moved step by step. There was not one satellite state where the Communist Party enjoyed a majority. It was not popular. Nevertheless, one by one the non-Communist members of the governments formed after liberation has been removed. The tactics employed varied: bogus treason charges, faked Fascist plots, sometimes outright terror. Eventually, in Bulgaria, Romania, Poland, Hungary and Czechoslovakia, the coalition governments were replaced by Popular Fronts in which the Communists held all the important jobs. Then the Popular Fronts were replaced by one-party Communist regimes.

Churchill, the man who had foreseen the Second World War, was now convinced that a similar process was about to roll around again. On 4 May 1945 he told Anthony Eden that the Soviet tide had to be stemmed: "All these matters can only be settled before the United States Armies in Europe are weakened. If they are not settled before the United States Armies withdraw from Europe and the Western world folds up its war machines, there are no prospects ... of preventing a third world war." The Soviet refusal to hold elections in Poland prompted Churchill to ask his military High Command to draw up a strategy to save Central Europe. They produced Operation *Unthinkable*, a plan to employ British, American, Polish and possibly German troops to eject the Red Army from Europe and "impose upon the Soviets the will of the United States and the British Empire". In other words, a Third World War in which the occupation of parts of the Soviet Union would not be ruled out. The British High Command, clearly unnerved by the prospect of Armageddon, warned, with massive understatement, that the invasion of Soviet Russia would be "hazardous".

Unthinkable was swiftly deemed impossible but it underlined the change in Churchill's thinking about Stalin. In the immediate aftermath of the war, the Prime Minister could not rely on the wholehearted support of President Truman, who was not privy to the deliberations on *Unthinkable*. Truman would come round to Churchill's point of view in time, but in May 1945 the President still regarded Stalin as a larger version of big-time American city bosses like Tom Pendergast, the political bruiser who had set Truman on the road to the White House. Indeed, he considered the Soviet leader as "near like Tom Pendergast as any man I know" and a moderating influence on the zealots around him. This was a trap into which Churchill had nearly fallen earlier in the war. Truman believed that he could sit down with Stalin and focus on immediate and long-term problems provided that lesser men like Molotov were confined to the sidelines. On the eve of the Cold War, this was a fatal misreading of Stalin, which in turn convinced Churchill, albeit temporarily, that the President was credulous and weak.

Nevertheless, it was Truman who extended an invitation to Churchill to deliver a lecture, "The Sinews of Peace", on 5 March 1946 at Westminster College in Fulton, Missouri, the President's home state. Churchill arrived at Fulton after six weeks of swimming and sunbathing in Cuba and Florida. He had taken the train to Fulton with Truman, a long journey that gave him the chance to get to know the President better after their brief acquaintance at Potsdam, although it seems they did not use the time to discuss Churchill's speech before it was delivered at Fulton.

In the speech Churchill painted a dramatic picture of a divided Europe:

From Stettin in the Baltic to Trieste in the Adriatic, an iron curtain has descended across the Continent. Behind that line lie all the capitals of the ancient states of Central and Eastern Europe. Warsaw, Berlin, Prague, Vienna, Budapest, Belgrade, Bucharest and Sofia, all these famous cities lie in what I must call the 'Soviet sphere', and all are subject in one form or another not only to Soviet influence, but to a very high, and in some cases, increasing measure of control from Moscow ... This certainly is not the liberated Europe we fought to build up, nor is it one which contains the essentials of permanent peace ... I do not believe that Soviet Russia desires war. What they desire is the fruits of war and the indefinite expansion of their power and doctrines... Our difficulties and dangers will not be removed by closing our eyes to them; nor will they be removed by a policy of appeasement.

Churchill went on to emphasise that there was nothing the Russians admired more than strength and nothing for which they had greater contempt than weakness, particularly military weakness.

The speech may have been well received by his audience in Fulton, but the response of the American press was more critical. The *Wall Street Journal*, a bastion of conservative thinking, observed that "The United States wants no alliance, or anything that resembles an alliance, with any other nation." The London *Times* drew attention to the Fulton speech's "less happy passages". In one of his rare interviews, to *Pravda*, Josef Stalin dismissed Churchill's analysis as the words of a bully. Referring to the former Prime Minister's call for the unity of the English-speaking peoples, Stalin compared Churchill with Hitler in his willingness to propagate racial theories: "In point of fact Mr Churchill and his friends in England and in America are presenting those nations who do not speak English with a kind of ultimatum – recognize our supremacy over you, voluntarily, and all will be well – otherwise war is inevitable."

President Truman remained equivocal about the Fulton speech, effectively distancing himself from it, claiming, with possible justification, that he had not known of its contents before it was delivered. However, it was more likely that he did not want to appear to the American public as a warmonger. When an opinion poll taken in the immediate aftermath of the speech showed that 60 per cent of Americans considered that Truman was being too soft on the Soviets, the President's attitude began to harden. In the meantime, Churchill was to make another significant speech, delivered on 19 September 1946 at Zurich University in Switzerland. The subject was a united Europe, a proposition which was to haunt successive British governments for generations to come. In his speech Churchill demonstrated with great clarity that such a Europe would depend at every level on close co-operation between two nations, France and Germany, which had recently been at war with each other. This was not universally welcome news. Churchill's son-in-law Duncan Sandys, a committed European who had been charged with investigating opinion across the Channel, particularly that held by de Gaulle, reported at the end of November that the speech had not gone down well with the French, most of whom did not consider that Germany any longer existed as a state. Fear and suspicion of a Fourth Reich were the dominant French national emotions, as were mistrust of British and American motives in pursuing this objective. In French eyes, a united Europe could only mean one eventually dominated by Germany. A balance had to be maintained by the inclusion of Britain in this process, and the two nations, Britain and France, had to hammer out a specific agreement on how to conduct this arrangement before any approach could be made to Germany.

Nevertheless, Churchill pressed on in spite of the Labour government's lack of enthusiasm for the project. He was the force behind the Hague Conference of May 1948, which again argued for a united Europe, and was attended by a 140-strong British delegation, headed by Churchill, which included 22 Labour MPs. In 1949, the Council of Europe was established in Strasbourg and a year later the Germans were invited to join, a year too late, as Churchill observed. Churchill attended both sessions, staying in a villa outside the city where he did much entertaining as well as addressing large outdoor gatherings. Questions remain as to whether this activity demonstrated a wholehearted commitment to the European project, but there is much evidence that at this stage in the debate he saw Britain at its heart rather than as a sympathetic bystander.

Where he differed from his European contemporaries was his conviction that the British Commonwealth, in his mind an essentially white construct, should play an integral part in this process. In November 1949 he told a European Movement rally:

Britain is an integral part of Europe, and we mean to play our part in the revival of her prosperity and greatness. But Britain cannot be thought of as a single state in isolation as she is the founder and centre of a world-wide Empire and Commonwealth. We shall never do anything to weaken the ties of blood, of sentiment and tradition and common interest which unite us with the other members of the British family of nations... The British Government have rightly stated that they cannot commit this country to entering any European Union without the agreement of the other members of the British Commonwealth. We all agree with that statement. But no time must be lost in discussing the question with the Dominions and seeking to convince them that their interests as well as ours lie in a United Europe.

Churchill's belief in the fostering of the closest relations with the United States proved less problematic as this ambition was to a large extent shared by the nations of Western Europe, who in the post-war years were the recipients of American aid. As the war drew to a close, traditional American isolationism began to reassert itself. In the summer of 1945, the United States' immediate aim was the speediest possible withdrawal from Europe. However, the nations of Western Europe remained financially dependent on American largesse. As the months went by, they showed little sign of struggling back to their feet. By 1947 they owed the International

Monetary Fund and the World Bank[57] $5.5 billion (something like $75 billion today). Unable to compete economically with the United States, they were in the grip of a "dollar shortage". Economic crisis brought political problems in its wake. The British were cutting back their commitments in Greece. There was unrest in Italy, where there was high unemployment and inflation. The Communist Parties in both Italy and France organized a series of damaging strikes aimed at bringing down the weak coalition governments in their countries. Economic collapse in Western Europe would leave a political vacuum that could be filled by the Soviet Union.

The Communist threat spurred American intervention. In a speech to the graduating class of Harvard University on 5 June 1947, the US Secretary of State, General George Marshall, offered aid to all the countries of Europe on the condition that they co-operated to produce a plan for recovery. Within hours the British Foreign Secretary, Ernest Bevin, seized on Marshall's offer. Acting on his own initiative, he cabled acceptance. He later told a group of American journalists that Marshall's speech was like "a lifeline to a dying man". For now, there was a conflict between pride and poverty. Poverty won. Without American aid, post-war rationing in Britain would have been savagely tightened.

The idea floated by Marshall was quickly fleshed out as the European Recovery Plan, popularly known as Marshall Aid. The $4 billion aid package was offered to all European states, including the Soviet Union and its Eastern European satellites. However, Stalin was not prepared to join a programme to revive the capitalist economies of Western Europe. On 2 July, the Soviet Foreign Minister, Vyacheslav Molotov, walked out of the Paris Conference on the Recovery Plan, dragging the reluctant Eastern European states with him. His exit confirmed the division of Europe into two hostile camps. The Soviets were blamed for

---

57. Both bodies were created in December 1945 to prevent a repetition of the Great Depression of the 1930s.

refusing an American offer of apparent generosity, although with heavy strings attached. Churchill called Marshall Aid "one of the most unsordid acts in the history of a nation". In reality, it had been motivated by more down-to-earth American political and economic interests. A poverty-stricken Europe was a Europe in which US-made goods could not be sold.

Marshall Aid was the economic arm of what became known as the "Truman Doctrine", in the President's words the provision of support for the "free peoples of the world". The Doctrine's military arm was represented by the integration of the atom bomb into the United States Air Force (USAF). It proved to be a painfully slow process. However, by mid-1948 the American Armed Forces Special Weapons Project – which supplied and controlled the technical teams assembling atomic weapons – could assemble two bombs per day for combat operations. Penetrating heavily defended Soviet airspace at high altitude to reach their targets presented formidable problems. It was not enough merely to possess atomic weapons. If they were to be used, overseas bases, intelligence and aircrews with the ability to fly their bombers through air defences would be needed.

While the Labour government navigated the choppy domestic and international waters of the post-war world, Churchill resumed his literary career. Throughout his life the business of writing, with its attendant army of researchers, advisers, secretaries and typists, had proved the surest salve to the menace of "Black Dog" depression and substitute for the ministerial red boxes when he was out of government. During the course of the First World War he had cheerfully declared that the verdict of history on the conduct of the war would be in safe hands, as they would be his own. Now the Second World War beckoned.

In January 1946 he met with his pre-war European press agent Emery Reves in Miami, where he indicated that Reves would have to handle the deal through Lord Camrose, the proprietor of the *Daily Telegraph*. Other individuals and publishers were also in the somewhat complicated picture, including Henry Luce, the owner of Time-Life, Houghton-Mifflin, the Boston publishers, and Cassells of London, with whom had had dealings over *A History of the English-Speaking Peoples*. Almost a year later Reves informed Churchill that Time-Life would pay him just over a million dollars for the US serial rights for the proposed six-volume history and that Houghton-Mifflin would cough up $250,000 for the book rights, the total worth some ten million dollars today. The first volumes were available for book and serial publication some 18 months later. The beneficiary of this cascade of money was the Chartwell Literary Trust.

Under the supervision of William Deakin, Churchill's pre-war research assistant and a wartime officer in the Special Operations Executive (SOE), an impressive panel of advisers was assembled, including Generals Ismay and Pownall, Commodore G.R.G. Allan RN, Air Chief Marshal Garrod, Air Chief Marshal Park, Field Marshal Alexander and the scientist Professor R.V. Jones, vanquisher of the V-weapons. Attlee gave Churchill permission to use Cabinet Office papers, with the exception of those relating to Bletchley Park's activities, and those of other principal players in the drama through which they all had lived. At first, it seemed as if the flood of documents and the contributions of numerous advisers would swamp the narrative. However, Deakin channelled the torrent into calmer waters while Churchill proved a skilful editor, trimming an unruly garden like a skilful topiarist. Much of this he undertook on holidays abroad, in France at Beaverbrook's villa in Cap d'Ail or at the Hôtel de Paris in Monte Carlo, or the Mamounis hotel in Marrakech. The first volume was on sale in New York in June 1948 and in London in the following October.

Churchill's account of the Second World War inevitably has the defect of an Anglo-centric view of the war against the Axis and his own role in it. And to many who fell foul of him during the war, notably Field Marshal Sir Archibald Wavell, his judgement in the war's aftermath was unkind. Nevertheless, his romantic immersion in Britain's past had enabled him to conduct a dialogue with its people which in the midst of disaster enabled both the people and the Prime Minister to endure. Whenever Churchill was asked to nominate his favourite year in a crowded life, his invariable reply was 1940 with all its attendant crises. In this he was an oddly shaped piece on the geopolitical chessboard. Cometh the hour, cometh the man; a man who in the 1920s had admired Mussolini but a doughty opponent who could not have been anticipated by Hitler in his 1940 pomp. A man who had only travelled on a bus once but who was recognised by every man and woman in the street. A man who had presided over, and largely inspired, a triumph by a nation which was on the point of transmogrifying into a country he would increasingly find it impossible to recognise. An Edwardian in the age of the atom bomb. As he reflected on the six volumes, "This is not history, this is my case."

By 1950 the Labour government was fast running out of steam. In the general election of that year, Labour seats were reduced to 315 and those of the Conservatives and their allies rose to 298. As Leader of the Opposition, Churchill had campaigned in more muted style than he had in 1945. There were no "Gestapo" blunders, although the sombre tone of a radio broadcast delivered in Scotland on 17 February caught his anxiety in the shadow cast by the atom bomb: "It is my earnest hope that we may feel our way to some more exalted and august foundation for our safety than this grim ... balancing power of the bomb. We must not, however, cast away our only shield of safety unless we can find something surer and more likely to last." He then struck a note which disinterred his wartime dealings with Stalin, that jovial despot, in the Kremlin at the height of the war: "Still I cannot help coming back to the idea of another talk with Soviet Russia upon the highest level. The idea appeals to me of a supreme effort to bridge the gulf between the two worlds, so that each can live their life, if not in friendship, at least without the hazards of the cold war."

The Labour government, beset by the ill-health of its leading Parliamentary lights, including Attlee, and buffeted by the economic cost of its participation in the Korean War under the banner of the United Nations, was put out of its misery in the general election called in the autumn of 1951. The Labour Party received just under 14 million million votes – the highest recorded by any British political party until 1997 – but the nationwide swing towards the

Conservatives and the vagaries of the "first past the post" electoral system returned the Conservatives to power with 321 seats against Labour's 295. Churchill was once again Prime Minister.

The four days Churchill spent assembling a new team amid associated bustle, the coming and going of secretaries, the conveyor belt of red boxes, and numerous congratulatory telephone calls from foreign statesmen, were among the happiest of his later years. However, in the words of Roy Jenkins, he was now a politician "gloriously unfit for office". The many faults to which Attlee had drawn attention in the closing months of the war were all too evident. Paperwork of all kinds was anathema to the Prime Minister, who preferred to play bézique rather than open his boxes. Cabinets became arenas of rambling and reminiscence rather than hard-headed discussion. Decisions were sometimes made by the Prime Minister without any prior discussion at all. The question of retirement soon raised its head, but the infirmity of Churchill's chosen successor, Anthony Eden, the result of botched abdominal operations, ruled this out. Moreover, just as Churchill had manoeuvred with some success in 1942-43 to push back the date of the Allied landings in France, so he also contrived to delay his departure from the premiership.

The principal planks of Churchill's premiership were the four visits he made to the United States. The first was in January 1952, when Truman was still president, during which he made his third address to Congress and also visited Ottawa. He had set sail in *Queen Mary*, on 30 December 1951, a mode of travel that was becoming increasingly rare for a world statesman but enabled Churchill to savour the delights of the Cunard liner's exclusive Verandah Grill, considered to be a cut above the ship's first-class restaurants. He was beginning to show signs of his advancing years. The First Sea Lord, Admiral Louis Mountbatten, who dined with him aboard the liner shortly before its departure, found Churchill "really past his prime. He was very deaf and kept having to have things repeated to him. He quoted poetry at great length." Leslie Rowan, a former secretary who met Churchill in New York, reflected that the Prime Minister had lost much of his former tenacity, no longer vigorously pushing things through and walking like an old man.

In Washington, Truman and his team prepared for the arrival of the "Old Boy", as they called the Prime Minister, with great care. The President was determined to avoid the free-wheeling nature of the discussions Churchill had enjoyed with Roosevelt and insisted on establishing a fixed agenda for the forthcoming talks. There were to be no rambling late-night negotiations. The American Secretary of State Dean Acheson later recalled: "President Truman approved some general conclusions we had reached about the visit. Of first importance would be the tone and atmosphere of the meetings. Mr Churchill should return home in a good mood. This did not require material concessions and changes in US policy, but long, intimate and frank discussions conducted with respect and goodwill."

On 5 January, on the evening of his arrival in the United States, Churchill set the cat among the pigeons while on the Presidential yacht on the Potomac dinning with Truman, Acheson and Harriman. He launched into a long digression about the NATO proposal for a European Army to foster the cause of European unity, a scheme which at the time enjoyed considerable American support. Churchill, however, regarded the idea as an impractical fudge. Dean Acheson recalled: "He pictured a bewildered French drill sergeant sweating over a platoon made up of a few Greeks, Italians, Germans, Turks and Dutchmen, all in utter confusion over the simplest orders. What he hoped to see were strong national armies marching to the defence of freedom singing their national anthems. No one could ever get up any enthusiasm singing, 'March NATO, march on!'" It required an intervention by Eden to point out that the Prime Minister was joking.

The nub of Britain's European problem lay in the differences between Churchill and his Foreign Secretary. The Prime Minister now wanted the European project to succeed while he and the British remained benevolent observers, on the outside looking in. Eden, whose responsibilities included our relations with Europe, adopted a basically hostile Foreign Office line about our European neighbours. This was made flesh in a report of December 1955 which concluded that "the United Kingdom cannot seriously contemplate joining in European integration." Later, Eden put it more pithily, telling American students at Columbia University, that formally joining the European community was something that the British in their bones knew they could not do.

In Washington there was to be no return to the wartime "special relationship". However, the Americans recognised that cordial relations remained vital to gain access to the worldwide network of British bases made all the more important by the onset of the Cold War. The delicate path which the Americans were determined to tread was highlighted by the row which blew up in an early meeting in Washington during Churchill's 1952 visit over the appointment of a NATO Supreme Commander Atlantic. The North Atlantic Treaty Organisation had been formed in April 1949 in the immediate aftermath of the failed Soviet attempt to isolate the city of Berlin from the four Western zones of Germany, the so-called "Berlin Blockade", which had been thwarted by a massive air shuttle, the Berlin Airlift. Twelve Western countries, including the United States, Canada and Great Britain, had signed NATO's founding charter. In the words of Frank Roberts, a future British ambassador to NATO: "The overall success of the Berlin airlift was first of all that it persuaded a lot of very frightened people throughout Europe that they had to come into the Atlantic Alliance, which provided security and a feeling that we are safe despite the presence of these very much larger Russian forces, which are next door."

When it came to the appointment of a NATO Supreme Commander Atlantic, the Americans, with the biggest navy in the world, favoured one of their own. This was vigorously opposed by Churchill, who argued for a joint Anglo-American command beholden to the US Chief of Naval Staff and the British First Sea Lord, the final court of appeal being the Prime Minister and the President, a completely unworkable arrangement. Sadly, things had changed since Churchill had, for the second time, been First Lord of the Admiralty. He was, inadvertently or otherwise, invoking the special relationship to which the British have been so poignantly devoted since the days of the Atlantic Charter. The Americans would not budge. This was doubly embarrassing as Truman was expected at a British Embassy dinner that evening. Also at the dinner was Dean Acheson. At one point Churchill, in an elephantine demonstration of bonhomie, turned to his neighbour, his wartime scientific adviser Lord Cherwell, now Paymaster General, and asked him to get out his slide rule and calculate the depth of champagne in the room if all that had been drunk were poured into it. Acheson recalled, "The result was very disappointing for the Old Man. He had expected that we would all be swimming in it like goldfish in a bowl. Whereas it would hardly cover our knees." An inadvertent comment, perhaps, on the diminished international status of Britain in the early 1950s.

In November 1952, Truman was succeeded as President by Dwight D. Eisenhower, whose post-war career had included a brief period as Commander of the Occupation Forces in Germany, then as US Army Chief of Staff before he retired. In 1951 he had returned to the service to become Supreme Commander Allied Forces in Europe, a NATO post from which he resigned in 1952 to enter politics. In that year he became the 34th President of the United States.

The immediate geopolitical problem confronting the West was dealing with the consequences flowing from the death of Stalin on 5 March 1953. Could a rapprochement with the new regime in Moscow be established? On 11 March 1953, Churchill had appealed to Eisenhower: "When there is no more Stalin ... I have the feeling that we might both of us or together or separately be called to account if no attempt were made to turn over a leaf so that a page would be started with something more coherent on it than a series of casual and dangerous incidents at the many points of contact between the two divisions of the world." He went on to suggest another summit.

Eisenhower was reluctant to commit himself, tending to doubt the wisdom of such a meeting, arguing that this would merely fuel the Soviet propaganda machine. It must be noted that this exchange took place at the height of the anti-Communist frenzy in America stoked by Senator Joseph McCarthy. Eisenhower was extremely wary of appearing to be "soft" on Communism while at the same time having no clear indication that the Soviets, in the post-Stalin era, would welcome a détente with the West, particularly as they now possessed the atom bomb. Eisenhower was further discouraged by his discovery that the Psychological Strategy Board set up by his predecessor to evaluate an eventuality like the death of Stalin had left behind no concrete conclusions. He berated a Cabinet meeting that after seven years of deliberation this august body had left behind precisely zero.

A month later, on 16 April, Eisenhower woke up. Addressing the American Society of Newspaper Editors, he told his audience: "The world knows that an era ended with the death of Josef Stalin... The new Soviet leadership now has a precious opportunity to awaken, with the rest of the world, to the point of peril reached and to help turn the tide of history. Will it do this?" Eisenhower's question was answered by his Secretary of State, John Foster Dulles, a slab-faced Cold War warrior happy to contradict his President at every turn, who insisted that the United States was arguing from a position of greater strength and would not "dance to any Russian tune". The British Foreign Office was alarmed at this display of belligerence. Lord Cranbourne, deputising for Eden, who had undergone surgery for a damaged bile duct, expressed the concern:

There seems now to be a new and more dangerous American tendency, which has its roots in the Republican election campaign and was illustrated in a recent statement by Mr. Dulles to interpret the situation behind the Iron Curtain as already very shaky and therefore to advocate new although unspecified measures to encourage and even promote the early liberation of the [Soviet] satellite countries. It is my intention to resist American pressure for new initiatives of this kind.

During the war Churchill had got on well with Eisenhower, although the military man's easygoing outward appearance masked a tetchy interior just below the surface. Shortly after Eisenhower's election as President, Churchill told Colville, "I am greatly disturbed. I think that this makes war more probable." These words were uttered after the testing by the Americans at Eniwetok Atoll in the South Pacific of the first hydrogen bomb, generating the equivalent of 10.4 million tons of TNT. Churchill regarded the development of the H-bomb as an entirely new and terrible phenomenon, which, if used, would bring about the end of the human race. However, at the four-day Bermuda conference held in December 1953, which was also attended by the French, Eisenhower had observed that far from being the harbinger of the end of civilisation the H-bomb was no more than the latest in the long line of improvements in military hardware. This implied that there was no distinction to be made between conventional and nuclear weapons, as all weapons in the long run become conventional weapons. In Eisenhower's mind the use of the H-bomb would be merely the Rhine Crossing writ extra large.

In Bermuda, Eisenhower compounded Churchill's alarm by a series of caustic observations on the Prime Minister's view of the Soviet Union. The President observed that Churchill's opinion that there was a New Look[58] to Soviet foreign policy was entirely mistaken. He then likened Russia to a prostitute who would never be changed by the mere application of another layer of make-up. The United States was set upon driving the Soviet hooker "off the streets". Eden, not for the first time attempting to smooth things over, enquired over the timing of the next meeting. Eisenhower replied that his next meeting was with a whisky and soda before leaving the room.

Colville, who was present at this exchange, considered that this undiplomatic language was highly unusual, if not unique: "Pained looks all round. Of course, the French gave it all away to the press."

---

58. A reference to Christian Dior's fashion innovations of the post-war period.

In contrast, Churchill seemed curiously relaxed about Eisenhower's apparent mulishness, blaming the President's Secretary of State, John Foster Dulles, for setting Prime Minister and President at cross purposes. Churchill had no time for Dulles, for whom he had a visceral dislike. He told Moran that in Dulles's hands the President was little more than a ventriloquist's dummy parroting anti-Soviet prejudice. The Prime Minister glumly reflected that although age was catching up with him, he was still capable of dealing with "this bastard". He was as determined as ever to secure another summit, which would be the crowning glory of his premiership and would also prolong his time in office, silencing the growing body of whisperers around him.

Churchill's obsession with summitry, placing him once again at the centre of world affairs, as he had been at Yalta and Potsdam, overrode the contradictions evident in his reaction to the second American explosion of an H-bomb at Bikini Atoll on 1 March 1954, describing it in the House of Commons as the essential guarantor of world peace. The Prime Minister was more candid in private, referring to the bomb as "the bloody invention". Nevertheless, this did not prevent him from giving the go-ahead to the manufacture of a British H-bomb, a development which he had assured Eisenhower in Bermuda would not happen. British H-bomb tests began in 1957, long after Churchill had ceased to be Prime Minister.

By March 1954, Churchill was nearing the end of the line. In June 1953, after a Downing Street dinner for the Italian Prime Minister Alcide De Gasperi, he had suffered a severe stroke, from which it took him several weeks to recover and news of which was hidden from press. In the spring of 1954, a highly critical article in *Punch* magazine by Malcolm Muggeridge was accompanied by a cartoon depicting the Prime Minister as an overweight dodderer, not an image calculated to restore the faith of Conservative voters waiting for appointments in doctors' and dentists' waiting rooms. On 11 March he had told R.A. Butler, the Chancellor of the Exchequer, that he felt like an aeroplane in a darkening sky, running low on fuel and searching for a safe landing. The hope of a renewed dialogue with the Soviets was the only thing that kept him going. On the same day he hinted to Eden that he intended to resign by the summer at the latest. However, his departure was delayed by an offer from Eisenhower for talks at the end of June. Eden, champing at the bit to succeed to the office of Prime Minister, was fobbed off once again, this time with a suggestion that there might be an autumn handover.

Accompanied among others by Eden and Cherwell, Churchill flew to Washington on 24 June. The principal aims of the visit were to convince Eisenhower that there should be closer co-operation between the Americans and the British in the sphere of nuclear weapons, and the convening of a summit with the Soviets to discuss the possibility of deploying the resources of both the West and East in fields more productive than the arms race. The visit began propitiously. Churchill spent the first three nights in the White House, where to his astonishment Eisenhower immediately agreed to talks with the Soviets. From the White House the Prime Minister travelled to Ottawa before sailing back to the United Kingdom aboard the liner *Queen Elizabeth* on 1 July, his last Atlantic voyage on a Cunard ship. Significantly, the grandeur of former crossings was much diminished. Colville noted that even the Verandah Grill had adopted an Americanised menu, a reflection of changing times, and the standard of service was notably slipshod.

Churchill's relations with his impatient would-be successor took a downward turn during the return voyage. If Churchill secured his cherished summit, this would block, or at least delay, Eden's path to the premiership, which on the outward voyage Churchill had promised him for the early autumn. Churchill then succeeded in exciting Eisenhower's ire by sending a telegram to Molotov about the summit without first consulting the President about its terms. In the event, these mishaps mattered little. On 25 July, the Soviets torpedoed any hope of a summit by demanding a 32-power meeting to discuss the Soviet plan for European security, which would have involved a NATO withdrawal from Germany. The Prime Minister's last great foreign policy initiative lay in ruins around him. Churchill nevertheless remained unabashed.

He retreated to Chartwell and having considered his position, put back the possibility of resignation by another six months.

The remainder of Churchill's time as Prime Minister was dominated by a prolonged period of trench warfare between himself and Eden, which, as they were both gentlemen, was conducted relatively decorously before erupting into outright hostility. Roy Jenkins accurately observed that the two men's rivalries resembled those of the Cold War superpowers, both capable of destroying each other but at the same time destroying themselves. Churchill, however, knew full well that his exit, and come it must, had to be handled with some dignity to prevent a descent into rancour and bitterness which would blight his own reputation but also that of the Conservative Party. At the same time, he dreaded the thought of a retirement that would end his active life as a politician. He told Moran, "I think I shall die quickly once I retire. There would be no purpose in living when there is nothing to do."

Churchill's Cabinet colleagues were of a mind that he should resign but collectively lacked the nerve to confront the Prime Minister with the unwelcome news. They were also nervously aware of the political perils of a mishandled operation both among Conservative activists and the public at large. The crisis simmered on as the Prime Minister approached his 80th birthday, an occasion which was to be marked by the unveiling of a portrait of Churchill by the artist Graham Sutherland, depicting the visibly ageing but uncharacteristically cruel-looking lion, which had been commissioned by the House of Commons. Churchill had seen the finished work two weeks before his birthday and had been appalled. At the presentation he described it, with heavy irony, as "a remarkable example of modern art". It was consigned to an attic and later burned by Clementine. A bizarre subsequent suggestion for another portrait, by the vulgar surrealist Salvador Dali, was mercifully abandoned, sparing us, no doubt, the ageing lion in a sea of suspended and sagging time pieces.

Christmas was spent at Chequers. It was ten years since Churchill had made the dramatic decision to fly to Greece, but this time he remained with family and friends until early January, there to consider the suggestion made by seven of his most senior cabinet colleagues the day before he left on his holiday, 22 December, that he should resign. It had not been an outright demand, the nominal item of discussion had been the date of the next election, but the question was left hanging in the air, prompting an angry outburst from the Prime Minister, who told his colleagues that he would think it over. Once again, he found solace in distraction, this time the detailed preparation of a speech delivered at a February meeting of Commonwealth Prime Ministers, in which he announced the British commitment to the building of the H-bomb. In a Cold War context the decision did little to affect the strategic balance between the United States and the Soviet Union, but doubtless Churchill had weighed up the pros and cons of hanging on to American coat tails in the Cold War conflict. In what was to be his last House of Commons speech, delivered on 1 March 1955, Churchill made this bleak appeal, striking for a man who was not a devout Christian: "Which way shall we turn to save our lives and the future of the world? It does not matter so much to old people, they are going soon anyway, but I find it poignant to look at youth in all its activity and ardour ... and wonder what could lie before them if God wearied of mankind." He finished with a phrase recalling his and Britain's finest hour: "Meanwhile never flinch, never weary, never despair."

The Prime Minister lingered on, the tattered old eagle on the wire, sustained by lingering hopes of a final summit with Eisenhower, and enduring snapping and snarling exchanges with an increasingly impatient Eden. His hopes were dashed in mid-March when it became clear that no such summitry was contemplated by the Americans. Rumours of his coming resignation, until now not in general circulation, were seeping into the public domain. At the end of March there was a momentary flare of anticipation sparked by an announcement by the Soviets that they were ready to entertain the prospect of four-power talks. This, combined with newspaper and dock strikes at home and the decision about the forthcoming election, temporarily convinced Churchill that he could further postpone the announcement of retirement. That night, during a visit to the Queen, he asked if she would object to his continuing as Prime Minister. She replied that she would not, although this would only have been an indication that her constitutional duty did not lay in adjudicating in a row between her Prime Minister and Foreign Secretary.

The meeting with Her Majesty was followed by a dinner with Eden, at which Sir Winston and Sir Antony observed all the requirements of civilised discourse. Eden, if anything, was pointedly amiable. By the next day, however, Churchill had reached a decision. At 6.30pm he informed Eden and Butler that he would resign on 5 April. Churchill spent his last days as Prime Minister in Downing Street. There was a royal dinner party at the end of which a moving photograph caught Churchill bidding goodbye to the Queen on the doorstep of No. 10. Afterwards, Colville went up to Churchill's bedroom to find him sitting on his bed clad in his Order of the Garter, Order of Merit and knee breeches. After a long silence, Churchill turned to him and said, correctly as it turned out, "I don't believe Anthony can do it."

15

SUNSET

Winston Churchill was a man of remarkable resilience, and his withdrawal from public life was a gradual and poignant process. Throughout his life he had been borne along by a surging tide of vitality which defied his frequently fragile physical condition. Willpower alone had carried him through the "Black Dog" melancholia which had plagued him in the 1930s when he was out of office, if not out of action. By the time he had reached 80, when he was nearing the end of his second term as Prime Minister, he had survived a traffic accident, a heart attack, three severe bouts of pneumonia, three strokes and two operations. During the Second World War, during which he was under unremitting strain, he seldom complained of fatigue.

Moran, who knew Churchill as well as anyone, observed, "I could see this sensitive boy, bullied and beaten at his school, grow up into a man, small in stature, with thin unmuscular limbs, and the white delicate hands of a woman; there was no hair on his chest, and he spoke with a lisp and a slight stutter." The poet Wilfred Scawen Blunt, who met Churchill in 1903, described him as "a little square-headed fellow of no very striking appearance". Churchill's toughness was acquired by a supreme effort of will. It sustained him at Omdurman and on the South African veldt; it carried him through his time in the trenches in 1915-16; it went with him on to the roof of Downing Street as the bombs rained down in the Blitz of 1940; and sustained him during the arduous and decidedly risky flights to wartime summits. He knew fear and mastered it.

There were to be no more summits. Instead, Churchill was given the cold shoulder by Anthony Eden in the run-up to the June 1955 General Election. His successor had decided to establish his own unchallenged authority as Prime Minister and in this he considered that he needed no help from Churchill. During the campaign Churchill gave only four local speeches, two in his own constituency, another in Bedford in support of his son-in-law Christopher Soames, and the fourth in West Walthamstow. However, Churchill kept himself busy in these slack days, tinkering with the final version of *A History of the English-Speaking Peoples*, a task which would occupy him, the work's contributors and his editors for the next two years.

Eden's unchallenged authority was not to last long. It failed to survive its first serious international test in the Suez crisis, which erupted in the autumn of 1956. The Arab-Israeli war of 1948-49 had been followed by a succession of border skirmishes, guerrilla activity and acts of terrorism. In 1955, Egypt's President Gamal Abdel Nasser, having secured by agreement the withdrawal of British troops from the Suez Canal zone, announced that the Canal would be closed to Israeli commerce. Furthermore, he warned that ships using the Israeli port of Eilat, at the head of the Gulf of Aqaba, might be shelled by guns commanding the Tiran Strait. It was not long before a British steamer was hit, prompting an Israeli counterstroke.

Having had his appeal for armaments to the British and French turned down, followed by their withdrawal from the Aswan dam project, Nasser turned to the Eastern bloc for assistance and nationalised the Suez Canal, whose major shareholders were the British and French. They then hatched a plan with Israel to invade Sinai and the Canal zone. Following a successful Israeli offensive launched at the end of October 1956 across the Sinai desert to the Canal, the British and French mounted an airborne operation, code-named *Musketeer*, to seize the Canal. The British

3rd Parachute Battalion, in conjunction with French airborne units, was ordered into action. Flying from Cyprus and landing 24 hours ahead of the seaborne force, the 3rd **Battalion secured** El Gamil airfield by a coup de main, cleared the **road** to Port **Said** and sealed off the native quarter. They then link**ed up with the 2**nd Battalion, who had arrived by sea and assisted in **the seizing of** the town and advanced down the Canal, halted **only by political** pressure brought to bear on the two governments, **principally** by the Americans, who prevailed on the United Nations to intervene, halting the Anglo-French advance and forcing a humiliating withdrawal in December.

Churchill had been in the South of France when *Musketeer* was launched, recovering from a stroke. He had been requested by the Eden government to issue a statement supporting *Musketeer* and duly complied, but he was less than happy with his successor's conduct during the crisis. A month later he told Moran that he would never have dared to move against the Canal zone but had he done so he would never have dared to stop. In the wake of the Anglo-French climb-down, Eden had fled to the West Indies to recover his health, prompting Churchill to observe that he now anticipated Harold Macmillan would become the next Prime Minister, which he duly did in the following January. Of one thing Churchill was sure. He would have done nothing before consulting the Americans, with whom he had expended so much time and energy in cementing collegiate relations throughout Second World War and the Cold War. During the immediate aftermath of the Suez crisis, Anthony Montague Brown, Churchill's private secretary seconded from the Foreign Office, fretted that his employer had not been consulted by the Queen. Others less eminent in standing had been summoned to Buckingham Palace. Montague Brown's prodding eventually paid off and a belated call came to a much-publicised audience. Whether it added to Churchill's fading prestige is a moot point.

During Churchill's decline, Montague Brown became more a travelling companion than a private secretary, ensuring that his employer enjoyed the maximum amount of sun and luxurious living, principally in the Mediterranean, which had featured throughout his life. In September 1955, Churchill's first port of call had been Beaverbrook's villa La Capponcina at Cap d'Ail, where he stayed for two months, painting and correcting proofs of *A History of the English-Speaking Peoples*. It was at La Capponcina that three years later Churchill celebrated his Golden Wedding Anniversary with Clementine. Another snug haven was La Pausa, some ten miles away in Roquebrune, built by Bendor, Duke of Westminster, for Coco Chanel and now owned by the Hungarian émigré Emery Reves, the agent for Churchill's post-war writings. Reves, a wealthy man through his Churchill connection, had embellished La Pausa with a stunning art collection, and Churchill's visits combined haute cuisine and connoisseurship in equal measure. Indeed, the raison d'être of Reves and his wife Wendy became for a short time the entertainment of the old lion. At La Pausa the cicadas thrummed as Churchill sank into a somnolent reverie interrupted only by expeditions to the celebrated restaurants and grand casinos for which this part of the Midi is famous.

In 1959, after a number of Churchillian visits to La Pausa, there had been a rupture in the relationship with Reves and his wife, in part caused by the arrival on the scene of the Greek shipping magnate Aristotle Onassis, who had been introduced to Churchill by his son Randolph in January 1956. Churchill wrote to Clementine: "Randolph brought Onassis (the one with the big yacht) to dinner last night. He made a good impression on me … and told us a bit about whales. He kissed my hand!" Thereafter Onassis made it his business to befriend Churchill, eventually hosting him in September 1958 on his first trip aboard the "big yacht" *Christina*, a converted Canadian anti-submarine frigate, on the first of many voyages in the Mediterranean and the West Indies. Two of the proposed guests, the Duke and Duchess of Windsor, were vetoed by Churchill, who had not revised his opinion of that "empty man", the former King.

Another former King, Farouk of Egypt, considered *Christina* "the height of opulence". When one considers the stools in the bar, upholstered with the foreskins of minke whales, one is tempted to suggest the height of vulgarity might be a more appropriate description. However, this lapse of taste was more than offset by the yacht's ten staterooms and Onassis's lavish personal suite, uniquely made over to the Churchills on this and subsequent trips, the mosaic swimming pool which at night became a dance floor, marble bathtubs, Louis XV furniture, and flotilla of gold and silver ashtrays. Although total opposites in character and background, Churchill and Onassis seemed genuinely to enjoy each other's company. Churchill even enlisted his new friend's help in spotting a retirement property in the South of France, a pointless exercise as there was no shortage of high-end property owners only too willing to accommodate one of the most famous men in the world for indefinite periods completely free of charge. The nearest Churchill came to taking the plunge was while pondering the acquisition of a plot owned by the Société des Bains de Mer de Monte Carlo overlooking the Beach Hotel in that resort. Controlling shareholder in the Society and the hotel was none other than Aristotle Onassis. As Churchill grew ever more decrepit, Onassis became the willing interpreter of his increasingly mumbled conversation. When the Greek tycoon became an unlikely member of the Other Club, he retained this function, at one point marshalling a conversation on the Middle East between Churchill and the former Chancellor and Foreign Secretary Selwyn Lloyd. Guests aboard the yacht for whom he performed the same service included the Morans, Margot Fonteyn, who scored a great hit, and Maria Callas, who was somewhat less successful.

In the spring of 1961, *Christina* sailed up the east coast of the United States to anchor, during a considerable storm, in the Hudson. There Churchill dined with Adlai Stevenson, the Democrats' forlorn Presidential hope in in the 1950s, who was escorting Marietta Tree, the second wife of his old Ditchley Park host Ronald Tree. President John Fitzgerald Kennedy, who had modelled much of his dashing political style on Churchill's literary output in the 1930s, was eager to meet the old warrior, but Montague Brown ruled out a visit to the White House without consulting his boss on the grounds that such task was now beyond Churchill's fading powers.

During these years Churchill retained his seat in the House of Commons, from June 1955 always sitting on the seat on the front bench below the gangway. He voted on occasion but never spoke again. In the summer of 1958, during a civil war in Iraq in which its King and Prime Minister had been assassinated, he made extensive preparations to address the House but decided against breaking his silence. However, he made sporadic public forays, including a May 1956 visit to Aachen to receive the Charlemagne Prize, where he warned the West Germans against seeking a union with their compatriots in the East, a move which he warned would lead to "ashes and death". In the winter of 1959, he planted a commemorative tree and laid the foundation stone of the new Churchill College in Cambridge, the brainchild of Cherwell and "Jock" Colville, the latter now the keeper of the vast Churchill archive.

A staging post on Churchill's long final journey came with a fall from his bed in the Hôtel de Paris in late June 1962, which resulted in a broken thigh. He was not found for an hour. He had always insisted that he be buried in England and was flown back to the land of his birth by an RAF Comet, then a symbol of lingering British aeronautical and technological achievement. Churchill was to live for another two and a half years but was never the same man again. He returned to the Hôtel de Paris; he made his last seaborne outing with Onassis; and he was created an honorary citizen of the United States but was unable to attend the ceremony. He made his last visit to Chartwell in October 1964. In London he celebrated his last birthday on 30 November that year. He slept his way through a final dinner with the Other Club at the beginning of December.

On 12 January 1964 he suffered another stroke. There were many callers at Hyde Park Gate in the twelve days before he died, among them his old friend Violet Bonham Carter and the new Prime Minister Harold Wilson; Edwardian England and a hint of the Swinging Sixties. The mighty spirit was stilled on

Sunday, 24 January. For three days Churchill's body lay in state in Westminster Hall. His funeral, the last great outpouring of British Imperialism was held, like that of the Duke of Wellington – a greater soldier but a less successful politician – in St Paul's cathedral. After the service the coffin was taken by boat down the Thames to Waterloo Station and thence by special train and route to Bladon churchyard on the edge of Blenheim Park. During his progress down the river the waterside cranes one by one bowed their heads in remembrance.

SELECTED READING

The best single-volume account of Winston Churchill's unique life and career is *Churchill* by Roy Jenkins (2001). Critical insights into his often idiosyncratic character can be found in *Winston Churchill as I Knew Him* by Violet Bonham Carter (1965), *Churchill: Four Faces and the Man* by A.J.P Taylor, Robert Rhodes James, J. H. Plumb, Basil Liddell Hart and Anthony Storr (1969) and W. H. Thompson's *I Was Churchill's Shadow* (1951). An invaluable source of Churchill's attitude to soldiering in World War I is to be found in *With Winston Churchill at the Front* by A.D. Gibb (1924) while his own *My Early Life* (1930) is an immensely stimulating picture of Imperial military life in the late 19th century and the Boer War. Churchill's often fraught relations with the Royal Navy in both World Wars is covered in *Churchill and the Admirals* (1977) by Stephen Roskill. A useful introduction to the Gallipoli campaign, and Churchill's advocacy of it, is Tim Travers' *Gallipoli* (2001). John Keegan, in Chapter 17 of his *History of The Second World War* (1989) provides a keen analysis of Churchill's strategic thinking at a decisive point in the conflict. Observations on Churchill's conduct of the war, both candid and warmly supportive, abound in Field Marshal Lord Alanbrooke's *War Diaries, 1939–1945* (2001). An account of Churchill's stewardship of Britain' s fortunes at a time of deep national crisis is provided by John Lukacs in *The Duel: Hitler v. Churchill 10 May-31 July 1940* (1991). A warm appreciation of Churchill's driving, indomitable spirit is the thread running through *Assignment to Catastrophe* by Edward Spears (1954), an on-the-spot account of the fall of France in 1940. Churchill's wartime relations with RAF Bomber Command are covered in Max Hastings' *Bomber Command* (1979) and *Fallen Eagle* by Robin Cross (1995) and his role in presiding over the creation of the Special Operations Executive in *SOE* by M.R.D. Foot (1984). Churchill's involvement in the D-Day operation is analysed in Max Hastings' *Overlord* (1993). An insightful portrait of Churchill at a high point of his career can be found in *Daughters of Yalta: The Churchills, Roosevelts and Harrimans – A Story of Love and War* by Catherine Grace Katz (2021). Churchill's state of mind at war's end is examined in *VE-Day: Victory in Europe 1945* by Robin Cross (1985). A compelling portrait of Churchill in 1940 and the immediate post-war years can be found in *Never Again* by Peter Hennessy (1992). An American point of view is presented by Dean Acheson in *Present at the Creation: My Years in the State Department* (1969). *The War of Nerves* by Martin Sixsmith (2021) devotes generous space to a discussion of Churchill and the Cold War. A history of one of Churchill's abiding social passions is told in *The Other Club* by Colin Coote (1971). Fascinating albeit waspish glimpses of Churchill in the social and political scenes of the years 1918 to 1938 are to be found in the Diaries of Henry "Chips" Channon (2021).

INDEX